Frommer's™

Nova Scotia, New Brunswick & Prince Edward Island
day BY day™

1st Edition

by Paul Karr

WILEY

John Wiley & Sons Canada, Ltd.

Contents

PHOTO **CREDITS**

p viii: © Barrett & MacKay/All Canada Photos; p 4, top: © Nova Scotia Museum; p 4, bottom: © Barrett & MacKay/All Canada Photos; p 5: © Barrett & MacKay/All Canada Photos; p 7: © Barrett & MacKay/All Canada Photos; p 10: © Andrew Hempstead; p 11: © Radius/SuperStock; p 13: © Nova Scotia Museum; p 14: © Andrew Hempstead; p 15: © Rolf Hicker/All Canada Photos; p 16: © Pictures Colour Library—PCL; p 17: © Andrew Hempstead; p 21: © W. Hayes; p 22: © Courtesy The Great Hall of the Clans; p 28: © Andrew Hempstead; p 29: © Barrett & MacKay/All Canada Photos; p 30: © Andrew Hempstead; p 31: © Stuart Dee/Alamy; p 33: © Courtesy Upper Clements Parks; p 34, top: © Nova Scotia Museum; p 35: © Courtesy Katherine Roze; p 39: © Andrew Hempstead; p 40: © Rolf Hicker/All Canada Photos; p 41: © Rubens Abboud/Alamy; p 43: © Andrew Hempstead; p 44: © Nova Scotia Tourism, Culture and Heritage; p 45, top: © Andrew Hempstead; p 45, bottom: © Andrew Hempstead; p 47: © Andrew Hempstead; p 48: © Andrew Hempstead; p 49: © Andrew Hempstead; p 52, top: © Pictures Colour Library—PCL; p 52, bottom: © Courtesy Art Gallery of Nova Scotia; p 53: © Andrew Hempstead; p 54: © Andrew Hempstead; p 55: © Andrew Hempstead; p 57: © Andrew Hempstead; p 58: © Nova Scotia Museum; p 59: © Andrew Hempstead; p 61: © Andrew Hempstead; p 63: © Andrew Hempstead; p 64: © Courtesy Rock Bottom Brewery; p 65: © Courtesy Propeller Brewing Company; p 67: © Andrew Hempstead; p 68: © Andrew Hempstead; p 69, top: © Andrew Hempstead; p 69, bottom: © Andrew Hempstead; p 71: © Andrew Hempstead; p 73, top: © Installation view of artwork by Steve Higgins at the Dalhousie Art Gallery, photo: Steve Farmer; p 73, bottom: © Andrew Hempstead; p 76: © Andrew Hempstead; p 77, bottom: © Andrew Hempstead; p 78: © Courtesy Ryan Duffy's Restaurant; p 79: © Courtesy Waverley Inn; p 83: © Andrew Hempstead; p 84: © Ryan Whalen, Shakespeare by the Sea; p 85: © W. Hayes; p 87: © Andrew Hempstead; p 89: © Andrew Hempstead; p 91: © Andrew Hempstead; p 93: © Courtesy Brier Island Lodge; p 94: © Andrew Hempstead; p 95: © Nova Scotia Museum; p 97: © Andrew Hempstead; p 98: © johncw/Frommers.com community; p 99: © Andrew Hempstead; p 101: © John Sylvester/All Canada Photos; p 105: © Barrett & MacKay/agefotostock; p 111: © Andrew Hempstead; p 112: © Andrew Hempstead; p 113: © Courtesy Rita's Tea Room and www.ritamacneil.com; p 115: © Courtesy Yolanta Christie; p 116: © Andrew Hempstead; p 117: © Courtesy Westin Nova Scotian and Keltic Lodge Resort and Spa; p 119: © Gaja Snover/Alamy; p 121: © Greg Vaughn/Alamy; p 127: © First Light/Alamy; p 134: © Thomas Kitchin & Victoria Hurst/All Canada Photos; p 135: © Brian Simpson, PEI Provincial Photographer; p 136: © Rodd Hotels & Resorts; p 141, bottom: © Courtesy Windows On The Water Restaurant; p 143: © Courtesy Barachois Inn; p 144: © Barrett & Mackay; p 145: © David Wilmer; p 146: © Courtesy Shipwright Inn; p 147: © Danita Delimont/Alamy; p 150: © New Brunswick Museum, Saint John, NB; p 153: © Barrett & MacKay/All Canada Photos; p 155: © Andrew Hempstead; p 157: © Courtesy of the Beaverbrook Art Gallery, Fredericton, New Brunswick; p 159: © Andrew Hempstead; p 163: © Courtesy of Fairmont Hotels & Resorts; p 164: © Courtesy of Kingsbrae Arms Relais & Chateaux ; p 165: © Tsuneo Nakamura/PhotoLibrary; p 167: © Rolf Hicker Photography/Alamy; p 171: © Reimar2/Alamy; p 173: © Sherab/Alamy

Published by:

John Wiley & Sons Canada, Ltd.

6045 Freemont Blvd.
Mississauga, ON L5R 4J3

ISBN 978-0-470-67833-6 (paper); 978-0-470-96398-2 (ebk);
978-0-470-96397-5 (ebk)

Editor: Gene Shannon
Production Editor: Pamela Vokey
Project Coordinator: Lynsey Stanford
Editorial Assistant: Katie Wolsley
Photo Editor: Photo Affairs, Inc.
Cartographer: Lohnes + Wright
Vice President, Publishing Services: Karen Bryan
Production by Wiley Indianapolis Composition Services

For information on our other products and services or to obtain technical support, please contact our Customer Care Department within the U.S. at 877/762-2974, outside the U.S. at 317/572-3993 or fax 317/572-4002.

Wiley also publishes its books in a variety of electronic formats. Some content that appears in print may not be available in electronic formats.

Manufactured in China

5   4   3   2   1

A Note from the Editorial Director

Organizing your time. That's what this guide is all about.

Other guides give you long lists of things to see and do and then expect you to fit the pieces together. The Day by Day guides are different. These guides tell you the best of everything, and then they show you how to see it *in the smartest, most time-efficient way.* Our authors have designed detailed itineraries organized by time, neighborhood, or special interest. And each tour comes with a bulleted map that takes you from stop to stop.

Hoping to drive the spectacular roads of Cape Breton Island or relax on the beaches of Prince Edward Island? Planning to walk the lively, historic streets of Halifax or marvel at the world's highest tides at Hopewell Rocks? Whatever your interest or schedule, the Day by Days give you the smartest routes to follow. Not only do we take you to the top attractions, hotels, and restaurants, but we also help you access those special moments that locals get to experience—those "finds" that turn tourists into travelers.

The Day by Days are also your top choice if you're looking for one complete guide for all your travel needs. The best hotels and restaurants for every budget, the greatest shopping values, the wildest nightlife—it's all here.

Why should you trust our judgment? Because our authors personally visit each place they write about. They're an independent lot who say what they think and would never include places they wouldn't recommend to their best friends. They're also open to suggestions from readers. If you'd like to contact them, please send your comments our way at feedback@frommers.com, and we'll pass them on.

Enjoy your Day by Day guide—the most helpful travel companion you can buy. And have the trip of a lifetime.

Warm regards,

Kelly Regan

Kelly Regan, Editorial Director
Frommer's Travel Guides

About the Author

Paul Karr is a prize-winning journalist and travel editor who has authored more than 25 guidebooks around the world, including *Frommer's Vermont, New Hampshire & Maine, Vancouver & Victoria For Dummies, Insight Guide: Switzerland, Driving Northern Italy & The Italian Lakes, USA On the Road,* and *Scandinavia: The Rough Guide.* Now based in New York and Tokyo, he has twice served as writer-in-residence for the National Parks Service and once dined in the White House at the President's personal invitation. For real.

An Additional Note

Please be advised that travel information is subject to change at any time—and this is especially true of prices. We therefore suggest that you write or call ahead for confirmation when making your travel plans. The authors, editors, and publisher cannot be held responsible for the experiences of readers while traveling. Your safety is important to us, however, so we encourage you to stay alert and be aware of your surroundings.

Star Ratings, Icons & Abbreviations

Every hotel, restaurant, and attraction listing in this guide has been ranked for quality, value, service, amenities, and special features using a **star-rating system.** Hotels, restaurants, attractions, shopping, and nightlife are rated on a scale of zero stars (recommended) to three stars (exceptional). In addition to the star-rating system, we also use a **kids icon** to point out the best bets for families. Within each tour, we recommend cafes, bars, or restaurants where you can take a break. Each of these stops appears in a shaded box marked with a coffee-cup-shaped bullet 🍵 .

The following **abbreviations** are used for credit cards:

AE	American Express	DISC	Discover	V	Visa
DC	Diners Club	MC	MasterCard		

Frommers.com

Now that you have this guidebook to help you plan a great trip, visit our website at **www.frommers.com** for additional travel information on more than 4,000 destinations. We update features regularly to give you instant access to the most current trip-planning information available. At Frommers.com, you'll find scoops on the best airfares, lodging rates, and car rental bargains. You can even book your travel online through our reliable travel booking partners. Other popular features include:

- Online updates of our most popular guidebooks
- Vacation sweepstakes and contest giveaways
- Newsletters highlighting the hottest travel trends
- Podcasts, interactive maps, and up-to-the-minute events listings
- Opinionated blog entries by Arthur Frommer himself
- Online travel message boards with featured travel discussions

A Note on Prices

In the "Take a Break" and "Best Bets" sections of this book, we have used a system of dollar signs to show a range of costs for 1 night in a hotel (the price of a double-occupancy room) or the cost of an entree at a restaurant. Use the following table to decipher the dollar signs:

Cost	Hotels	Restaurants
$	under $100	under $10
$$	$100–$200	$10–$20
$$$	$200–$300	$20–$30
$$$$	$300–$400	$30–$40
$$$$$	over $400	over $40

An Invitation to the Reader

In researching this book, we discovered many wonderful places—hotels, restaurants, shops, and more. We're sure you'll find others. Please tell us about them, so we can share the information with your fellow travelers in upcoming editions. If you were disappointed with a recommendation, we'd love to know that, too. Please write to:

Frommer's Nova Scotia, New Brunswick &
Prince Edward Island Day By Day, 1st Edition
John Wiley & Sons Canada, Ltd. • 6045 Freemont Blvd. •
Mississauga, ON L5R 4J3

16 Favorite **Moments**

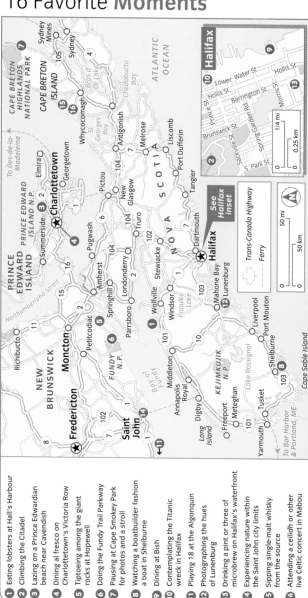

1. Eating lobsters at Hall's Harbour
2. Climbing the Citadel
3. Lazing on a Prince Edwardian beach near Cavendish
4. Dining al fresco on Charlottetown's Victoria Row
5. Tiptoeing among the giant rocks at Hopewell
6. Doing the Fundy Trail Parkway
7. Pausing at Cape Smokey Park for photos and a stroll
8. Watching a boatbuilder fashion a boat in Shelburne
9. Dining at Bish
10. Contemplating the Titanic wreck in Halifax
11. Playing 18 at the Algonquin
12. Photographing the hues of Lunenburg
13. Drinking a pint or three of microbrew on Halifax's waterfront
14. Experiencing nature within the Saint John city limits
15. Sipping single-malt whisky from the source
16. Attending a *ceilidh* or other live Celtic concert in Mabou

Previous page: A beautiful sunset at Hopewell Rocks in eastern New Brunswick.

The Atlantic provinces of Canada are big, spread-out, and thinly populated, which means you'll very likely log quite a few miles during your visit to the region's greatest hits. But if you think big, rural places like this are devoid of special, incandescent experiences, think again—this region is chock-full of magical moments, from quiet coves and sandy beaches to historic forts and sublime seafood meals. Here are a few of my favorite Eastern Canadian experiences.

The beaches around Cavendish, PEI are some of the best in the Maritimes.

❶ Eating lobsters at Hall's Harbour. It's one thing to come upon a secret little cove full of fishing boats, sunset moments, and not all that many tourists. It's quite another to discover great lobsters, fresh off the boat, right on those same docks. You can find both at Hall's Harbour, a little inlet at the end of a rural road from Kentville and Wolfville at the top of Nova Scotia's Annapolis Valley. *See p 30,* ㉓.

❷ Climbing the Citadel. You haven't seen Halifax 'til you've climbed to the top of the Citadel, the fort-on-a-hill that both defines and reveals the city to the expectant traveler. It's a 5- to 10-minute clamber that almost everyone can make without any difficulty at all (and you can also park almost at the top, if you're so—er—inclined). Once here, you see the city's past and present spread out before you. *See p 55,* ❿.

❸ Lazing on a Prince Edwardian beach near Cavendish. The best beaches in Eastern Canada are along the northern shore of Prince Edward Island, and Brackley Beach is one of the best of those. This national park is everything families are looking for: safe, clean, attractive, uncomplicated, and stocked with just enough campgrounds, concessions, changing areas, and boardwalks to keep everyone happy. *See p 128,* ❺.

❹ Dining al fresco on Charlottetown's Victoria Row. Victoria Row isn't an official designation, but Charlottonians all know where it is: It's the little stretch of Richmond Street in front of the Confederation Centre of the Arts that's happily blocked off to vehicular traffic in summer. This is one of Eastern Canada's best spots for an outdoor beer, coffee, sandwich, or full meal. *See p 122,* ❻.

In Shelburne, boat builders hand-make amazing new wooden boats.

⑤ Tiptoeing among the giant rocks at Hopewell. I guarantee you've never done this before: walked on the sea floor while the tide was out, marveling at giant, beautiful ochre rocks—then skedaddled safely back to shore before high tides submerged the whole thing. But at Hopewell Rocks, in eastern New Brunswick, you can. *See p 153,* ③.

⑥ Doing the Fundy Trail Parkway. You can do the Parkway—a privately held park bordering spectacular coastal scenery just north of Saint John, New Brunswick—by car, bike, or foot. I don't care which route you take, but get there: These are among the best views on the Eastern Canadian mainland. The park admission fee is well worth paying. *See p 170.*

⑦ Pausing at Cape Smokey Park for photos and a stroll. If I were allowed to recommend but a single experience in all of Eastern Canada, it would probably be the obvious one: a clockwise drive around Cape Breton, mostly passing through Cape Breton Highlands National Park; you get stupendous photo opportunities in exchange for a bit of white-knuckle driving. This free provincial park is a good stopping point before the last of the stunning descents in the park, and views from here are amazing—you feel like you can see all the way to Europe. *See p 168.*

⑧ Watching a boat builder fashion a boat in Shelburne. The Shelburne Historic Complex is one of Eastern Canada's best

The Fundy Trail Parkway has miles of spectacular coastal scenery.

Lunenburg's harbor yields beautiful views of the colorful town.

historic attractions, for my money: compact, family-friendly, and uncrowded. And the Dory Shop is one of its best features, as expert boat builders hand-make new wooden boats in the old style before your amazed eyes. *See p 14.*

9 Dining at Bish. Halifax is full of restaurants, a lot of them good and a few of them legitimately great; locals argue about it, but I've still yet to find anyone who feels like Bish *isn't* in the "great" category. Right on the city's historic waterfront and across the street from its best complex of public markets, the kitchen here supplies tons of imagination while drawing from the region's prodigious strengths in seafood and farm produce. Don't miss dessert, either— it's spectacular. *See p 76.*

10 Contemplating the *Titanic* wreck in Halifax. Since we mentioned Halifax, here's one more thing you'll want to do there: think about the shipwreck that launched a legend (and a Hollywood blockbuster). You can still stand a few feet away from a deck chair from the doomed luxury liner in a Halifax museum, and you can pace rows

and rows of marked and unmarked graves in several city cemeteries. *See p 50,* **2** *& 69.*

11 Playing 18 at the Algonquin. Each of the maritime provinces of Canada is over-supplied with good-to-great golf courses; in fact, I've devoted an entire tour (see p 36) to golfing in this region. But if I had time for a single round, I'd head for the Algonquin in little St. Andrews, New Brunswick. This links-style course is home to some of my favorite seaside holes on the eastern shore of the continent. And there's something about this town and its sea breezes that just feels like Scotland, too. *See p 37,* **5***.*

12 Photographing the hues of Lunenburg. Lunenburg, Nova Scotia, is a wedding-cake of a historic town that's worth time on any itinerary through the eastern provinces, short or long. You can see historic homes and museums, eat fresh seafood, tour one of the most impressive churches in Atlantic Canada . . . *and* get a Stairmaster-like workout as you ascend and descend the town's orderly grid of streets on its hillside. But for the best photos, head around the harbor along Tanyard Road and shoot the multicolored town across the water. *See p 96.*

13 Drinking a pint or three of microbrew on Halifax's waterfront.

There are so many locally brewed beers in Halifax that I've dedicated an entire tour to them; North America's first brewery, after all, was established right here (Alexander Keith's; and it still brews beer today). For starters, seek out waterfront bars with plenty of local taps marked with names like Propeller, Garrison, Granite, and Rock Bottom. I recommend Maxwell's Plum (1600 Grafton St.; ☎ 902/423-5090) and Henry House (1222 Barrington St.; ☎ 902/423-5660), for starters. *See p 62.*

14 Experiencing nature within the Saint John city limits.

It's amazing how many parks lie within or just outside this New Brunswick city's orbit. And the best of them is Irving Nature Park, a huge seaside spread (which was, yes, donated by the Irving oil company) that's unusually well-stocked, both with things to do and with guided programs to help families do them. You'll see wildlife, bird life, and maybe even some aquatic life. *See p 151,* 9.

15 Sipping single-malt whisky from the source.

I don't normally pimp for commercial establishments when they can do the job well enough themselves, but I think the continent's only single-malt whisky distillery is worth mentioning. This one was situated just north of Mabou, on Cape Breton Island, Nova Scotia, to take advantage of the clear local groundwater. Take a tour and a taste. *See p 101,* 2.

16 Attending a *ceilidh* or other live Celtic concert in Mabou.

I'm changing my vote. Sure, driving Cape Breton (moment 7, above) is spectacular, but you can't take it with you. While on Cape Breton, do not miss a chance to attend either a *ceilidh* (a sort of music party) or a live gig by local musicians in one of the area pubs. The best place to do this is in Mabou, though there are plenty of musicians scattered throughout the island. You'll remember the experience forever. *See p 101,* 1. ●

Attending a ceilidh on Cape Breton Island is a truly memorable experience.

1

Strategies for Seeing
Atlantic Canada

Atlantic Canada

Previous page: Getting off the beaten track while you travel will yield many hidden treasures.

I'm not going to lie to you: **Atlantic Canada is big.** Big enough that seeing it on a short schedule is difficult, if not impossible. It's also different from many other tourist destinations—quieter, more spread out, and more ruggedly natural than almost anywhere else on the east coast of the continent. You'll find fewer tourist services but friendly people. Here are a few strategies and rules of thumb to help you get more enjoyment out of this unique place.

Traveling by boat is one of the best ways to get around Atlantic Canada.

Rule #1: Get yourself some wheels.

Public transit in these provinces exists, but it's pretty spotty. (This is a surprisingly large and mostly rural region.) Unless you're planning to confine yourself to Halifax—in which case, you could certainly use city buses and your own two feet—you're going to need a rental car to get anywhere you want to go.

Rule #2: Get out on the water. Literally.

Eastern Canada is almost all about the sea, so at some point, you need to feel that salty, bracing sea spray on your face to really experience the place. Whether it's on a ferry boat, a whale-watching excursion boat, or a tall ship, it doesn't especially matter; just get out there.

Rule #3: Pay more for a view (or don't).

It's up to you, but find out before you arrive what you'll be looking at. Even the simplest, least expensive motel on Cape Breton Island's Cabot Trail often looks out on top-dollar ocean vistas. Other times, you might be lodging in a city hotel with a view of parking lots. Prices sometimes reflect these differences in scenery, but sometimes don't. My advice? When booking, *always* ask about your view (and try to negotiate a better one, if possible). Going to Eastern Canada and then skipping the views to save a few loonies doesn't make much sense.

Rule #4: Don't try to do too much.

After all, Eastern Canada is a place to relax. That means traveling and sightseeing slowly. Some of my very best memories here involve slow, solitary walks around harbors or village streets when I had no itinerary and no watch on my wrist, and the next day's plans weren't pressing me to hurry back to my room or campsite. Staying in one town—and one room—for two nights in a row isn't a bad idea at all.

Don't forget to pack a good camera—you'll be rewarded with some once-in-a-lifetime photos.

Rule #5: Don't try to see too much.
Though it looks cute in pictures, you'll be surprised by how big Eastern Canada is. Between the major tourist points (Yarmouth and Halifax, Halifax and Cape Breton, Halifax and Prince Edward Island), it's often a 3-to-5-*hour* drive—sometimes with little company en route but spruce trees. Trying to see everything in this book in a short period of time is a recipe for disaster.

Rule #6: Get off the beaten track.
Throughout this book, I've tried to nudge you toward a few experiences that aren't obvious tourist stops—local coffee shops, little-known historical spots, somewhat-secret beaches. You can see just the "greatest hits" if you want, but you'll probably have a better story to tell afterward if you deviate from them.

Rule #7: Bring a good camera.
You'll probably visit places like stunning Cape Breton, Prince Edward Island's purple-and-red lupine fields, and Lunenburg's wedding-cake-like vertical town grid just once in your lifetime; make sure you capture it in the digital equivalent of Kodachrome. Even little point-and-shoot cameras are doing amazing things these days.

Rule #8: Be prepared.
I'm talking about weather here. We all dream of perfect, sunny days on the beach, but these provinces stick out into the Atlantic Ocean—the hemisphere's champion weather-maker. You can expect to be dealing with rain maybe a third of the time in summer, more often than that in a wet year. In spring or fall, weather could be anything from a lovely stretch to a miserable 3-day blow of a typhoon-like Northeaster—it could even snow. Bring umbrellas, a sweater, a change of dry shoes, puzzles, a laptop, and a thick novel, just in case.

Rule #9: Adjust your expectations slightly downward.
There are certainly enough luxury inns and gourmet restaurants here to build a luxe trip, but many other lodgings and eats in these provinces (especially in the non-tourist towns) are a throwback to the old days—days when a traveler would sleep in a sparely furnished room, sharing hallway bathrooms and communal breakfasts with fellow travelers, and eat a basket of fried fish for dinner. That's not an unpleasant experience at all—if you come in expecting it. ●

The Best in **3 Days**

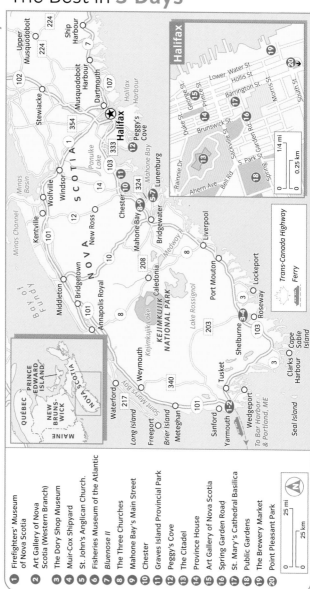

Halifax

Trans-Canada Highway

Ferry

1. Firefighters' Museum of Nova Scotia
2. Art Gallery of Nova Scotia (Western Branch)
3. The Dory Shop Museum
4. Muir-Cox Shipyard
5. St. John's Anglican Church
6. Fisheries Museum of the Atlantic
7. Bluenose II
8. The Three Churches
9. Mahone Bay's Main Street
10. Chester
11. Graves Island Provincial Park
12. Peggy's Cove
13. The Citadel
14. Province House
15. Art Gallery of Nova Scotia
16. Spring Garden Road
17. St. Mary's Cathedral Basilica
18. Public Gardens
19. The Brewery Market
20. Point Pleasant Park

Previous page: The Cape Breton Highlands boasts many postcard-like views.

The Atlantic provinces of Canada are so big that 3 days aren't nearly enough to understand or appreciate them. Sometimes, though, that's all you've got. In that case, I'd restrict myself to Nova Scotia—apologies to Prince Edward Island and New Brunswick—and its southeastern coast. Fortunately, between Halifax and Lunenburg, lovely towns abound. START: **Yarmouth, Nova Scotia.**

Yarmouth's Firefighter's Museum has vintage equipment and memorabilia.

DAY 1

1 kids **Firefighters' Museum of Nova Scotia.** You might be able to channel some of your children's energy into this firefighters' museum, right in downtown Yarmouth. As expected, the displays feature firefighting memorabilia and some vintage equipment. ⏱ *30 min. See p 95,* **8**.

Continue .3km (¼-mile) along Main St. to the

2 ★ **Art Gallery of Nova Scotia (Western Branch).** An offshoot of the larger official provincial museum up in Halifax (see below), Yarmouth's gallery is filled with historical items and art depicting the history of the province (but also contemporary looks at it) through the eyes of some of the region's most notable visual artists, such as Halifax video artist Emily Vey Duke and New Brunswick husband-and-wife painters Mary and Christopher Pratt. ⏱ *45 min. See p 95,* **9**.

From Yarmouth, drive 80km (50 miles) north on Rte. 103 to Shelburne.

Turn right off Rte. 103 to reach Dock St. (by the waterfront), which has

3 ★★ **The Dory Shop Museum.** Right on the waterfront, this is just what it says: a working boatbuilding shop that captures the town's heritage best among the four stops. On the first floor, you can see examples of the simple, elegant dories (which some say were invented here) and view videos of the late Sidney Mahaney, a master builder who worked in this shop from the time he was 17 until he was 96. Upstairs, where all the banging is going on, see the craft not as history, but as a still-living art: You can order a dory, if you like. ⏱ *45 min. 11 Dock St.* ☎ *902/875-3219. June–Sept daily 9:30am–5:30pm.*

Visiting the Shelburne Historic Complex

The two museums described in stops 3 and 4 run along and near several blocks of Shelburne's water-front Dock Street (1 short block off Water St.); all four are administrated together, and all are within walking distance of each other. Visiting all of them costs C$8 adults (free for children under 16); individual museums are C$3 adults (free for children); and Sunday mornings are always free. ☎ *902/875-3219; www. historicshelburne.com.*

2 blocks farther, at the very end of Dock St., is the

❹ ★ **Muir-Cox Shipyard.** This is the most recent addition to the complex. It features displays of barks, sailboats, yachts, and more—all of which were once built here at one time or another, amazingly. And the craftspeople here are still active: in 2008, to mark Shelburne's 200-year anniversary, two longboats were built here and launched. Their proud sails can still be seen in Halifax harbor during the summer. ⏱ *30 min. Dock St. (south end).* ☎ *902/875-3219. June to mid-Oct daily 9:30am–5:30pm.*

Drive 85km (53 miles) north on Hwy. 103 to Rte. 3 and the town of Bridgewater; exit onto Rte. 3 & continue 32km (20 miles) to Lunenburg.

❺ ★★ **St. John's Anglican Church.** What a wonderful intro-duction to Lunenberg! One of East-ern Canada's finest churches, in my opinion, is this restored wonder (which was torched by an arsonist in

2001 but rebuilt quickly to the origi-nal design several years later). It's interesting to note how the church began as a plain house of worship but became progressively more elaborate over subsequent decades—perhaps reflecting the town's increasing prosperity from its fisheries. ⏱ *1 hr. See p 97,* ❷.

DAY 2
Still in Lunenburg, descend to the waterfront, site of the

❻ ★★ kids **Fisheries Museum of the Atlantic.** One of the prov-ince's two best sea-related museums (see also the Maritime Museum of the Atlantic, in Halifax, below), this one focuses on the fish that gave (and still, to some extent, give) Nova Scotia its economic vitality. You learn about the life cycles of the major spe-cies of fish living in the North Atlantic waters here—but also the life cycles of local fishermen. In addition to good aquariums and exhibits, the museum's trump card is its collection of boats. ⏱ *1¼ hr. See p 97,* ❸.

The rebuilt St. John's Anglican Church is one of the most beautiful in Atlantic Canada.

The Bluenose II *in Lunenburg's harbor.*

In summer, docked on the waterfront, is the

7 ★ ***Bluenose II.*** During summer, on Lunenburg's harbor near
the Fisheries Museum, the popular
Bluenose II schooner is often tied
up. The schooner was built in 1963
from the same plans as the original
Bluenose, in the same shipyard. The
ship, now owned by the province,
sails throughout Canada and
beyond as a sort of seafaring
ambassador. Whenever it's in port
here, visitors can sign up for 2-hour
harbor sailings. *Note: The* Bluenose
*will be closed for restoration in the
2011 season.* ⏲ *2 hr. Lunenburg
waterfront.* ☎ *866/579-4909, ext.
234, or 902/634-4794, ext 234. http://
museum.gov.ns.ca/bluenose. Free
admission for viewing.*

Drive 11km (6¾ miles) north on
Rte. 3 to Mahone Bay. Along the
waterfront, facing the bay, stand

8 ★★ **The Three Churches.**
You may not find three churches
this beautifully arrayed together
anywhere else on the continent.
Take time to photograph St. James

Anglican, St. John's Lutheran, and
Trinity United from all available
angles. You can also take an official
tour of one of the churches, St.
James (the one closest to downtown). ⏲ *1 hr. See p 98,* **5***, p 99,*
6 *& p 99,* **7***.*

Also take time to walk along

9 ★★ **Mahone Bay's Main
Street.** A stroll through Mahone
Bay's pleasant downtown is a must
before departing for points north.
Look for arts and crafts shops, such
as **Amos Pewter** (589 Main St.;
☎ 902/624-9547 or 800/565-3369),
and culinary adventures, such as
**Jo-Ann's Deli Market & Bake
Shop** (9 Edgewater St.; ☎ 902/624-
6305). ⏲ *1 hr. See p 96.*

Continue 22km (14 miles) north
on Rte. 3 to

10 ★★ **Chester.** For New England–
style towns set in Canada, Chester
is as good as it gets. This compact,
former seafaring town now looks
like a Cape Cod summer retreat—
people are low-key, but don't be
fooled. A lot of money has passed
through this town. Today, it's full of
quiet attractions like the top-rate
Chester Playhouse (22 Pleasant
St.; ☎ 800/363-7529 or 902/275-
3933), a gentle harbor with good
views, and cafes and bakeries like
the **Kiwi Café** (19 Pleasant St;
☎ 902/275-1492) and **Julien's**
(43 Queen St.; ☎ 902/275-2324).
A perfect place to unwind. ⏲ *2 hr.
See p 96.*

3km (1¾ miles) north of Chester
on Rte. 3 is

11 **kids** **Graves Island Provincial Park.** This big, estate-like park
is one of the province's more ele-
gant-looking parks, as befits mon-
eyed Chester—views out to sea and
the spruce-clad islands of Mahone
Bay are splendid. It's also a campground, with 80-plus sites, many

dotting a high, grassy bluff. And there's a boat launch, swimming area, and playground for the kids. Good spot for a picnic break from the road. ⏲ *1 hr. Rte. 3, East Chester.* ☎ *902/275-4425. Free admission. Camping mid-May to early Sept.*

Continue 35km (22 miles) northeast on Rte. 3/103 to Tantallon; exit onto Rte. 333 (Peggy's Cove Rd.) & continue 25km (16 miles) to

⑫ ★★ **Peggy's Cove.** Considered by many to be the single most picturesque fishing village in Atlantic Canada, Peggy's Cove (population around 120) offers postcard-like views, an octagonal lighthouse, little fishing shacks, and fishing boats bobbing in a tiny harbor. In other words: Bring an extra memory stick for your camera. This bonsai-like perfection hasn't gone unnoticed by the tour operators, though, so in summer, it's invariably crowded with other day-trippers and their buses, vans, and cars. The village is also home to a handful of B&Bs; the **Jo Beale Gallery** (154 Peggy's Point Rd.; ☎ 902/823-1960); and a simple seafood restaurant, the **Sou'Wester** (178 Peggy's Point Rd.; ☎ 902/823-2561). ⏲ *1½ hr. Peggy's Cove Rd. (Rte. 333).*

DAY 3
Continue 55km (34 miles) east on Rte. 333 & Rte. 3 to return to Halifax.

⑬ ★★ **The Citadel.** An historic fort, with a view of Halifax's waterfront, old battlements, costumed interpreters, and big green lawns. This is the first stop in town for history-lovers or those wanting an overview on the city. ⏲ *1 hr. See p 55,* ⑩.

Travel 6 blocks downhill to Barrington St. From either Prince or Duke sts., turn onto Hollis St. Mid-block is

⑭ ★★ **Province House.** Halifax is the capital of the province of Nova Scotia, and Province House is the seat of government—where provincial laws are hashed out in Parliamentary chambers. Take a tour and learn the fun stories about the building's history and architecture, then watch the provincial legislature in action if they're in session during your visit. ⏲ *30 min. See p 53,* ⑥.

Directly across the street from Province House is the fine

⑮ ★★ **Art Gallery of Nova Scotia.** The province's major museum of visual arts is filled with provincial and Canadian work, and it conceals a

The octagonal lighthouse at scenic Peggy's Cove.

Halifax's Public Gardens feel like a little piece of London.

wonderful little cafe for snacking (see p 52, ④). ⏱ 1¼ hr. See p 53, **5**.

Return to Barrington St. & turn left. Continue to

16 ★ Spring Garden Road. This is arguably the city's prime shopping and eating spot, despite the more obvious draw of the waterfront area. En route, you'll pass several shopping malls, restaurants galore, coffee shops, and outdoor art vendors and buskers. ⏱ 1 hr. See p 56.

Near the foot of Spring Garden Rd. is

17 ★ St. Mary's Cathedral Basilica. The city's most impressive church is this massive, 19th-century edifice featuring solid doors, stained-glass work, and a spire that's one of the tallest in Eastern Canada. Architecture, history, and religion buffs: Take time to savor it, as most of the rest of Nova Scotia's churches are of the country-plain variety. ⏱ 45 min. See p 57, ②.

At the top of Spring Garden Rd. are the

18 ★ Public Gardens. Genteel Haligonians love to congregate in these quiet gardens, created in the mid-18th century and gradually improved. They really do feel like a little piece of London. The Sunday bandstand concerts help create atmosphere, too. ⏱ 1 hr. See p 59, ⑦.

Descend back down Spring Garden Rd. & continue all the way to the waterfront. Turn right & walk along Water St. until you reach

19 ★ The Brewery Market. Originally a brewery (obviously), Halifax's primary public market consists of a series of spaces, warehouses, and a courtyard filled with fine dining, drinking, and shopping. The famous **daMaurizio** restaurant (☎ 902/423-0859; www.damaurizio.ca) is here, as is a good crepe shop, **La Centrale** (☎ 902/981-4010). ⏱ 1½ hr. See p 51, ①.

Walk or drive 2.5km (1½ miles) south along Lower Water St., which becomes Marginal Rd., past the train station & into

20 ★★ Point Pleasant Park. Almost 80 hectares (200 acres) of parklands, with lovely paths, water views, al fresco theater performances, and the remains of colonial battle towers? Check. Often overlooked by tourists intent on exploring only downtown's sights, this park is well worth a detour. ⏱ 1¼ hr. See p 61, ④.

The Best in 1 Week

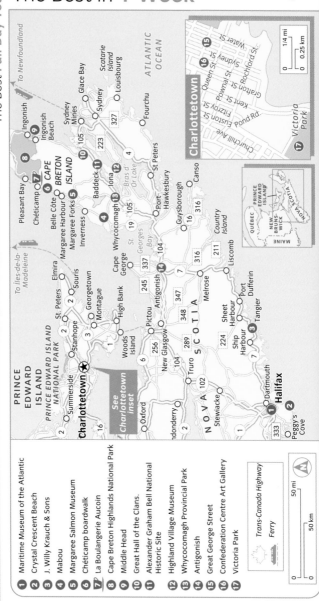

1 Maritime Museum of the Atlantic
2 Crystal Crescent Beach
3 J. Willy Krauch & Sons
4 Mabou
5 Margaree Salmon Museum
6 Chéticamp boardwalk
7 La Boulangerie Aucoin
8 Cape Breton Highlands National Park
9 Middle Head
10 Great Hall of the Clans.
11 Alexander Graham Bell National Historic Site
12 Highland Village Museum
13 Whycocomagh Provincial Park
14 Antigonish
15 Great George Street
16 Confederation Centre Art Gallery
17 Victoria Park

Trans-Canada Highway
Ferry

0   50 mi
0   50 km

A week is probably the minimum time you need to attack Atlantic Canada. This tour takes you from Halifax along Nova Scotia's wild, empty eastern shore to stunning Cape Breton Island, which we'll explore in depth for several days. Then we'll head west to touch upon another, much gentler island—Prince Edward Island. Begin this 1-week tour by first following my "Best in 3 Days" tour, described on p 12. START: **Halifax.**

DAY 4

❶ ★★★ kids Maritime Museum of the Atlantic. This is one of the great museums in Eastern Canada—testifying to Halifax's and Nova Scotia's seafaring origins and history. The exhibits here are involving and well executed, and there's even a smidge of sadness—there's information about (and artifacts from) the *Titanic* shipwreck and rescue. ⏱ 1½ hr. See p 51, **❷**.

Exit Halifax via Rte. 3 (Quinpool Rd.). Turn left onto Rte. 349 & then left again onto Rte. 306. Continue south for 20 min. At West Pennant Rd., turn right & enter

❷ ★ kids Crystal Crescent Beach. If your idea of a vacation includes swimming, beachcombing, and possibly seeing whales or dolphins in a cove, Crystal Crescent is the best place to do that in the Halifax region. It's down a long peninsula, about a half-hour south of the city. The park offers clean sand, trails, and views, but there are no snacks, facilities, or lifeguards. ⏱ 45 min. 223 Sambro Creek Rd., Sambro Creek. No phone. http:// parks.gov.ns.ca. Free admission. Mid-May to mid-Oct dawn–dusk.

Backtrack to Halifax. At the Quinpool rotary, follow Joseph Hyde Rd. to Rte. 111 (cross the bridge) to Dartmouth, which merges with Rte. 7 East. Continue on Rte. 7 80km (50 miles) to Tangier &

❸ ★ J. Willy Krauch & Sons. Often called the best fish-smoking outfit in Eastern Canada, Krauch's (pronounced "craw," not "crotch") sells its own home-smoked Atlantic salmon, mackerel, and eel in an unpretentious little store by the side of the road. (Willy was a Dane, by the way.) They'll also give you a tour of the premises, if you like, where you can check out the old-style smoking process in action. Take some to go for a picnic. ⏱ 30 min. 35 Old Mooseland Rd. (at Rte. 7), Tangier. ☎ 800/758-4412 or 902/772-2188. Daily 9am–6pm.

Travel 170km (106 miles) on Rte. 7. Turn right onto Rte. 104 East & go 50km (31 miles) to Cape Breton; cross the bridge. Immediately turn left on Rte. 19 (Ceilidh Trail) & continue 55km (34 miles) to

At J. Willy Krauch & Sons you can take a tour of the facility and take home some excellent smoked fish.

The scenic boardwalk in the Acadian town of Chéticamp.

④ ★★ **Mabou.** As Cape Breton villages go, they don't get much smaller, cuter, or more musical than this one. Mabou is a wonderful stop or overnight for some fiddle music and a pint of ale at **The Red Shoe** (11573 Hwy. 19; ☎ 902/945-2996), a bite to eat at a place such as **The Mull** (11630 Hwy. 19; ☎ 902/945-2244), or a scenic stroll on Mabou's resident beach (turn onto Little Mabou Rd. at the south end of the town bridge and drive 8km/5 miles). ⏲ *2–3 hr. See p 101,* ❶.

Overnight in Mabou, Glenville, or the Margarees.

DAY 5
Travel 50km (31 miles) north on Rte. 19 to Margaree Forks. Turn right onto the Cabot Trail & immediately left onto East Margaree Rd. to find the

⑤ ★ **Margaree Salmon Museum.** A museum dedicated to a fish? Hey, on Cape Breton Island, it works. That's because fly-fishing is one of the favored pastimes of travelers and locals alike in these parts, particularly on the little Margaree River. You'll see art, exhibits on ecology, and plenty of famous fly rods and ties. Not for everyone, but great for those *A River Runs Through It* types. ⏲ *45 min. See p 102,* ❸.

Return to the Cabot Trail & turn right (north), then travel 30km (19 miles) to the

⑥ **Chéticamp boardwalk.** The Acadian town of Chéticamp's boardwalk follows the working harbor's edge through much of the downtown, and it's a good spot to stretch out your legs before attacking the two most dramatic, switch-backing sections of the national park. Chéticamp Island sits just across the water, while the mighty coastal hills of the national park peek above the horizon just up the coast. ⏲ *15 min.*

⑦ **La Boulangerie Aucoin.** This small-town bakery has been a staple of Chéticamp life since the 1950s. Just off the Cabot Trail between the town and the national park (look for signs), the place is full of fresh-baked goods; ask what's out of the oven when you get to the counter. Among the potential options: croissants, scones, fresh bread, and (yum) berry pies. This is a great place to fuel up on snacks before setting off into the park. *14 Chemin Lapointe (just off Main St.), Chéticamp.* ☎ *902/224-3220. $.*

Continue 120km (75 miles) along the scenic Cabot Trail through

8 ★★★ **Cape Breton Highlands National Park.** The granddaddy of all parks in the provinces covered in this book is surely Cape Breton, which features awe-inspiring sea views from atop rugged cliff tops; hikes short and long, easy and difficult; and postcard-like vistas at many points along the way. (Thankfully, there are a number of turnouts en route.) For a much more detailed tour of the park area, see p 100. ⏱ *4–5 hr.* ☎ *902/224-2306. www. pc.gc.ca. Entry C$7.80 adults, C$6.80 seniors, C$3.90 children, C$20 families. Park July & Aug daily 8am–8pm; mid-May to June & Sept to mid-Oct daily 9am–5pm; Mid-Oct to mid-May park offices Mon–Fri 8am–4pm, info center closed.*

Cape Breton Highlands National Park is home to many hikes with outstanding views.

1.6km (1 mile) past Ingonish Centre, turn left on Keltic Inn Rd. at signs for Keltic Lodge. Park at the lodge & hike out to

9 ★★ kids **Middle Head.** This stony peninsula sticks a few miles out into the sea, giving you one last shot at glory—or, rather, at views and photographs of those famous Cape Breton highlands you've just driven up, over, and through. ⏱ *1–2 hr. See p 169.*

Overnight in the Ingonishes.

DAY 6

Travel 75km (47 miles) south on the Cabot Trail (turning right at Celtic Tea Room to stay on it) to St. Anns. Just before Rte. 105 (the Trans-Canada Hwy.), on the left, is the

10 ★ **Great Hall of the Clans.** At this good museum inside a low-slung, brown building, visitors get a lesson in Scottish culture via interactive displays. Exhibits provide answers to burning questions like "why plaid?" and "what do Scotsmen wear under a kilt?" Even better, one of Scot poet Bobby Burns's (1759–1796) walking sticks is on display here. Buy a clan history if you've got Scottish blood running through your veins. There's a fiddle display and sometimes even live music. ⏱ *45 min. C$7 adults, C$5.50 children, C$20 families. June–Sept Mon–Fri 9am–5pm.*

Continue 1.1km (¾ mile) to Rte. 105; turn right. Travel 19km (12 miles) south to Baddeck & the

11 ★★ kids **Alexander Graham Bell National Historic Site.** The inventor Bell's family may have been Scottish, but he spent many summers at this mansion just north of lakeside Baddeck and its little main street. Today, it's a museum that serves as a memorial to the man and

The Great Hall of the Clans gives visitors lessons in Scottish culture.

his genius, while imparting some information about the science and natural history with which Bell was so fascinated. ⏱ *1½ hr. See p 108,* ❶.

Continue south on Rte. 105 for 27km (17 miles) to Rte. 223. Turn left & continue 25km (16 miles) south to

⓬ ★ kids **Highland Village Museum.** A "village" occupying a lovely panoramic post just outside Iona, this museum purports to recreate life from colonial times in the highlands of Nova Scotia—though it sometimes feels like Scotland, instead. Buildings are a mix of the restored and the recreated. ⏱ *1 hr. See p 109,* ❺.

Backtrack north & west along Rte. 223 for 25km (16 miles) south to Rte. 205. Turn left & continue about 7km (4¼ miles) to

⓭ ★★ kids **Whycocomagh Provincial Park.** This tucked-out-of-the-way park isn't far at all from

Baddeck, and it's the perfect place to get an eagle's eye view—literally—of big Lake Bras D'Or. As for the eagles? They live here, too, and you might see 'em. ⏱ *1 hr. See p 109,* ❹.

Travel west about 50km (31 miles) on Rte. 105 (the Trans-Canada Hwy.) to the Cape Breton Bridge. Cross & travel 50km (31 miles) on Rte. 104 to exit 34. Exit & drive into

⓮ **Antigonish.** This town (ahn-TIG-oh-nish) can trace its European roots back to the 1650s (the French came first; the British later), and today it's still the local market town, with a bustling main street thanks mainly to attractive **St. Francis Xavier University** (☎ 902/863-3300), which occupies a chunk of the downtown off West, James, Church, and St. Niman streets. Stroll around it for a bit. The town is also a good spot in which to grab a bite in one of the several cafes lining Main Street, such as **Sunshine on Main** (332 Main St.; ☎ 902/863-5851). ⏱ *30 min. Rte. 4/337 (at Rte. 104).*

The Highland Games

If you're in Antigonish in mid-July, check out the 3-day Highland Games, staged here annually since 1861—the oldest continuously played Highland games in North America. You'll see everything from piping and dancing to feats of strength and dexterity like "tossing the caber" (a heavy pole tossed for accuracy, not distance). Contact the Antigonish Highland Society for details and tickets; expect kilts aplenty. ☎ *902/863-4275; www.antigonishhighland games.ca. Tickets C$5-C$15 per day or C$50 for entire event.*

DAY 7

Continue west on Rte. 104 60km (37 miles) to exit 22 (Pictou). Exit & follow Rte. 106 for 12km (7½ miles) to the Wood Island ferry (www.peiferry.com). Take the ferry (1¼ hr., C$63/car plus C$16/person; C$14 seniors, kids under 12 free). Drive off the boat onto Rte. 1 & travel 60km (37 miles) northwest into Charlottetown. Park by the waterfront & stroll up

⑮ ★★ **Great George Street.** It's only 4½ blocks long, yet this is one of the best-looking streets in all of Eastern Canada. Stroll beneath big shady trees, alongside

handsome Georgian townhouses, and past more churches than you ever thought you'd find in one city, including two-towered **St. Dunstan's Basilica** (45 Great George St.; ☎ 902/894-3486). One of the city's premier inns, **The Great George** (58 Great George St; see p 144), is also here. ⏱ *15 min. See p 121,* ❸.

Ascend Great George St. 5 blocks to the top, where you'll find the Confederation Centre of the Arts. Inside is the

⑯ ★★ **Confederation Centre Art Gallery.** A terrific, modern art museum, housed inside an unfortunate block of a structure. But the art is terrific. There are even sketching classes for the little ones. ⏱ *1 hr. See p 123,* ❽.

From the gallery, walk west along Richmond St. 4 blocks to the edge of

⑰ ★★ **Victoria Park.** Our 1-week tour concludes at this quiet, lovely city park with water views, which also happens to be surrounded by historic structures, including **Beaconsfield** (2 Kent St.; ☎ 902/368-6603) and **Government House** (1 Government Dr.; ☎ 902/368-5480). Allow time for strolling, picnicking, boat-watching, and ice cream eating, as well as the history. ⏱ *1–2 hr. See p 125,* ⑯.

The Confederation Centre Art Gallery displays excellent modern works.

The Best in 2 Weeks

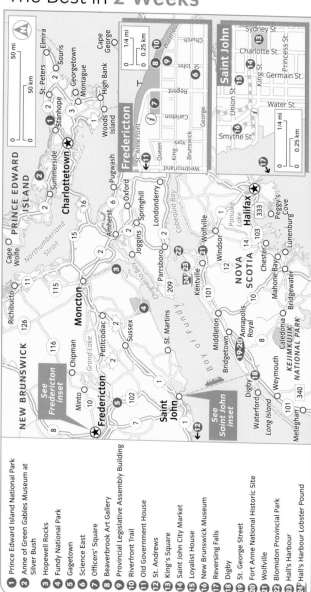

Two weeks is a more reasonable amount of time for a trip that covers the region fully. This tour continues a sort of "great circle" around the Bay of Fundy (with its whales, high tides, and many other natural wonders) to Prince Edward Island's beaches and golf courses, then south through New Brunswick, where there's plenty of great dining, good museums, and more water views. We conclude in the Annapolis Valley, one of the continent's most historic regions—and a great place to eat an apple or a lobster, too. START: **Charlottetown.**

The Anne of Green Gables Museum at Silver Bush is where author Lucy Maud Montgomery was married.

DAY 8

From Charlottetown, drive northeast 14km (8¾ miles) on Rte. 2 to Rte. 6. Turn left & travel 10km (6¼ miles) north into

1 ★★★ **kids** **Prince Edward Island National Park.** PEI's national park occupies two beachfront sections along the island's northern shore. It's the perfect family holiday, or for the person or couple intent on nothing more stressful than reading books, riding bikes, and combing beaches. Highlights include the **Greenwich Intepretation Centre** (☎ 902/961-2514 or 902/672-6350); the dunes and boardwalks at **Greenwich Beach; Brackley**

Beach; and the beach at **Cavendish East,** which is near many of the "Anne of Green Gables" attractions. You will need a park pass to enter (see p 129). ⏱ *4–5 hr. See p 34,* **4**.

Follow Rte. 6 west through the national park to Rte. 20 and the town of New London. Turn right at the intersection of Rtes. 6 and 20 & continue 10km (6¼ miles) to the

2 ★★ **kids** **Anne of Green Gables Museum at Silver Bush.** There are plenty of sights with legitimate and tenuous connections to author Lucy Maud Montgomery (1874–1942) and her character Anne. This is one of the few worth a visit: a simple home that belonged to

At Fundy National Park you can witness the world's highest daily tides.

Montgomery's relatives. She loved it so much, she got married here—and there's memorabilia to prove it. The grounds are attractive. 🕐 *1 hr. See p 131,* **16**.

DAY 9

From Cavendish, follow Rte. 13 about 40km (25 miles) to Rte. 1. Cross the PEI Bridge (which becomes Rte. 16) & continue 80km (50 miles) to Rte. 2 (Trans-Canada Hwy.); turn right & travel west 45km (28 miles) to Moncton. Take exit 467A & follow Rte. 15 downtown. Exit the large traffic circle at Main St. & continue along Rte. 106 to the next traffic circle; exit onto Rte. 114 & continue 30km (19 miles) to

3 ★★ **Hopewell Rocks.** A stranger sight you'll rarely see: rocks that look like Easter Island statues, later mostly submerged by huge sea tides. The fact that you can reach out and hug these rocks makes it all the more mystical an experience. 🕐 *2½ hr. See p 153,* **3**.

Continue 45km (28 miles) south on Rte. 114 into Alma & then into

4 ★★ **Fundy National Park.** Any trip to the Maritime provinces must include a stop in Fundy, where the attractions include (but aren't limited to) the world's highest daily tides. There's also plenty of hiking, biking, or kayaking (with **FreshAir Adventure;** ☎ 800/545-0020 or 506/887-2249), ranger-led beach walks for everyone, and 1-hour nature walks for kids 6 to 12. I recommend walking either the **Caribou Plain Trail**, a 3km (1.9-mile) loop past a beaver pond, over a raised peat bog (via boardwalk), and through a lovely forest; or **Third Vault Falls Trail**, a 9km (5.6-mile) hike into the park's highest waterfall. Read the visitor's guide closely when you pay the entry fee at the gate—it's full of more information and suggestions. 🕐 *4–5 hr. See p 152,* **1**.

DAY 10

From Alma, travel 40km (25 miles) west to Rte. 1. Turn south & travel for 16km (10 miles) before exiting onto Rte. 10; follow it 45km (28 miles) to Youngs Cove. Bear left on Rte. 105 & continue 15km (9¼ miles) to Rte. 2. Take exit 330 & follow Rte. 102 for 10km (6¼ miles) to

5 ★★ **Gagetown.** Often called one of the prettiest villages in Canada, Gagetown has somehow remained mostly unchanged through the years. It's still backed by farm fields and cozied up to by Gagetown Creek. The peaceful surroundings and simple country architecture here have attracted art galleries, the **GAS Station crafts cooperative** (17 Mill Rd.), potters such as **Greig Pottery** (36 Front St.; ☎ 506/488-2074), and souvenir shops such as **Village Boatique** (50 Front St.; ☎ 506/488-6006), among other businesses. ⏱ *2 hr. Rte. 102.*

Return to Rte. 2 & continue 35km (22 miles) to Fredericton &

6 ★★ Kids Science East. One of the best science museums in Canada, even if it's located inside a jail. (A *former* jail, that is.) Ignore the creepy implications and dive in with the little ones; this is a great hands-on experience. ⏱ *1¼ hr. See p 35,* **7**.

Walk 2 blocks to Queen St. Turn left and continue 3 blocks to

7 ★ Officers' Square. This open square was once used by the Brits to practice formations, but now it's the nearest thing Fredericton has to an open theater. The human kind. Everybody—tourists, locals, mutts,

The pretty village of Gagetown has attracted many art galleries and craft studios.

guys in costumes—show up here to congregate, entertain, and people-watch. ⏱ *15 min. See p 155,* **2**.

Follow Queen St. south to the

8 ★★ Beaverbrook Art Gallery. A fantastic little provincial art museum by the river, and it even holds a Dalí. It's also one of the best places in Atlantic Canada to see native Canadian-produced works of art in a museum setting. ⏱ *1½ hr. See p 156,* **6**.

Directly across Queen St. is the

9 ★ Provincial Legislative Assembly Building. The business of New Brunswick is carried out within these halls, in a stunning architectural space. Look for the picture of Queen Elizabeth—she was a *lot* younger when they painted it. ⏱ *45 min. See p 157,* **7**.

Overnight in Fredericton.

DAY 11
In the morning, walk to the Saint John River's edge (it nearly encircles the downtown) & hike the

10 ★ Riverfront Trail. A good morning workout is a walk along Fredericton's walking path trail, a 5km (3.1-mile) system that clings to the river bank. ⏱ *45 min. See p 156,* **5**.

Walk west on the Riverfront Trail to its terminus. Or, by car, follow King St. all the way west to where it becomes Woodstock Rd. This is the

11 ★ Old Government House. Built in 1828 as the official residence of governors and lieutenant governors of the province, the Old Government House features a Palladian symmetry and intricate plasterwork. Bilingual tours begin in a basement interpretive center; you climb sweeping staircases and view extraordinarily high-ceilinged

St. Andrews' blockhouse is just one of the historic elements in this pretty town.

reception rooms. There's a little art gallery on the second floor, and the rooms are full of intriguing period pieces and fixtures. ⏱ *1 hr. 51 Woodstock Rd.* ☎ *506/453-2505. www.gnb.ca/lg/ogh. Free admission. Tours mid-May to Aug Mon–Sat 10am–4pm & Sun noon–4pm; no tours Sept to mid-May, but occasionally open for public events.*

Follow Rte. 2 (Trans-Canada Hwy.) west out of the city 20km (12 miles) to Rte. 3. Exit & continue 65km (40 miles) south to Lawrence Station. Bear left onto Rte. 127 & continue 40km (25 miles) to

⑫ ★★ **St. Andrews.** Little St. Andrews is one of the best little towns in Eastern Canada. Why? It might be the sea breezes and views, the laid-back pace along Water Street (tall ships and whale-watching boats included), or the lovely **Algonquin Golf Course** (☎ 506/529-8165). There's also a mix of simple and gourmet restaurants such as **Europa** (48 King St.; ☎ 506/529-3818), the attractive **Kingsbrae Gardens** (220 King St.; ☎ 866/566-8687 or 506/529-3335), the historic **blockhouse** (Joe's Point Rd.; ☎ 506/529-4270), and top-notch inns and resorts such as the **Algonquin** (184 Adolphus St.; ☎ 800/441-1414 or 506/529-8823). ⏱ *3 hr. See p 158.*

DAY 12

Drive north 10km (6¼ miles) on Rte. 127 to Rte. 1. Turn east & continue 85km (53 miles) to downtown Saint John &

⑬ ★ **King's Square.** The center of Saint John is this handsome square, which became a formal, planned park (as opposed to a drill area and grazing area) in the 1800s. It's British through and through, from its shape (try to guess) to the statuary, and even, perhaps, the landscaping. ⏱ *45 min. See p 149,* ❶.

Just off the square, on Charlotte St., is the

⑭ ★★ **Saint John City Market.** When you're hungering for a bite, or a little gift or souvenir to take home, there's no better place on the Bay of Fundy to do it than at Saint John's market building, which was constructed in the late 19th century. Not only is it appropriately London-looking; vendors hawk everything from fresh meat and cheese to coffee and flowers inside. ⏱ *1½ hr. See p 150,* ❺.

Continue 1 block on Charlotte St. to Union St. Turn left & continue 2 blocks to

⑮ ★ **Loyalist House.** Once a private home, this is now Saint John's most historic edifice—look for original furniture, as well as classic architectural touches (hand-shaped wooden staircase rails, for instance) that you'll probably never see incorporated into new homes in this lifetime. 🕐 *45 min. See p 150, ⑥*.

Walk 2 blocks south on Germain St.; turn right on King St. & continue 3 blocks to the

⑯ ★ kids New Brunswick Museum.

This museum really delivers a convincing sense that oft-overlooked New Brunswick is actually a happening place—geologically and ecologically speaking, at least. You get to experience a little bit of the fisherman's and sea captain's life, and learn about the fascinating natural history, geology, and biology of this province. 🕐 *1 hr. See p 150, ⑦*.

From downtown Saint John, follow Main St. west to Douglas Ave.; turn onto Douglas & merge onto Rte. 100. In about 1.6km (1 mile), turn right on Fallsview Avenue into

⑰ kids Reversing Falls.

Just west of Saint John's are the Reversing Falls, which reverse themselves several times a day in a deep gorge as huge local tides surge inland and run smack into the Saint John River. Big, slurping whirlpools sometimes form, reverse, and disappear. View them from aptly named Fallsview Park. 🕐 *1 hr. Fallsview Ave. (off Rte. 100), Saint John.* ☎ *506/658-2937. Free admission. Daily dawn–dusk (best at low or high tide); call for tide schedule.*

DAY 13
From the Saint John ferry docks at the foot of Lancaster St., catch a ferry (3 hr.; summer one-way fares C$40 adult, C$30 senior, C$25 kids 6 to 13, C$5 child under 6, C$100 and up per vehicle, off-season cheaper) to

⑱ ★ Digby.

A working-class town with a ton of history and great scallops, Digby makes a fine off-the-boat stop. Stroll the town's bayside boardwalk, snap photos, or check out **the Digby Anglican Church** (109 Queen St.; ☎ 902/245-6744) and the **Digby County Courthouse** (119 Queen St.). 🕐 *2½ hr. See p 90.*

Follow Rte. 303 a few miles south to Rte. 1. Turn north onto Rte. 1 & travel north about 30km (19 miles) into Annapolis Royal. Park & stroll along

⑲ ★★★ St. George Street.

This street can legitimately lay a claim to being the oldest colonial street in Canada: The French first set up shop here in 1605. Less than a mile long, it packs a historic punch. Visit buildings such as the graceful, whitewashed **St. Luke's Anglican Church** (342 St. George St.; ☎ 902/532-0913); the barn-red **Sinclair Inn** (230 St. George St.; ☎ 902/532-0996), now a museum; and the sturdy **Annapolis Royal Courthouse** (377 St. George St.; 902/245-4567). 🕐 *2 hr. See p 89, ⑤*.

Fallsview Park is the best place to take in the Reversing Falls.

Also on St. George St. is the

20 ★ kids **Fort Anne National Historic Site.** The French constructed 17th-century fortifications here, and then the British did; today, kids do. Pretend you're a gunner on the wall, or just look over old mementoes. The downtown district is just steps away. ⏱ *1 hr. See p 88,* **4**.

DAY 14

Continue north on Rte. 1 about 25km (16 miles) to Rte. 101. Merge with Rte. 101 & continue 80km (50 miles) north to

21 ★★ **Wolfville.** This handsome village has a New England feel to it, both in its architecture and its compact layout. So it's not surprising to learn the town was settled by transplanted New Englanders (who forced off the original Acadian settlers, it should be added). Visit the campus of **Acadia University** (University Ave.; ☎ 902/542-2201 or 902/585-2200), which maintains both an excellent system of walking trails and the pleasing little **Acadia University Art Gallery** (10 Highland Ave.; ☎ 902/585-1373). ⏱ *1½ hr. See p 87.*

Travel 5km (3 miles) west on Rte. 1 to Rte. 358. Turn right (north) & go 12km (7½ miles) to Canning; turn left onto Pereau Road & continue 16km (10 miles) to

22 ★★ **Blomidon Provincial Park.** Miles of trails in this provincial park take you through forests to the coast; the 6km (3.7-mile) **Jodrey Trail** is the star, following towering cliff tops with stunning views over the Minas Basin. (Keep back from the cliff edges.) But travelers short of time can also simply drive to viewpoints along the ridge and to a picnic area on the park's scenic beach, instead. ⏱ *1 hr. Pereaux Rd.,*

The secret cove of Hall's Harbour is a great place to enjoy a lobster supper.

Blomidon. ☎ *902/582-7319. Free admission. Mid-May to early Sept.*

Backtrack 7km (4¼ miles) to Stewart Mountain Green Bridge Rd. Turn right. Go 3km (1¾ miles), then turn left onto Rte. 358. Travel 5km (3 miles), bear right (uphill) on Gospel Woods Rd. & travel 13km (8 miles) to the end. Turn right on Rte. 358 & go 5km (3 miles) to

23 ★★ **Hall's Harbour.** Well out of the way yet incredibly scenic, Hall's Harbour is the secret Canadian cove you dream about. When the tide comes in, you actually *see* it rising inch by inch up the piers: amazing. Walk the harbor and catch a sunset, which can be spectacular under the right conditions. The drive down to this sliver of coast also runs through pleasant green fields, farms, and woods. ⏱ *1½ hr. Rte. 359.*

★ **24** **Hall's Harbour Lobster Pound.** Lobster picked out by the traveler, steamed in a cook-shack, and served by the docks? I'm in. An attached family restaurant serves fried fish, pasta, and burgers. *1157 W. Hall's Harbour Rd.* ☎ *902/679-5299. $$$.*

Backtrack 15km (9¼ miles) to Rte. 1 & Rte. 101, then turn east. Follow Rte. 101 East 95km (59 miles) into Halifax. ●

Atlantic Canada for Families

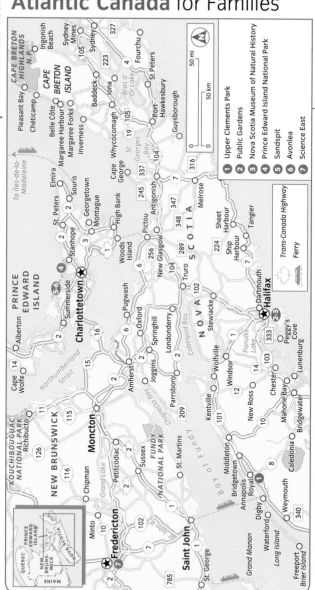

1 Upper Clements Park
2 Public Gardens
3 Nova Scotia Museum of Natural History
4 Prince Edward Island National Park
5 Sandspit
6 Avonlea
7 Science East

Trans-Canada Highway
Ferry

Previous page: Avonlea recreates a village from the time of the Anne of Green Gables stories.

The Maritime provinces are a great place for a family vacation. The summer weather is (usually) temperate; there's little to no crime; and you'll rarely encounter crowds, lines, or traffic jams—except, perhaps, in the highest summer season. I've divided this tour up into regions of Eastern Canada—but it takes time to travel from region to region. If I had to pick just *one* province to visit with kids, I'd choose Prince Edward Island. START: **Upper Clements (8km/5 miles south of Annapolis Royal).**

Day 1

❶ **Upper Clements Park.** Just 5 minutes south of Annapolis Royal on Route 1 (the local road, not the expressway) is this old-fashioned amusement park full of low-key attractions for young kids. Highlights include a flume ride (originally built for Expo '86 in Vancouver) and a wooden roller coaster that twists and winds through treetops. Corny? Yep. Kid-friendly? Definitely. 🕐 *1 hr. Rte. 1, Upper Clements.* ☎ *888/248-4567 or 902/532-7557. www.upperclementsparks.com. Admission C$9 adults, free for children under 2; C$3.50 single rides. Spring–fall daily 11am–7pm.*

Drive 8km (5 miles) north to Annapolis Royal; turn east on Rte. 8 & continue to Rte. 101. Drive 180km (112 miles) northeast into Halifax & the

❷ ★ **Public Gardens.** Halifax's primmest, most Victorian park (thanks to its orderly flower beds, carefully kept pond, gazebo, and august Lord Nelson hotel standing beside it) also turns out to be a great place to take the kids. Each Tuesday and Thursday morning from spring through fall, there's storytelling for children in the park's **Horticultural Hall.** (Toys and puzzles are also available for the more restless kids who don't want to listen to the stories.) Afterward, push that baby buggy around the park, enjoying the wildlife, impromptu and scheduled music concerts, and cultivated grounds if the weather's nice enough. 🕐 *1½ hr. South Park St. (at Spring Garden Rd.), Halifax.* ☎ *902/423-9865. www.halifaxpublicgardens.ca. Free admission. Park year-round daily dawn–dusk; stories spring–fall Tues & Thurs 10:30am.*

From the southern border of the park (Spring Garden Rd.), drive west along Spring Garden Rd. for

The roller coaster at Upper Clements Park winds through treetops.

The Nova Scotia Museum of Natural History has lots of hands-on exhibits for kids.

10 blocks (becomes Coburg Rd.) until you reach the

❸ Nova Scotia Museum of Natural History.
Kids love science, right? Most of 'em do, anyway, and the province's premier science museum—founded in 1868—has undergone several upgrades and expansions to freshen its exhibits and reflect present-day science interests more closely. The little ones can view working beehives, a wise old tortoise named Gus (you'll be surprised just how old he is), whale bones, tide-pool creatures, an eagle's nest, Micmac relics, and more. ⏱ 1½ hr. 1747 Summer St., Halifax. ☎ 902/424-7353. http://museum.gov.ns.ca/mnhnew. Admission C$5.75 adults, C$3.75 children 6–17, free for children 5 & under,

C$12–C$17 families. Tues & Thurs–Sat 9am–5pm, Wed 9am–8pm, Sun noon–5pm. Closed Mon.

Overnight in Halifax.

Day 2
Follow Rte. 102 north out of Halifax 70km (44 miles) to Rte. 104; turn west on Rte. 104 & travel 100km (62 miles) to Rte. 16; exit & follow Rte. 16 for 110km (68 miles) across the PEI Bridge into Charlottetown, then take Rte. 2 for 50km (31 miles) to reach

❹ ★★★ Prince Edward Island National Park.
Long, clean, sandy beaches; lovely sunsets; great cottages and campgrounds; friendly locals; and a lost-in-time feeling—PEI's national park is hands-down the best place in Eastern Canada to take a carload of kids. I cover this park in much more detail in chapter 6. Stop first at the modern Greenwich Interpretation Centre (p 133, ❸). ⏱ 1–2 days. ☎ 902/961-2514 (June–Sept) or 902/672-6350 (Oct–May). Admission July–Sept C$7.80 adults, C$6.80 seniors, C$3.90 children 6–16, C$20 families; June 50% discount; Oct–May free. Multiday passes available. Park open year-round.

Overnight in the Cavendish or Brackley areas, near the beach.

Day 3
On Rte. 6, between Cavendish's boardwalk & its tourist office (just

Sandspit has go-karts and lots of other rides.

Science East has more than 150 interactive displays.

west of the big Rte. 6/13 intersection), is

5 Sandspit. This is a good spot to take the kids *if* you don't mind amusement parks. We're talking go-karts, a big Ferris wheel, a roller coaster, bumper cars, and games of chance. There's no admission charge; pay as you go. 🕐 *1½ hr. 8986 Cavendish Rd. (Rte. 6), Cavendish Beach.* ☎ *902/963-2626. www. sandspit.com. Rides C$3–C$5 each; all-inclusive bracelet C$12–C$22 adults, according to height. Late June–early Sept, daily 10am–11pm; mid to late June, daily 9am–3:30pm. Closed early Sept to mid June.*

Continue 1.6km (1 mile) west on Rte. 6. On the left is the entrance to

6 Avonlea. This historic park is a bit pricey and kitschy. (It's supposed to recreate a village from Anne's time, but the real Cavendish never has had a main street.) It's a legitimate stop, though, for kids or adults with a deep interest in the *Anne of Green Gables* tale. The property includes a one-room schoolhouse Lucy Maud Montgomery (1874–1942) taught in and a church she attended, among other buildings. There's also a campy musical, hayrides, and staff in slightly ridiculous period costumes. 🕐 *1 hr. 8779 Rte. 6, Cavendish.* ☎ *902/963-3050.*

www.avonlea.ca. Admission mid-June to Aug C$19 adults, C$17 seniors, C$15 children, C$65 families; Sept C$10 adults. Mid June to Aug, daily 10am–5pm, early to mid Sept daily 10am–4pm. Closed mid Sept to mid June.

From Cavendish, follow Rte. 13 about 40km (25 miles) to Rte. 1. Cross the PEI Bridge (Rte. 1 becomes Rte. 16) & continue 80km (50 miles) to merge with Rte. 2 (Trans-Canada Hwy.). Travel west 170km (106 miles) to exit 333; exit & continue 45km (28 miles) to Fredericton &

7 ★★ Science East. The inside of this science center is much more exciting than the plain exterior. It's located inside an old stone jail built in the 1840s, but it's quite modern within. Kids can fool around with more than 150 interactive displays, including a huge kaleidoscope, a periscope for people-watching, a solar-powered water fountain, and a laser beam that draws. The "dungeon museum" will also probably catch many kids' fancy. 🕐 *1½ hr. 668 Brunswick St., Fredericton.* ☎ *506/457-2340. www.scienceeast.nb.ca. Admission C$8 adults, C$7 seniors, C$5 children under 16, C$22 families. June–Aug Mon–Sat 10am–5pm, Sun noon–4pm; Sept–May Mon–Fri noon–5pm, Sat 10am–5pm, closed Sun.*

Atlantic Canada for Golfers

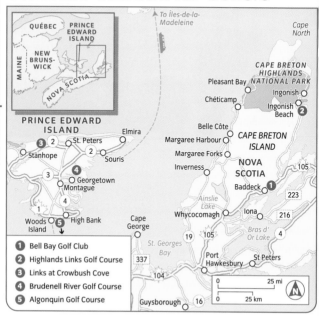

1 Bell Bay Golf Club
2 Highlands Links Golf Course
3 Links at Crowbush Cove
4 Brudenell River Golf Course
5 Algonquin Golf Course

Eastern Canada offers some of the best golfing in the country: If you're serious about big views and professionally landscaped, links-style courses, don't miss them. All are open roughly May to October. If you can't get a tee time, don't despair: Many of the eastern provinces' *public* golf courses are spectacular, too, and cost a fraction of what semi-private courses do. START: **Cape Breton Island, Nova Scotia.**

1 ★★ **Bell Bay Golf Club.** This 7,000-yard tester is wonderfully scenic and was selected by *Golf Digest* magazine as the "best new Canadian course" when it opened in 1998; it has hosted the Canadian Amateur Championships, among other tournaments. *761 Rte. 205 (1.6km/1 mile north of downtown), Baddeck.* ☎ *800/565-3077.* www.bellbay.ca. *Greens fees C$65–C$79, twilight C$45; discounts for children.*

A 90-min. drive north, at the western end of the Cabot Trail loop, is the

2 ★★★ **Highlands Links Golf Course.** *Golf Digest* ranks this seaside course one of the best 100 in the world, mostly thanks to its dramatic coastal setting. Owned by the province of Nova Scotia, it was laid out by noted course architect Stanley Thompson to complement Keltic Lodge (p 117) and restored to Thompson's original design in 1997. It only stretches 6,600 yards from

the blue tees—but you might see eagles circling overhead as you line up a putt. *275 Keltic In Rd., Ingonish Beach (at Keltic Lodge). ☎ 800/441-1118 or 902/285-2600. www.highlands linksgolf.com. Greens fees C$72–C$91, twilight C$43–C$55; discounts for children.*

Prince Edward Island has the best concentration of courses in Eastern Canada. The best on the island is just outside Morell, the

③ ★★ Links at Crowbush Cove. Open only since 1994, this 6,900-yard course in a provincial park is considered by most to be PEI's finest for both its lovely aesthetic and stiff challenge. It's a link-style course in the best Scottish tradition, with lots of water and dunes—even the dreaded "pot bunkers." Persistent winds off the Gulf of St. Lawrence increase the challenge further. *Rte. 350 (3.2km/2 miles from Rte. 2), Morell. ☎ 902/961-5600. Greens fees C$75–C$90; discounts for children, free for children after 3pm.*

About 30 minutes north via Rte. 4 is the

④ ★ Brudenell River Golf Course. This 6,500-yard course

opened in 1969 and was later updated by Graham Cooke; it's very pastoral, running through woods along the river it's named for. Tournaments are often hosted here, and it's known to be a favorite of LPGA pro (and PEI native) Lorie Kane (1964–). *86 Dewars Lane, Georgetown Royalty (6.5km/4 miles west of Georgetown, off Rte. 3). ☎ 902/652-2232. Greens fees C$55–C$70; discounts for children.*

On the Bay of Fundy in New Brunswick, about 4½ hr. south of PEI by car, St. Andrews is home to the

⑤ ★★ Algonquin Golf Course. More than a century old, this 6,900-yard resort course was retouched by architect Donald Ross (1872–1948) in the 1920s but only expanded to 18 holes in the 1990s. The front nine are newest; the back (original) nine become increasingly spectacular as you approach the point of land separating New Brunswick from Maine. *184 Adolphus St., St. Andrews. ☎ 506/529-8165. Greens fees C$49–C$99, twilight rates lower; 50% discount for children.*

Brudenell River Golf Course is a favorite of PEI pro Lorie Kane.

An Acadian History Tour

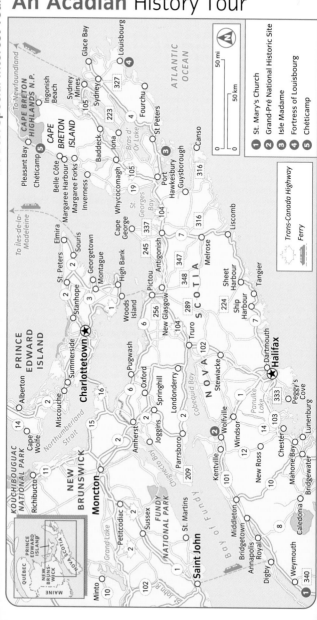

1 St. Mary's Church
2 Grand-Pré National Historic Site
3 Isle Madame
4 Fortress of Louisbourg
5 Chéticamp

Trans-Canada Highway
Ferry

The settlement and subsequent expulsion of Canada's Acadians is one of the saddest stories in the history of this region, even if it had a curious ending—today, the "Cajuns" thrive in the state of Louisiana. But it's often forgotten that French explorers were the first to settle large parts of Canada. This tour touches on this legacy. START: **Yarmouth, Nova Scotia.**

Day 1

From Yarmouth, drive north 50km (31 miles) to exit 29 (Church Point); turn left & continue to Rte. 1. Turn right & travel 4km (2½ miles) to

1 ★★ **St. Mary's Church.** Many Acadian towns along this west coast are proud of their churches, but *none* is quite so amazing as this one. The imposing, gray-shingled church has the feel of a European cathedral made of stone—yet it's made entirely of wood. It's said to be the tallest and largest wooden building on the entire continent. How big? *Tree trunks* serve as columns inside. A small museum offers glimpses of its history. ⏱ *45 min. 1713 Hwy. 1, Church Point. Free admission (donation requested).*

Follow Rte. 1/101 north 210km (130 miles) to Wolfville. Take exit 10; turn left onto Rte. 1, then right on Grand-Pré Rd. to find the

2 **Grand-Pré National Historic Site.** Before Loyalists arrived here, Acadians conquered the

landscape Dutch-style: by diking marshes and converting them to farms. At Grand-Pré, you learn about Acadians who populated this valley from 1680 until their expulsion in 1755. ⏱ *2 hr. 2241 Grand-Pré Rd., Grand-Pré. ☎ 902/542-4040. www.grand-pre.com. Admission C$7.80 adults, C$6.55 seniors, C$3.90 children 6–16, C$20 families. Daily mid-May to mid-Oct 9am–6pm. Closed mid-Oct to mid-May.*

Overnight nearby in Wolfville or Kentville.

Day 2

Follow Rte. 101 about 75km (47 miles) southeast (toward Halifax) to Rte. 102. Merge with Rte. 102 North (away from Halifax) & continue 70km (44 miles) north to Rte. 104 (the Trans-Canada Hwy.) & travel 180km (112 miles) east. Cross the bridge onto Cape Breton Island & turn onto Rte. 4; continue east on Rte. 4 25km (16 miles) to Rte. 320, the turnoff for

A stained glass window depicting Acadian history at Grand-Pré National Historic Site.

The Fortress of Louisbourg has been rebuilt to show life as it might have been in 1744.

3 ★ **Isle Madame.** Actually a group of small islands, Isle Madame is as authentic as modern Acadiana gets. These village and islands are almost entirely French. Drop by a local eatery such as the **Corner Bridge Bakery** (3648 Hwy. 206; ☎ 902/226-3225) for a croissant or sit down for dinner at a typical local restaurant such as that in the **L'Auberge Acadienne Inn** (2375 Hwy. 206, Arichat; ☎ 902-226 2200). ⏱ *2 hr. Rte. 320 (off Rte. 4).*

Travel 2 hr. (145km/90 miles) east of Isle Madame, via Rte. 4 & Rte. 22, to Louisbourg. Overnight in Louisbourg.

Day 3

4 ★★ **kids Fortress of Louisbourg.** A French fort once stood here; it has been rebuilt to show life as it might have been in 1744. You wander narrow lanes past faux-historic buildings while barnyard animals cluck and vendors hawk fresh bread from wood-fired ovens. ⏱ *2 hr. Wolfe St., Louisbourg NS.* ☎ *902/733-2280 or 902/733-3546. Admission June–Sept C$18 adults, C$15 seniors, C$8.80 children, C$44 families; May & Oct 60% discount.*

July & Aug daily 9am–5:30pm; mid-May to June & Sept to mid-Oct 9am–5pm.

It's a 2- to 3-hr. drive from Louisbourg via Rte. 22, Rte. 105 west (the Trans-Canada Hwy.) & the Cabot Trail to the capital of the Highlands region, the town of

5 ★★ **Chéticamp.** Chéticamp is living history: the center of Franco culture on this island, with bakeries, eateries, and galleries reflecting its heritage. The town is famous for hooked rugs; view them at the **Elizabeth LeFort Gallery and Hooked Rug Museum** (15584 Cabot Trail; ☎ 902/224-2642) and the artist-owned **Co-operative Artisanale de Chéticamp** (15067 Main St.; ☎ 902/224-2170). There's also a traditional eatery, **Restaurant Acadien** (☎ 902/224-3207), attached to the co-op. ⏱ *2¼ hr. Rug museum: Admission C$5 adults, C$4 seniors, C$3.50 children 6 to 18, C$12 families. Mid-May to mid-Oct daily 9am–5pm (July & Aug to 7pm). Co-operative & restaurant: Closed mid-Oct to mid-May, Mid-May to mid-Oct daily 9am–5pm (July & Aug to 7pm).* ●

Halifax in **1 Day**

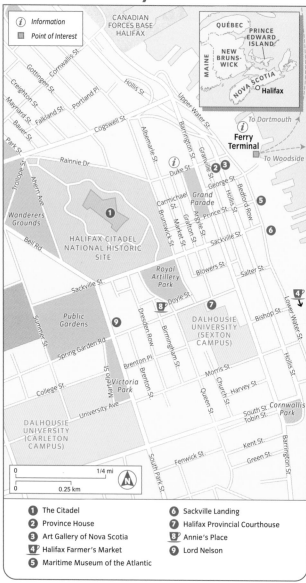

(i) Information

■ Point of Interest

CANADIAN FORCES BASE HALIFAX

QUÉBEC

PRINCE EDWARD ISLAND

MAINE

NEW BRUNS-WICK

NOVA SCOTIA

Halifax

Gottingen St.

Cornwallis St.

Creighton St.

Maynard St.

Falkland St.

Portland Pl.

Bauer St.

Hollis St.

Upper Water St.

To Dartmouth

(i) Ferry Terminal

To Woodside

Park St.

Rainnie Dr.

Cogswell St.

Albemarle St.

Barrington St.

Granville St.

(i) Duke St.

2 **3**

George St.

Bedford Row

Hollis St.

Trollope St.

Ahern Ave.

Wanderers Grounds

Bell Rd.

1

HALIFAX CITADEL NATIONAL HISTORIC SITE

Carmichael St.

Grand Parade

Brunswick St.

Market St.

Grafton St.

Argyle St.

Prince St.

Sackville St.

5

6

Sackville St.

Royal Artillery Park

Blowers St.

Salter St.

8 Doyle St.

7

4 ↓

Lower Water St.

Summer St.

Public Gardens

9

Spring Garden Rd.

Dresden Row

Birmingham St.

DALHOUSIE UNIVERSITY (SEXTON CAMPUS)

Bishop St.

Hollis St.

College St.

Martello St.

Victoria Park

Brenton Pl.

Brenton St.

Morris St.

Queen St.

Church St.

Harvey St.

University Ave.

DALHOUSIE UNIVERSITY (CARLETON CAMPUS)

South St.

Tobin St.

Cornwallis Park

Barrington St.

Fenwick St.

Kent St.

Green St.

South Park St.

0 — 1/4 mi

0 — 0.25 km

N

1 The Citadel

2 Province House

3 Art Gallery of Nova Scotia

4 Halifax Farmer's Market

5 Maritime Museum of the Atlantic

6 Sackville Landing

7 Halifax Provincial Courthouse

8 Annie's Place

9 Lord Nelson

Previous page: The popular Halifax waterfront.

Halifax is a resilient place. The *Titanic* wrecked off its shores in 1912, and it became famous for all the wrong reasons *again* just a few years later when a huge explosion leveled most of downtown. Yet the city bounced back with vigor: Today, this is the artistic, economic, and culinary capital of Atlantic Canada. You can see much of it in a day. START: **Citadel Hill (north side of Sackville St.).**

1 ★★ The Citadel. This ruined fort is the best single place to grasp Halifax's past. Views are splendid from the hilltop, and the history is equally impressive. Learn about it from costumed interpreters on-site. ⏱ *1 hr. Citadel Hill (btwn. Rainnie Dr. & Sackville St.). ☎ 902/426-5080. www.pc.gc.ca. Admission June to mid-Sept C$12 adults, C$10 seniors, C$5.80 children 6–16, C$30 families; May & mid-Sept to Oct discounted 30–40%; free admission Nov–Apr. Citadel July & Aug daily 9am–6pm; May, June, Sept & Oct daily 9am–5pm; Nov–Apr only grounds open (no guides or tours). See p 55, ⑩.*

Travel 6 blocks downhill to Barrington St. From either Prince or Duke St., turn onto Hollis St. Mid-block is

2 ★ Province House. All Nova Scotia's laws have been made within these walls for almost 200 years, reason enough to check this off your list of sights. A well-written free booklet is available inside, describing the Georgian building's history and architecture. It's said the headless falcons in several rooms were decapitated by a lawmaker with a cane who mistook them for eagles during a period of anti-American sentiment. I can't confirm that, but it's fun to recount. ⏱ *30 min. 1726 Hollis St. (near Prince St.). ☎ 902/424-4661. www.gov.ns.ca/legislature. Free admission. July & Aug Mon–Fri 9am–5pm; Sat, Sun & holidays 10am–4pm; Sept–June Mon–Fri 9am–4pm, closed Sat & Sun. See p 122.*

Directly across the street is the

3 ★★ Art Gallery of Nova Scotia. Any serious exploration of the city's artistic treasures begins

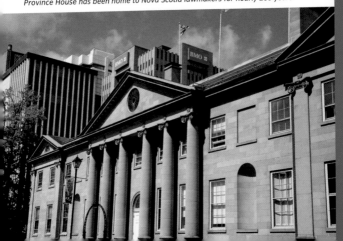

Province House has been home to Nova Scotia lawmakers for nearly 200 years.

The Halifax Farmers' Market is the oldest in Canada.

here, at the province's biggest and best museum. Holdings include lots of regional and Canadian art, plus a *house:* In 1998, during an expansion, the gallery reassembled the entire home of Nova Scotia folk artist Maud Lewis (1903-1970) here. ⏱ 1¼ hr. 1723 Hollis St. ☎ 902/424-5280. www.artgalleryofnovascotia. ca. Admission C$10 adults, C$8 seniors, C$5 students, C$3 children 6–17, C$20 families. Thurs 10am– 9pm, Fri–Mon 10am–5pm. Guided tours (no extra charge) daily 2:30pm, extra tour Thurs 7pm. See p 52, ④.

★★ **4⁷ Halifax Farmer's Market.** The Saturday morning farmer's market held within the Brewery Market (p 51,①) is a highlight of the week for many Haligonians. It's Canada's oldest farmer's market—and its most interesting. The market runs every Saturday until early afternoon; get there early for the best choice of crepes, donuts, fruits, vegetables, coffee, baked goods, smoked meats, pastries—and the free samples of wine, chocolate, cold cuts, or whatever else is being put out. *Pier 20. (Lower Water St. at Marginal Road). $.*

Walk 1 block south along Hollis St. & turn right on Sackville St. Continue downhill to the waterfront & the

⑤ ★★★ **kids** **Maritime Museum of the Atlantic.** This is one of the great museums of Canada—testifying to the city's and province's seafaring origins and history. The exhibits are involving and well executed. ⏱ 1½ hr. See p 51, ②.

Next to the museum is

⑥ ★ **Sackville Landing.** A waterfront stroll along Sackville Landing is probably the best single way in all of Halifax to absorb history and culture in one compact shot. In addition to several important historic attractions—which include Atlantic Canada's best maritime museum (see the previous stop) and a restored naval boat, the **HMCS *Sackville*** (see p 48, ④), berthed here from June through October—the walkway here features a city information kiosk, small historical plaques, and monuments to Canadian and Norwegian war dead. ⏱ 45 min. Foot of Sackville St.

Climb 4 blocks uphill along Sackville St. to Barrington St. Turn left on Barrington St., travel 2 blocks

& turn right on Spring Garden Rd. Just past the cemetery is the

7 Halifax Provincial Courthouse.
Almost continuously since the mid-19th century, this imposing 2½-story building has been the place where Nova Scotia metes out justice in Halifax-area matters. With its classically Palladian proportions, windows, and triangular roof, it's a fine example of the form. (Check out the bearded lions carved into the keystones.) The detailing inside includes oak furniture, plaster work, and arched entranceways. Spooky note: Public hangings were conducted at a gallows behind the courthouse until the 1930s. ⏲ 15 min. 5250 Spring Garden Rd. ☎ 902/424-8716. No formal guided tours; self-guided tours and tours from Sherriff's office possible by appointment or drop-in, Mon–Fri 9am–5pm.

A stroll along Sackville Landing encompasses several important historical attractions.

8 Annie's Place.
Good for a quick bite when walking along Spring Garden Road, Annie's Place serves pastries, coffees, teas, and light meals. (Look for the big CAFE sign.) Outstanding bargain lunch specials include offerings that could run to a slab of grilled meatloaf on focaccia or a chicken sandwich. It opens early. 1513 Birmingham St. (at Spring Garden Rd.). ☎ 902/420-0098. $.

Continue .6km (¼ mile) uphill along Spring Garden Rd. to Park St. & the lovely Public Garden (p 59, 7). Before entering the

park, duck into the hotel across the street, the

9 ★ Lord Nelson.
This boxy, brick hotel, erected in 1927 by the Canadian Pacific Railway during one of its grand hotel-building sprees, is one of the city's toniest lodging addresses. (Touring rock stars often stay here.) Though basic on the outside, inside a giant mural of Nelson (1758–1805)—a British naval hero—carries historic weight. And both the gold leaf on the ceilings and the crystal chandeliers in the ballroom testify to the opulence of the roaring '20s. It's also a good place to stay (see p 78). ⏲ 30 min. 1515 South Park St. ☎ 800/565-2020 or 902/423-6331. www.lord nelsonhotel.com.

Annie's Place is a popular choice for coffee and snacks.

Halifax in **2 Days**

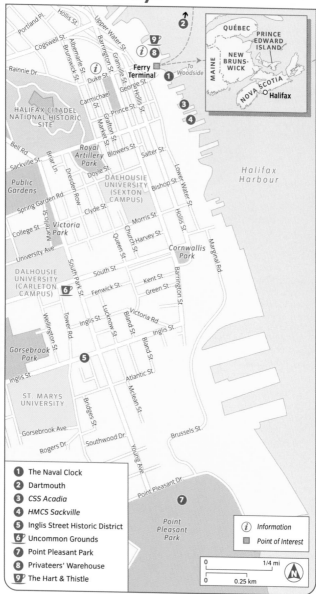

1 The Naval Clock
2 Dartmouth
3 CSS Acadia
4 HMCS Sackville
5 Inglis Street Historic District
6 Uncommon Grounds
7 Point Pleasant Park
8 Privateers' Warehouse
9 The Hart & Thistle

i Information
■ Point of Interest

Given a second day in Halifax, first thank your lucky stars. There are so many eateries, bars, and entertainment options here that you'll *need* that second day and night. We'll focus on finding some of the slightly more off-the-track charms, places that shed additional light on this fascinating city's history, architecture, and British-polite yet oh-so-creative vibe. START: **On the waterfront, at the foot of George St. (below Water St.).**

The Naval Clock marks the spot where the British first landed on the waterfront in the 1750s.

1 ★ The Naval Clock. This section of Halifax's waterfront, known as Chebucto Landing, was the very *spot* where the British landed and colonized in the 1750s. There had long been little here to commemorate that event—too much clutter from the waterfront businesses—but North America's oldest operating naval clock now marks the spot. Built in London in the late 18th century, the clock kept time for more than 200 years at a nearby dockyard. It's a bit incongruous, sitting

starkly on the pier—like a steeple without a church under it—but the golden weathervane on top is striking. ⏱ *10 min. Foot of George St. (below Water St.).*

Also at Chebucto Landing is Halifax's ferry terminal, your ticket to

2 Dartmouth. The city's ferry terminal gets hectic during morning and evening rush hours—but the rest of the time, it's an outstanding way to get a quick, cheap sweeping city-and-harbor view, plus some sea air. The passenger ferry runs every 15 minutes (every 30 min. midday) to and from the twin city of Dartmouth, right across the harbor, until almost midnight; the trip takes only 15 minutes. Get off and walk around Dartmouth a bit, snap pictures of the Halifax skyline or islands in the harbor, and get right back on. ⏱ *45 min. Ferry terminal foot of George St. (beyond Water St.).* ☎ *902/490-4000. www.halifax.ca/ metrotransit/ferries.html. Ferry one-way C$2.25 adults, C$1.50 seniors & children 5–15.*

Walk 2 blocks south along Water St. to Sackville Landing (p 44, **6**). Docked at the landing is the

3 CSS *Acadia*. This steam-powered vessel is part of the Maritime Museum (they call it "our largest artifact"); it was used by the Canadian government to map the bottom of the Atlantic for years. Much of the ship is open for self-guided tours, including the captain's

The CSS Acadia was used to map the bottom of the Atlantic Ocean.

quarters, upper decks, wheelhouse, and an oak-paneled chart room. If you want to see more, take a guided tour—it gives you access to the lower decks, engine room, and other restricted areas. 🕐 *30 min. 1675 Lower Water St. (in front of the Maritime Museum).* ☎ *902/424-7490. Admission C$2 adults (free w/Maritime Museum ticket). Mon–Sat 9:30am–5:30pm, Sun 1–5:30pm; free guided tours daily, 1:30–4:30pm every half-hour.*

Also at Sackville Landing, farther out along the pier, is the

④ **HMCS Sackville.** This blue-and-white "corvette" (a speedy warship that's smaller than a destroyer) is tied up along a wood-planked wharf behind a small visitor center. There's a short multimedia presentation to provide some background about the ship, which is outfitted just as it was in 1944. It serves chiefly as a memorial to Canadians who served in World War II. 🕐 *15*

min. Sackville Landing (on the water). ☎ *902/429-2132. Admission C$4 adults, C$2 seniors & children, C$9 families. June–Oct daily 10am–5pm. Closed Nov–May.*

Drive or take a taxi along Lower Water St. south to its end. Cross in front of the Westin hotel; turn left on Barrington St. & right on Inglis St. Continue .5km (¼ mile) to the

⑤ ★ **Inglis Street Historic District.** Halifax is painfully thin on beautiful streets, so anytime you're in the South End, there are two I recommend making quick passes by simply to gawk at architecture. One is Oxford Street, a leafy boulevard of professor's homes; the other is Inglis Street, a little Victorian wonderland in spots. The block from Young Avenue to McLean Street is especially nice, filled with colorful late-19th-century wooden homes in fine Queen Anne and Second Empire styles; steep mansard roofs,

Palladian and bay windows, dormers, and even bits of stained glass abound. ⏱ *30 min. Inglis St. (from Young Ave. to McLean St.).*

⑥ Uncommon Grounds. What's a walking tour without some lofty thoughts scribbled in a journal over a cup of locally roasted coffee? There are numerous coffee shops in which to indulge your java habit, but the Uncommon Grounds chain is especially well-positioned. This location is on South Park Street. Yes, they serve food and maintain a Wi-Fi hotspot. *1030 South Park St. ☎ 902/431-3101. www.coffeesold here.com. $.*

Turn left onto Tower Rd. & walk to Point Pleasant Dr., gateway to

⑦ ★★ Point Pleasant Park. Curiously, Halifax's biggest, best park is often overlooked by travelers. But locals know all about it—for its historic structures, quiet wooded pathways, harbor views, and summertime al fresco performance programs. ⏱ *1 hr. Entrance at Young Ave. & Point Pleasant Dr.; parking lot at Black Rock Beach (end of Point Pleasant Dr.). Daily dawn–dusk. See p 61, ④.*

Retrace your path by car 4km (2½ miles) along Tower Rd., South St.,

Barrington St. & Water St. to the Historic Properties complex at 1869 Upper Water St. Perhaps the best building in the complex is the

⑧ Privateers' Warehouse. This appealing, connected series of granite-and-ironstone warehouses dates from 1813 but looks even older than that. Privateers (legalized pirates, essentially) did some serious plundering in Halifax's heyday, and the Crown looked the other way. They stashed some of that contraband in this very warehouse, but today, it's notable not for pirate booty, history exhibits, nor peg legs (there are none), but shops and pubs. ⏱ *1 hr. 1869 Upper Water St. (in the Historic Properties). ☎ 902/429-0530. www. historicproperties.ca. Open daily; hours vary by season.*

★ ⑨ The Hart & Thistle. While inside the Historic Properties and the Privateers' Warehouse, take a break at this new "gastropub," brewing beer on premises (check with the bartender about daily beer specials) and serving food a notch above the usual pub grub. There are tons of Alexander Keith's beers on tap, too. *1869 Upper Water St. (in the Historic Properties). ☎ 902/407-4278. www.hartandthistle.com. $$.*

The Hart & Thistle brews its own beer on the premises.

The Waterfront & Downtown

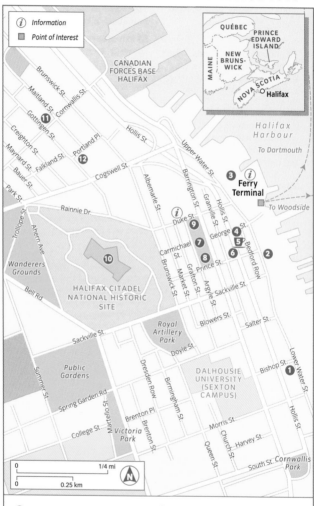

- (i) Information
- ■ Point of Interest

1. The Brewery Market
2. Maritime Museum of the Atlantic
3. Historic Properties
4. Art Gallery of Nova Scotia
5. Cheapside Cafe
6. Province House
7. Grand Parade
8. St. Paul's Anglican Church
9. Halifax City Hall
10. Halifax Citadel National Historic Site
11. Cornwallis Street Baptist Church
12. Eye Level Gallery

Halifax begins and ends with its waterfront. This has been a seafaring town ever since the British founded the city in 1749 as a beachhead against the Acadians occupying the area. Once a huge British naval base and later a wartime supply depot, this waterfront has seen layer after layer of history and culture. START: **Lower Water St. at Bishop St.**

❶ ★ The Brewery Market. On the uphill side of Lower Water Street, just above the city docks, this is the city's most interesting one-stop shopping-and-dining experience. Originally the site of North America's first true commercial brewery, the space here was eventually redesigned to enclose courtyards and link the various sections of the brewery. Some of the city's finest restaurants reside here, plus a range of shopping and imbibing options. Though navigating the labyrinthine courtyards to find a particular shop can be a little confusing, it's a fun and interesting introduction to the modern face of the city. 🕐 1 hr. 1496 Lower Water St.

Walk 2 blocks north along Lower Water St. to Sackville Landing & its undisputed star attraction, the

❷ ★★★ kids Maritime Museum of the Atlantic. Visitors are greeted by a cool 3m (10-ft.) lighthouse lens, then walk through shipbuilding and seagoing displays, like the deckhouse of a coastal steamer. (Learn about Samuel Cunard [1787–1865], the Nova Scotian who founded a steamship line.) But the most poignant exhibit here is the single deck chair from the ill-fated *Titanic*, which sank offshore. Also memorable are an "Age of Steam" exhibit; Queen Victoria's barge; a shipwreck section; and recreations of a ship's chandlery, sail loft, and carpenter's shop. 🕐 1½ hr. 1675 Lower Water St. ☎ 902/424-7490. www.maritime.museum.gov. ns.ca. Admission May–Oct C$8.75 adults, C$7.75 seniors, C$4.75 children 6–17, C$23 families; Nov–Apr 50% discount. May–Oct Tues

Myriad shops and restaurants can be found inside The Brewery Market, originally the site of North America's first commercial brewery.

The Maritime Museum of the Atlantic has a poignant exhibit on the Titanic, which sank offshore.

9:30am–8pm, Wed–Mon 9:30am–5:30pm; Nov–Apr Tues 9:30am–8pm, Wed–Sat 9:30am–5:30pm, Sun 1–5pm, closed Mon.

Continue 3½ blocks north along Lower (becomes Upper) Water St. to the

❸ ★ **Historic Properties.** The Halifax waterfront's shopping core is difficult to locate, but one of the densest concentrations of shops is in and around the three blocks known as the Historic Properties. The late-18th-century buildings of wood and stone here are Canada's oldest surviving warehouses, and were once the heart of the city's thriving shipping trade. Today, their historic details are a bit lost on the slightly precious boutiques, pubs, galleries, coffee shops, and restaurants housed inside. Still, history buffs might get excited about the 2-century-old architecture. 🕐 *1 hr. 1869 Upper Water St. (beside Marriott hotel).* ☎ *902/429-0530. www. historicproperties.ca. Shops open daily; hours vary.*

From the Historic Properties, walk a short block uphill to Hollis St. Turn left & walk 2½ blocks south to the

❹ ★★ **Art Gallery of Nova Scotia.** This pair of sandstone buildings houses what is arguably the premier art museum in the Maritimes, with a focus on local and regional art plus work by other Canadian, British, and European artists, and well-chosen exhibits of folk and Inuit art. Overwhelmed by all the art? Sign up for the once-a-day guided tours. 🕐 *2 hr. 1723 Hollis St.*

The Art Gallery of Nova Scotia is arguably the premier art museum in the Maritimes.

The Cheapside Café, inside the Art Gallery of Nova Scotia.

☎ 902/424-5280. www.artgalleryof novascotia.ca. Admission C$10 adults, C$8 seniors, C$5 students, C$3 children 6–17, C$20 families. Thurs 10am–9pm, Fri–Wed 10am– 5pm. Guided tours daily at 2:30pm (extra tour Thurs 7pm).

★ 5️⃣ **Cheapside Cafe.** Inside the Art Gallery of Nova Scotia, this cafe's name actually comes from the open market that once occupied this street. It's a great find, run by the proprietress of the late, lamented Sweet Basil Bistro. The interior is almost like a small museum, too, with fun artwork on both the walls and table settings. The soups, sandwiches, and baked goods are outstanding. *1723 Hollis St.,* ☎ *902/425-4494. $.*

Nearly across the street from the art gallery is

6️⃣ ★★ **Province House.** You're looking at Canada's oldest seat of government. The three-story Province House has been home to the tiny Nova Scotian provincial legislature since 1819. A stone Georgian building featuring symmetrical Palladian architecture, it conceals fine ornamental detailing and artwork

within. If the legislature is in session (it's not always) and government floats your boat, you can get a visitor's pass and sit up in the gallery, watching the official business of the province unfold. The province also offers guided tours of the building, which you must book in advance by phone. 🕐 *30 min. 1726 Hollis St.* ☎ *902/424-4661. www.gov.ns.ca/ legislature. Free admission. July & Aug Mon–Fri 9am–5pm; Sat, Sun & holidays 10am–4pm; Sept–June Mon–Fri 9am–4pm.*

Continue to Prince St. & turn right. Continue 2 blocks to Barrington St. Just past it is the open space known as the

7️⃣ ★ **Grand Parade.** A good spot to take a breather, or at least get some fresh air, is this open expanse in the heart of the downtown district. British military recruits once practiced their drills here, but today, it's a lovely piece of urban landscape: a broad terrace carved into the hillside. The city restored and slightly lengthened the space in 1978, and it was upgraded and retouched with nice detailing right before the 1995 G-7 summit. Most remarkable of all, it understatedly ties together downtown's three most important attractions: St.

Memories of the Big Bang

The lovely St. Paul's Anglican Church (see below) on the Grand Parade is well worth exploring. But there's an interesting piece of trivia at the lovely St. Paul's Anglican Church—literally. A chunk of flying debris from the great Halifax explosion of 1917 is *still* lodged in the wall over the doors to the nave. (You can find another tossed object—a huge, heavy anchor—in Sir Sandford Fleming Park around the Northwest Arm)

Paul's and City Hall (the next two stops) preside over opposite ends of the Parade, while the Citadel (p 55, ⑩) lords over the scene. Bring a picnic and people-watch. 🕐 *30 min. Prince to Duke sts. (btwn. Argyle & Barrington sts.).*

At the south end of the Grand Parade is

⑧ ★★ St. Paul's Anglican Church.
Forming one end of the Parade, this handsome white Georgian building was the first Anglican cathedral established outside Great Britain; that makes it Canada's oldest Protestant place of worship.

St. Paul's Anglican Church was the first Anglican cathedral established outside Great Britain.

How old is it? Part of the 1749 structure was fabricated in Boston, then shipped here and erected with the help of funds from King George II (1683–1760). Notice the great stained-glass work and take a summertime guided tour. 🕐 *30 min. 1749 Argyle St. (on the Grand Parade near Barrington St.).* ☎ *902/429-2240. www.stpauls halifax.org. Mon–Fri 9am–4:30pm; Sun services 8, 9:15 & 11am. Free guided tours June–Aug Mon–Sat; call for scheduling.*

Walk 2 blocks north along the Grand Parade to reach

⑨ ★ Halifax City Hall.
This handsome, gray-sandstone municipal building was constructed between 1887 and 1890—which were boom times in these parts—and exuberantly overdone with the usual Victorian flourishes: a prominent clock tower, dormers and pediments, arched windows, pilasters, and some Corinthian columns for good measure. (The inside is surprisingly bland, however.) About that severe clock tower—yes, it does contain two clock faces, and one is permanently set to 9:04 a.m. Why? That's the moment when the 1917 Halifax Explosion (see p 187) occurred. 🕐 *15 min. 1875 Barrington St.* ☎ *902/490-1520. www. halifax.ca. Open to the public Mon–Fri 8:30am–5pm.*

One of the clock faces at Halifax City Hall is permanently set to the moment when the 1917 Halifax Explosion occurred.

Backtrack 1 block along the Parade to George St. & turn right. Walk north 3 blocks & cross Brunswick St. If you're in good shape, ascend the stairs leading to the

⑩ ★★ Halifax Citadel National Historic Site.

Even if a big stone fort weren't at the top of this hill, it would still be worth the trek just for the astounding views of city, harbor, and sea. Four forts occupied this height; the one displayed dates from the 1850s. Its sturdy granite walls topped by grassy banks form a star. In a courtyard, costumed interpreters in kilts and bearskin hats march, play bagpipes, and fire a cannon at noon. The barracks showcase exhibits about life at the fort. ⏱ *1 hr. Citadel Hill.* ☎ *902/426-5080. www.pc.gc.ca. Admission June to mid-Sept C$12 adults, C$10 seniors, C$5.80 children 6–16, C$30 families; May & mid-Sept to Oct C$7.80 adults, C$6.55 seniors, C$3.90 children 6–16, C$20 families; free admission Nov–Apr. July & Aug*

daily 9am–6pm; May, June, Sept & Oct daily 9am–5pm. Nov–Apr grounds open for self-guided tours; free.*

From the foot of the Citadel (Brunswick St.), walk or drive 2 long blocks north to Cornwallis St. Turn left & continue 2 blocks to the whitewashed

⑪ Cornwallis Street Baptist Church.

Just a few blocks north and downhill of the Citadel, there's a fascinating slice of Halifax's little-told African-American history. This Baptist church was built in 1832 by Richard Preston (1791–1861), an American slave's son who had bought his own way out of servitude, become a theologian, and emigrated north to Canada to live with his mother in the Halifax area. Amazingly, this church building came through the huge waterfront explosion in 1917 (which leveled most of the rest of the North End) more or less unscathed—and did yeoman's work as a city shelter for months afterward. The congregation still meets here for regular Sunday services; the interior features lots of blond wood. ⏱ *15 min. 5457 Cornwallis St.* ☎ *902/429-5573. Office Mon–Thurs 10am–4pm. Tour by appt.*

From the church, turn left on Gottingen St. to reach the

⑫ Eye Level Gallery.

Just steps from the Baptist church is this excellent little downtown gallery, cooperatively run by local artists working in various genres. You might run across anything from an exhibit of works in collaboration with the electronics and new media center CFAT to an exhibit highlighting storytelling and oral histories in the provinces. There's always something that makes you think. *2063 Gottingen St.* ☎ *902/425 6412. www.eyelevel gallery.ca. Tues–Sat noon–5pm.*

Spring Garden Road

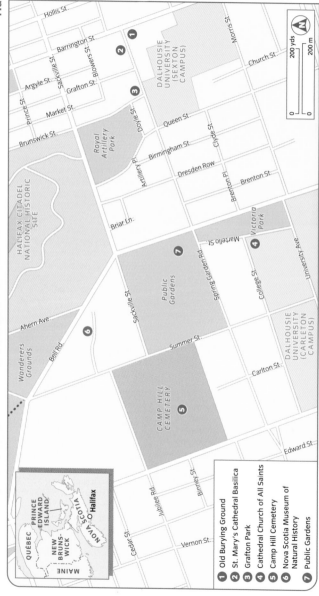

1 Old Burying Ground
2 St. Mary's Cathedral Basilica
3 Grafton Park
4 Cathedral Church of All Saints
5 Camp Hill Cemetery
6 Nova Scotia Museum of Natural History
7 Public Gardens

When you think of Halifax, you probably don't think of Spring Garden Road—but you should. This hill-climbing street has developed into one of Halifax's central arteries, shunting life-blood between the office towers and ships at water's edge and the lively pubs, buskers, restaurants, malls, and public gardens higher uphill. START: **Corner of Barrington St. & Spring Garden Rd.**

❶ Old Burying Ground.
Restored in 1991, this was the first burial ground in Halifax, and between 1749 and 1844, some 12,000 local residents were interred here, though only ¹⁄₁₀th of the graves are actually marked. It's chiefly of interest to aficionados of 18th- and 19th-century gravestone art—think winged heads and skulls—even if taking rubbings is prohibited. The Welsford-Parker Monument honors Nova Scotians who fought in the Crimean War, and another statue near the entrance features a lion with a Medusa-like mane. ⏱ *15 min. Corner of Spring Garden & Barrington sts.* ☎ *902-429-2240. Free admission. June–early Sept, free guided tours 9am–5pm (no set schedule; donation requested). Closed early Sept–May.*

Directly across the street is the impressive

❷ ★★ St. Mary's Cathedral Basilica.
Talk about a sleeper attraction: This huge cathedral is believed to sport the tallest granite spire on the continent. Ships steer by it. Who knew? It's also got heavy wooden double doors, triple rose windows, another rose on the door, loads of Gothic Revival detailing all over its facade, and truly outstanding stained-glass work. The church was constructed of local stone in 1820 and, over an 80-year period, became progressively more grandiose. During the summer, volunteers give free guided tours. ⏱ *45 min. 5221 Spring Garden Rd.* ☎ *902-423-4116. Self-guided tours Mon–Fri*

7:30am–6pm except during Mass (12:15 & 5:15pm). Guided tours June–Sept; call for times.

Continue 1½ blocks north to the public library on the right. In front is

❸ ★★ Grafton Park.
This is probably the most bohemian of all of this city's parks; you half expect to discover the next Sarah McLachlan strumming on a guitar or kicking a hackeysack around here. That's a big, weirdly oversized statue of Winston Churchill (1874–1965) in the park, though the students and folks on the benches may not realize it. This was once the burial ground for the city's poor; thousands of bodies lie shoveled beneath it, all in

The granite spire at St. Mary's Basilica is believed to be the tallest on the continent and is used to guide ships.

The Nova Scotia Museum of Natural History is a good introduction to the province's flora and fauna.

unmarked graves. ⏱ *30 min. 5381 Spring Garden Rd. (in front of the library).*

Continue 6 blocks north to Tower Rd. Turn left & walk 1 block to

④ ★ **Cathedral Church of All Saints.** This stone Anglican church with triple-arched doors was erected in 1910 just off Spring Garden Road, assimilating three local churches beneath one roof; the stone for it was quarried very nearby. The woodwork within the church is exceptional (see the bishop's chair and amazing ornate screens behind the altar, for example), and the total effect of the High Altar probably rivals that of any such altar in Eastern Canada. The stained-glass work here, which began in the 1940s and has been added to gradually during the decades ever since, is likewise striking. ⏱ *30 min. 5732 College St. (access from Martello St.).* ☎ *902/ 423-6002.*

Backtrack to Spring Garden Rd. & continue uphill 1 block to Summer St. Turn right. On the left, after 1 block (at Sackville St.), is an entrance to

⑤ **Camp Hill Cemetery.** A lovely, peaceful little cemetery tucked off away from the bustle of Spring Garden Road, this burial ground is newer than the "Old" burial grounds (p 57, ①). But it's no less impressive. It was carved out of a huge town-common green in 1844. Among the famous Canadians buried here are Alexander Keith (1795–1873), the Scotsman who served as mayor of this city for a short term (but is more famous for his beer); look for bottle caps marking his grave in early October, Keith's birthday. William Young (1799–1887) and Robert Stanfield (1914–2003), two former Nova Scotia premiers from different eras, are also buried here. ⏱ *15 min. Entrance at corners of Summer & Sackville sts., Robie & Binney sts.*

Continue along Summer St. less than a block to the fine

⑥ ★ **kids Nova Scotia Museum of Natural History.** This modern, mid-sized museum offers a good introduction to the province's flora and fauna. Its galleries include sections on geology, botany, mammals, and birds, plus

Shopping 'Til You Drop

One of the singular facts of Spring Garden Road is the sheer number of shops, eateries, and shopping malls (in little, British-style mews and squares off the main drag) along its length. On the stretch between Dalhousie University and the Cathedral Church (p 58, ❹), two of these tiny malls even square off across the road from each other. I describe the street's malls in a little more detail in the "Shopping" section of this chapter (p 82).

exhibits of archaeology and Mi'kmaq (native) culture. There's a very popular butterfly house open from July through September, as well as an extensive collection of lifelike ceramic fungi and a colony of honeybees that come and go from an acrylic hive via a tube connected to the outdoors. ⏱ 1¼ hr. 1747 Summer St. ☎ 902/424-7353. Admission C$5.75 adults, C$5.25 seniors, C$3.75 children 6–17, C$12–C$17 families; free Wed 5–8pm. June to mid-Oct Mon, Tues & Thurs–Sat 9:30am–5:30pm; Wed 9:30am–8pm; Sun noon–5:30pm; mid-Oct to May closed Mon.

Backtrack to Sackville St. & turn left. Go 1 block & turn right onto South Park St. At the end of the block are the city's

❼ ★★ kids **Public Gardens.** The Public Gardens sit at the top of Spring Garden Road, and they're the street's single best attraction. Founded in 1753 as a private venture, these gardens assumed their present look around 1875—the height of the Victorian era, a fact that quickly becomes evident in the deliberately winding walks, ornate fountains, duck ponds, and band shell. (There's a free concert every Sun afternoon in summer.) Come here for the leafy trees, lush lawns, ducks that have lost their fear of humans, and people-watching: everyone, from octogenarians to kids feeding pigeons and smartly uniformed guards, walking the grounds. ⏱ 1 hr. Main entrance at corner of Spring Garden Rd. & South Park St. Free admission. Spring to late fall daily 8am–dusk.

The popular Public Gardens are designed in a Victorian style.

The South End

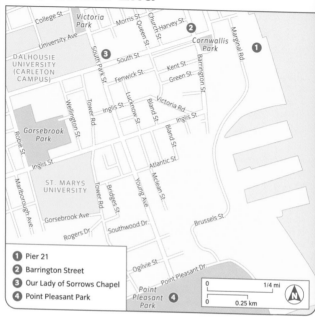

College St.

Victoria Park

Morris St.

Harvey St.

University Ave.

Cornwallis Park

1

2

DALHOUSIE UNIVERSITY (CARLETON CAMPUS)

South Park St.

South St.

Kent St.

Fenwick St.

Green St.

Wellington St.

Tower Rd.

Inglis St.

Lucknow St.

Bland St.

Victoria Rd.

Inglis St.

Bland St.

3

Gorsebrook Park

Robie St.

Inglis St.

Atlantic St.

Marlborough Ave.

ST. MARYS UNIVERSITY

Tower Rd.

Mclean St.

Young Ave.

Bridges St.

Gorsebrook Ave.

Southwood Dr.

Brussels St.

Rogers Dr.

Ogilvie St.

Point Pleasant Dr.

Point Pleasant Park

1 Pier 21
2 Barrington Street
3 Our Lady of Sorrows Chapel
4 Point Pleasant Park

4

0   1/4 mi
0   0.25 km

Loosely defined, the South End is everything south of Quinpool Road (west of Robie) or South Street (east of Robie). It's one of my favorite neighborhoods in the whole city: Halifax at its most natural and erudite, holding three universities, a huge green park, the city's train station, several intriguing churches, and numerous artsy diversions within its boundaries. START: **The south end of the waterfront, near the train station.**

1 **Kids** **Pier 21.** Between 1928 and 1971, more than 1 million immigrants arrived at Pier 21, Canada's version of New York City's Ellis Island. In 1999, the pier was restored and filled with exhibits. One section depicts the boarding of ships in far-off lands, another the Atlantic crossing (a half-hour multimedia show), another the dispersion of immigrants throughout Canada. It's said that one in five present-day Canadians have links to this dock. ⏱ 45 min. 1055 Marginal Rd. (on the waterfront,

behind the Westin hotel). ☎ 902/425-7770. www.pier21.ca. Admission C$8.50 adults, C$7.50 seniors, C$5 children 6–16, C$21 families. May–Nov daily 9:30am–5:30pm; Dec–Mar Tues–Sat 10am–5pm; Apr Mon–Sat 10am–5pm.

Head around the point & uphill to the Westin hotel. Continue 1 block & turn right to find

2 **Barrington Street.** Barrington is worth a block's detour north. This is one of the reasons you come to this city, after all: to graze upon its block after block of breweries, pubs, vintage shops, boutiques, and ethnic restaurants, and Barrington has one of the densest and best concentrations. It somehow feels much more appealing and authentic than the shops lined up along Spring Garden Road. Check out places like the gastropub **Henry House** (1222 Barrington St.; ☎ 902/423-5660), **Bearly's House of Blues & Ribs** (1269 Barrington St.; ☎ 902/423-2526), **Talay Thai** (1261 Barrington St.; ☎ 902/404-3700), the elegant **Café Chianti** (1241 Barrington St.; ☎ 902/423-7471), and the **Hostelling International youth hostel** *(1253 Barrington St.; ☎ 902/422-3863; www.hihostels.ca).* ⏱ *1 hr. South St. to Spring Garden Rd.*

Turn onto South St. Between Queen and South Park sts. is the small whitewashed

❸ ★ Our Lady of Sorrows Chapel. This chapel, set within the expansive Holy Cross Cemetery, is one of the coolest historical footnotes in town. The chapel was built in a *single day* in August of 1843. It's said that about 2,000 local volunteers showed up at the city cathedral about a mile away that morning, then walked together to the site and raised the barn, as it were. The stained-glass work is impressive. Prime Minister John Sparrow David Thompson (1845–1894), a local, was buried here when he unexpectedly died of a heart attack just 2 years into his term, while visiting Queen Victoria (1819–1901) in England. The interior is normally closed to the public year-round, but you might be able to score a walk-through. ⏱ *30 min. 1259 South Park St.* ☎ *902/423-4116, ext. 406. www.ccchalifax.com. Generally closed to the public; but Sat morning tours sometimes possible, or other times by appointment.*

At the Victoria General Hospital, turn left & go 8 blocks (about 1.6km/1 mile) to

❹ ★★ Point Pleasant Park. Point Pleasant is one of Canada's best urban parks, great for a long quiet walk on a warm day. The 73-hectare (180-acre) park occupies a wooded peninsula that was once home to a fort. You can still see the ruins of battlements and a so-called British Martello tower. (Officially, Halifax leases the park from Great Britain for about C10¢ per year.) Follow the lovely gravel carriage road around the point and enjoy the small beach and groves of graceful fir trees. Take note that no bikes are allowed here on weekends or holidays. ⏱ *1½ hr. Entrance at corner of Young Ave. & Point Pleasant Dr.; parking lot at Black Rock Beach (end of Point Pleasant Dr.). Daily dawn–dusk.*

More than one million immigrants arrived in Canada at Pier 21.

Halifax for Beer Lovers

(i) Information

▪ Point of Interest

QUÉBEC — PRINCE EDWARD ISLAND

MAINE — NEW BRUNSWICK

NOVA SCOTIA ○ Halifax

Brunswick St.

Hollis St.

Gottingen St.

Cogswell St.

7

Upper Water St.

Rainnie Dr.

(i) Ferry Terminal

To Dartmouth

To Woodside

Albemarle St.

Barrington St.

Granville St.

(i)

Duke St.

George St.

Bedford Row

HALIFAX CITADEL NATIONAL HISTORIC SITE

Carmichael St.

Grand Parade

Hollis St.

Prince St.

Brunswick St.

Market St.

Grafton St.

Argyle St.

Sackville St.

6

Royal Artillery Park

Blowers St.

Salter St.

1

Sackville St.

Doyle St.

2

Bishop St.

Lower Water St.

South Park St.

Dresden Row

Public Gardens

5

Spring Garden Rd.

Birmingham St.

DALHOUSIE UNIVERSITY (SEXTON CAMPUS)

Brenton Pl.

College St.

Victoria Park

Brenton St.

Morris St.

Church St.

Harvey St.

Hollis St.

University Ave.

Queen St.

4

South St. *Cornwallis Park*

3

Tobin St.

Marginal Rd.

DALHOUSIE UNIVERSITY (CARLETON CAMPUS)

Fenwick St.

Kent St.

Green St.

Barrington St.

South St.

Tower Terr.

Bland St.

Victoria Rd.

Inglis St.

Bland St.

1 Alexander Keith's Nova Scotia Brewery

2 Red Stag Tavern

3 Garrison Brewery

4 Henry House

5 Rock Bottom Brewery

6 Maxwell's Plum

7 Propeller Brewing Company

0 — 1/4 mi

0 — 0.25 km

Halifax is practically a paradise for beer drinkers, especially those who enjoy hopped-up, British-style ales. There are a half-dozen micro- and macro-breweries within city limits, plus dozens of great pubs with good beers on tap—often including special, one-time brews from local brewers. START: **Brewery Market (on Lower Water St.).**

① Alexander Keith's Nova Scotia Brewery.

Come here for the atmosphere, not the town's best beer. Alexander Keith's says it's the oldest working brewery on the continent. Impressive. The tour, though? Singing tour guides in period costumes—a period that's a few centuries old. You do get a couple of beers, but the whole thing feels a bit like being on a cruise ship. ⏱ 30 min. 1496 Lower Water St. ☎ 902/455-1474. www.keiths.ca. Tours C$16 adults, C$14 seniors, C$8 children. Tours June–Oct Mon–Sat noon–8pm, Sun noon–5pm; Nov–Apr Fri 5–8pm, Sat noon–8pm; May Sun–Thurs noon–8pm, Fri & Sat noon–5pm. Tours summer every half-hour; fall–spring every hour.

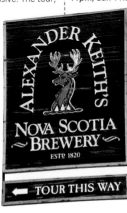

Alexander Keith's claims to be the oldest working brewery on the continent.

Also in the Brewery Market is the

② Red Stag Tavern.

The house organ, so to speak, of the Keith's brewery serves up the brewer's predictable beers, plus a helping of camaraderie—think open-mic nights, for starters—and decent fried food. You can also buy Keith's glasses, coasters, shirts, and the like; but I'd save my bullets for a smaller, lesser-known brewery if I were collecting memorabilia. The rooftop patio is everlastingly popular in summer. ⏱ 15 min. 1496 Lower Water St. ☎ 902/422-0275. www.redstag.ca. Mon–Sat 11:30am–11pm, Sun 11:30am–10pm.

Follow Water St. 2 blocks south (away from the attractions) & turn left. Downhill, on the water behind the Westin, is the

③ ★ Garrison Brewery.

Local college kids like this seaside micro-brewery, which has injected new life into the water-front area. You can tour the brewing operations if you like (tickets are a bit steep, but they do include a sample of the brewer's Irish red ale at the end). Or you can just show up at the brewery's gift shop (three tasting samples for a buck) and try examples of styles such as a raspberry wheat beer, an amber ale, a nut-brown ale, an IPA, a prize-winning porter (dark beer)—there's even sometimes a jalapeno ale. ⏱ 30 min. 1149 Marginal Rd. ☎ 902/453-5343. www.garrison brewing.com. Store hrs. Mon–Thur 10am–8pm, Fri–Sat 10am–10pm, Sun noon–8pm. Tours C$12–C$15 adults (must book in advance; no schedule).

When Someone Else Is Driving . . .

Not all Halifax's best beers are so easy to find—for one, you'll need wheels, and in that case, I recommend a designated driver. ★★ **Granite Brewery** (6054 Stairs St., btwn. Robie and Kempt sts.; ☎ 902/422-4954; www.granitebreweryhalifax.ca), founded in 1985 but newly relocated to an industrial area among train tracks and car dealerships, happens to brew some of the best beer in the province. It's open Monday to Wednesday from 9:30am to 6pm, Thursday to Saturday from 9:30am to 7pm, and Sunday from noon to 6pm. There are still no tours of the plant at press time (that may change someday), but you can visit the adjacent beer store to pick up growlers and kegs of Best Bitter, Peculier, Ringwood, Greenman Organic, IPA, and seasonal brews. The cask-conditioned ales are exceptional. The best place to drink this beer in *downtown* Halifax? It's Henry House (see below), where Granite's brewers specially create up to a half-dozen beers for the place at any given time.

Climb back uphill 2 blocks to Barrington St. & turn right. On the left side of the street is

④ ★★ **Henry House.** One of my favorite drinking spots in all of Halifax is the tri-level Henry House, inside a handsome stone 19th-century building at the foot of the South End. There are as many as a half-dozen top-fermented and unpasteurized ales on tap here at any given time, brewed in town by the folks over at Granite Brewery.

(See above.) The food's really good for a pub, too. Better still? There's live Irish music on Saturday nights. ⏱ *1 hr. 1222 Barrington St.* ☎ *902/423-5660. www.henryhouse.ca. Mon–Sat 11:30am–12:30am, Sun noon–11pm.*

Go north along Barrington St. 3½ blocks to Spring Garden Rd. Turn left & continue 6½ blocks to the

⑤ **Rock Bottom Brewery.** The latest entry in Halifax's beer sweepstakes, Rock Bottom looks to be off

Rock Bottom Brewery serves beer in most of the major styles.

The Propeller Brewing Company's "Prop Shop" sells specialties like pumpkin ale and ginger-flavored beer.

to a good start. To begin with, it's situated right underneath a popular bar. The menu runs to full dinner items like lobster-stuffed haddock and mussels, while Asian stir-fries and pasta all make appearances. And the beers? Most of the major styles are covered with a broad brush here—IPA, wheat, red ale, golden ale, stout—while the card is thankfully free of distractions like herbed or fruited beers. After all, sometimes you just want a beer that tastes like a beer. ⏲ *1 hr. 5686 Spring Garden Rd.* ☎ *902/423-2938. www.rockbottombrewery.ca. Sun–Wed 10am–midnight; Thurs–Sat 10am–1am.*

Turn around & descend Spring Garden Rd. 6 blocks to Grafton St. Turn left & walk almost 2 blocks to

6 Maxwell's Plum. This is one of the city's most crowded bars, an in-your-face English pub where peanut shells litter the floor and patrons, upstairs and down, quaff from a staggering list of some 150 import and Canadian draft and bottled beers, 60 of those on tap! How do they do it? The nightly happy-hour and pitcher specials can cut the cost of imbibing, and the burgers are practically free; sampler platters of six quarter-glasses of beer are also a popular option. And on Friday afternoons, a cask is cracked open and tapped on the spot. ⏲ *45 min. 1600 Grafton St.* ☎ *902/423-5090. Daily 11am–2am.*

Continue north 3½ blocks to Duke St. & turn left; continue 3 blocks (Duke St. becomes Rainnie Dr.) to Gottingen St. Turn right to find

7 ★★ Propeller Brewing Company. Some hop-heads insist Propeller—founded in 1997 by a Hollywood-prop-expert-turned-home-brewer—makes the best beer in Eastern Canada. Too bad you need to bring nine or more buddies to tour it. But anyone can visit the attached "Prop Shop" store and buy "growlers" (a 1.9-liter/½-gallon refillable jug) or a six-pack. Varieties include a *hefeweizen*, an ESB, and specialties like a pumpkin ale, ginger-flavored beer, and deep black "Revolution" beer. They bottle sodas at the same plant. ⏲ *15 min. 2011–2015 Gottingen St.* ☎ *902/422-7767. www.drinkpropeller.ca. Tours C$15 adults. Store open Mon–Thurs 10am–8pm, Fri & Sat 10am–10pm, Sun noon–10pm; self-guided tours Wed 7-9pm, groups of 10 or more also daily at 4:30, 7:00, and 9:30pm.*

Halifax History & Architecture

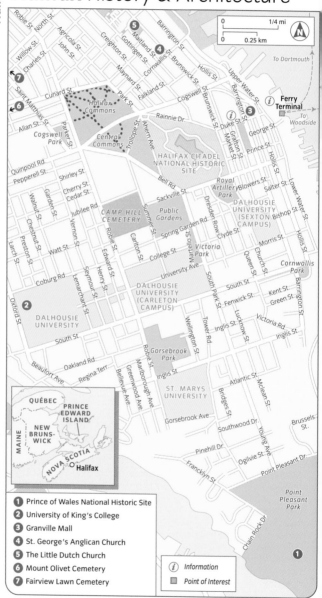

1 Prince of Wales National Historic Site
2 University of King's College
3 Granville Mall
4 St. George's Anglican Church
5 The Little Dutch Church
6 Mount Olivet Cemetery
7 Fairview Lawn Cemetery

ⓘ Information
■ Point of Interest

If there's one thing Halifax has in spades, it's history. The British ruled the North Atlantic naval roost from here; shipping and fisheries wealth flowed in, providing the funds for impressive works of commercial and residential architecture; and the province of Nova Scotia established its capital here. Upshot? There's plenty for history buffs to see. START: **The southern tip of the city peninsula, at the end of Tower Rd., in Point Pleasant Park.**

1 ★ Prince of Wales National Historic Site. Strap on your walking shoes. Within Point Pleasant Park (p 61, **4**) is this so-called "Martello" tower—a fortification popular in the 18th century throughout the British Empire. This one was built around 1796, the first in North America, to protect the city's guns; it consisted of thick, multi-tiered stone towers with infantrymen living right inside. Towers like this were considered difficult, even impossible, to capture. It's about .5km (⅓ mile) into the woods from the Tower Road parking lot on the park's southwestern corner. ⏱ *30 min. Point Pleasant Park.* ☎ *902/426-5080. www.pc.gc.ca. Free admission. Tower open July & Aug 10am–6pm; grounds open year-round.*

Follow Tower Rd. 1km (½ mile) north to Inglis St. Turn left & continue .8km (½ mile) west to the end. Turn right on Beaufort Ave. (which becomes Oxford St.) & go 1.2km (¾ mile) to the

2 ★ University of King's College. Canada's first chartered university? You're looking at it. The University of King's College was founded in 1789 in Ontario by Loyalists fleeing from American revolutionaries in New York City. After a 1920 fire, the university moved to this quiet southwest-Halifax corner. It has remained small ever since (just 1,100 students today), but the stone structures—the cupola-topped, Georgian-columned main building was designed by local architect Andrew R. Cobb (1876–1943)—remain suitably impressive.

The University of King's College is Canada's first chartered university.

🕐 *15 min. Main entrance on Coburg Rd. (at Oxford St.). www.ukings.ca.*

Continue 7 blocks north to Quinpool Rd. Turn right. Travel 2km (1¼ miles) downhill along Quinpool Rd. (which becomes Cogswell St.) to the Hollis St. ramp. Exit left; turn right onto Duke St. At Duke & Barrington sts. is the

③ **Granville Mall.** These attractive, Italianate-style buildings were built late in the 19th century to replace a group that had burned to the ground. Today it's a pleasing pedestrian mall, filled with narrow shops, restaurants, and bars, vaguely reminiscent of Boston's Back Bay or New York's Greenwich Village. The overall impression is far more attractive than that of neighboring malls such as Scotia Square. Part of the campus of the Nova Scotia College of Art and Design is also here. 🕐 *30 min. Granville St. (at Duke & Barrington sts.).*

St. George's Anglican Church is known to locals simply as "the Round Church."

Follow Barrington St. to Cogswell St. & turn left, then make the first right onto Brunswick St. In 2 blocks, on the left, is the unique

④ ★ **St. George's Anglican Church.** It's officially called St. George's, but nobody here knows it as that; this is "the Round Church." The entryway is angular, but the worship space itself is beautifully constructed as a layer-cake of three stacked circles, using Palladian proportions. Originally built in 1800 to handle overflow from the Lutheran church nearby (see below), the church later became Anglican. Its historic interior was scorched during a mid-1990s fire. Restoration followed. 🕐 *30 min. 2222 Brunswick St. (at Cornwallis St.). ☎ 902/423-1059 or 902/421-1705. www.round church.ca. Free tours Wed–Sat 11am–3pm, Sun 1–4pm by prior appointment.*

Continue another block along Brunswick St. to

⑤ ★ **The Little Dutch Church.** Built as the first Lutheran church in all of Canada, this (yes) little house of worship dates all the way back to 1756. How long ago was that? This peninsula had only been settled by the British for 7 years at the time, and it wouldn't become a city for nearly another century. You can request a tour from the clergy at St. George's, and they might well give you one if they've got the time. (Offer a donation afterward.) 🕐 *30 min. Gerrish St. (at Brunswick St.). ☎ 902/423-1059. Free tours (donations recommended). June–Sept tours by appointment only.*

Backtrack to Cogswell St. Turn right & drive 2.8km (1¾ miles; Cogswell St. becomes Quinpool Rd.) to MacDonald St. Turn right; continue 1.6km (1 mile; MacDonald St. becomes Mumford Rd.) to

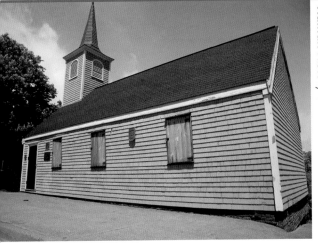

The Little Dutch Church dates back to 1756.

6 Mount Olivet Cemetery.

When the *Titanic* went down on April 15, 1912, almost 2,000 perished, and captains from Halifax were recruited for the grim task of retrieving the corpses. Dating from 1896, this is one of three cemeteries in Halifax where victims of the disaster were buried—the Catholic cemetery—and it holds 19 bodies from the tragedy. Victims of the Halifax explosion of 1917 were also buried here. It's chilling and a bit sad to contemplate the rows of squat, blocky stones. ⏱ *30 min. 7076 Mumford Rd. (at Olivet St.). Daily dawn–dusk.*

Continue a few blocks to Joseph Howe Dr. & turn right. Go 1.6km (1 mile) and merge right onto Rte. 2 (Kempt Rd.); shortly afterward, bear right onto Windsor St. On the right, you'll come upon

7 ★★ Fairview Lawn Cemetery.

This is another of the city's *Titanic* cemeteries. It's by far the most famous: More than 120 victims, mostly crew members, were buried here, and row after row of black-gray stones mark their final resting places. Some of the simple graves have names, but many of these stones bear only numbers. Plaques and signs highlight poignant individual stories from the tragedy, including that of an "unknown child" finally identified in 2007 through DNA techniques. ⏱ *45 min. Windsor St. (at Connaught Ave.).* ☎ *902/490-4883. www.halifax.ca. Daily dawn–dusk.*

More than 120 victims of the sinking of the Titanic are buried at the Fairview Lawn Cemetery.

Halifax for Art Lovers

- *i* Information
- ◼ Point of Interest

QUÉBEC
PRINCE EDWARD ISLAND
MAINE
NEW BRUNS- WICK
NOVA SCOTIA
○ Halifax

CANADIAN FORCES BASE HALIFAX

Provo Wallis St.

Creighton St.
Maitland St.
Brunswick St.
Cornwallis St.
Harris St.
Gottingen St.
Woodill St.
Maynard St.
Park St.
Falkland St.
Portland Pl.
Hollis St.
Cogswell St.
Albemarle St.
Brunswick St.
Barrington St.
Upper Water St.

Halifax Commons

Rainnie Dr.

i Duke St.
Granville St.
Prince St.
Hollis St.

i ③ Ferry Terminal

To Dartmouth

To Woodside

Central Commons

Trollope St.
Ahern Ave.

Carmichael St.

Wanderers Grounds

HALIFAX CITADEL NATIONAL HISTORIC SITE

Bell Rd.
Briar Ln.

Market St.
Grafton St.

④

Royal Artillery Park

Blowers St.
Salter St.

Jubilee Rd.
Sackville St.
Dresden Row

Doyle St.

DALHOUSIE UNIVERSITY (SEXTON CAMPUS)

Bishop St.

Lower Water St.

CAMP HILL CEMETERY

Public Gardens

Spring Garden Rd.

Clyde St.

Morris St.

Summer St.
Robie St.
Carlton St.

College St.
Maynard St.

Victoria Park

Queen St.
Church St.

Harvey St.
Hollis St.

Cornwallis Park

Marginal Rd.

Bliss St.
Edward St.

University Ave.

South Park St.

South St.
Kent St.
Green St.

Barrington St.

⑤

Henry St.

DALHOUSIE UNIVERSITY (CARLETON CAMPUS)

⑦

Fenwick St.
Luckmow St.

Bland St.

Victoria Rd.

Seymour St.
Cartaret St.
Waterloo St.
Fraser St.

Wellington St.
Tower Rd.

Inglis St.
Young Ave.

Bland St.
Inglis St.

Regina Terr.
Belmont Rd.
Bellevue Ave.
Greenwood Ave.
Marlborough Ave.

Gorsebrook Park

Robie St.
Inglis St.

Atlantic St.

Mclean St.

ST. MARYS UNIVERSITY

⑥

Bridges St.

Brussels St.

Roxton Rd.
Gorsebrook Ave.

① Anna Leonowens Gallery
② Seeds Gallery
③ Argyle Fine Art
④ Khyber Institute of Contemporary Arts
⑤ Nova Scotia Centre for Craft and Design
⑥ Saint Mary's University Art Gallery
⑦ Dalhousie Art Gallery

Halifax is a city of commerce, history (p 66), and beer (p 62). But it has *also* become the place where many of the top working artists in Atlantic Canada gravitate for an arts-friendly atmosphere. Their many galleries and studios are tucked into converted buildings all over town; this tour, of galleries plus a few university museums, supplements the city's must-see museum, the Art Gallery of Nova Scotia (p 52, ④). All stops on this tour are free.
START: **The Granville Mall (at Granville & Duke sts.).**

---

① ★ Anna Leonowens Gallery. Named for the British world traveler who founded the Nova Scotia College of Art and Design, this is NSCAD's official student and faculty art gallery—a must-see, since it's the province's largest visual arts school. The gallery claims to hang an astounding 125 exhibitions every year in its halls, with a new show or two opening every Monday; how can you *not* find something you like? ⏱ 45 min. 1891 Granville St. ☎ 902/494-8223. http://nscad.ca. Tues–Fri 11am–5pm, Sat noon–4pm. Closed Sun & during school breaks.

Half a block downhill is the

② Seeds Gallery. Only steps from the Anna Leonowens Gallery is Seeds, the "other" gallery operated

by NSCAD, with additional works from that university's busy student and alumnae artists. Unusually, this gallery space showcases and sells fashion items, fabric art, and textiles, but you can also find the usual visual-arts works you'd expect: jewelry, ceramic work, paintings, photography. Look for the seasonal sale announcements. ⏱ 30 min. 1892 Hollis St. ☎ 902/494-8301. http://nscad.ca. Tues–Sat 11am–6pm. Closed Sun & during school breaks.

Half a block downhill on the waterfront, in the Historic Properties, is

③ Argyle Fine Art. Inside the Historic Properties' Collins Bank building, this gallery draws heavily from a local stable of artists. Some

The Seeds Gallery is operated by the Nova Scotia College of Art & Design.

Take a Detour: Agricola Street

The North End of Halifax houses a surprising number of artists' studios. Hours tend to be highly variable (the artists are busy making, you know, art), but it's worth visiting if you're in the area. Agricola Street, in particular, has become a hotbed of arty activity; it's less than a mile from either the Citadel or Historic Properties. **Lost & Found** (☎ 902/446-5986), at 2383 Agricola St., is a good shop collecting a group of local designers' work beneath a single roof; **Finer Things** (p 81), at 2797 Agricola St., is the city's best antiques mall.

of the work is conventional: coastal painter Vaughn Gray, landscapist Paul Chester, and streetscape painter Shelley Mitchell. But there's also offbeat work from the likes of acrylic artist Sara Caracristi and New Brunswick ceramic artist Mary Jane Lundy. Most of Argyle's artists have close ties to NSCAD. 🕐 *30 min. 1869 Upper Water St. (in the Historic Properties).* ☎ *902/425-9456. www.argylefa.com. Mon noon–5pm, Tues–Sat 10am–6pm. Closed Sun.*

Walk 3 blocks uphill to Barrington St. Turn left & continue 3½ blocks to the

④ ★ **Khyber Institute of Contemporary Arts.** It's got some of the shortest hours in town, but the tri-level collective known as "The Khyber" is one of the leading lights of Halifax's art scene. Inside a striking 19th-century Gothic Revival building owned by the city of Halifax, it's home to performance art, mind-bending installations, art classes, and talks that always keep you on your toes. Note that the city was renegotiating its lease agreement with Khyber at press time; check the website for updates. 🕐 *1 hr. 1588 Barrington St.* ☎ *902/422-9668. www.khyber.ca. Tues–Sat noon–5pm.*

Backtrack past South St. to Terminal Rd. Turn right & continue around the point onto Marginal Rd. In .4km (¼ mile), you reach the

⑤ ★ **Nova Scotia Centre for Craft and Design.** Nova Scotia's provincial government runs this arts and crafts center, next to **Pier 21** (p 60, ①), with a specific goal: to develop crafts- and design-based industries and artists throughout the province. It's working. The Mary E. Black Gallery, inside the center, is the public face of that effort and showcases constantly changing exhibits of the best work that Nova Scotia craftspeople are currently producing in silver, pewter, ceramic pottery, precious jewelry, fabric, needlepoint—even whalebone. 🕐 *45 min. 1061 Marginal Rd., Ste. 140.* ☎ *902/492-2522. www.craft design.ns.ca. Tues–Fri 9am–5pm, Sat & Sun 11am–4pm.*

Return to South St. & turn west. After .8km (½ mile), turn left onto Tower Rd. Go .8km (½ mile) & turn right on Gorsebrook Ave. Enter the Loyola building, home of the

⑥ ★★ **Saint Mary's University Art Gallery.** This gallery is a find. It does not focus exclusively on work produced by its own students on its own campus. Rather, it also reaches

The Dalhousie Art Gallery has an ongoing program of modernist art exhibitions.

out to the Canadian art community at large, and brings back some sur- prisingly thought-provoking concep- tual art: Torontonian Nina Levitt's installation of ASCII code, projected images of heroic women, and found objects, for instance. It also hosts excellent traveling exhibitions from other museums in Eastern Canada

St. Mary's University Art Gallery has thought-provoking conceptual art from artists across Canada.

and Ontario. Very well done. ⏲ *1 hr. 5865 Gorsebrook Ave. (inside Loyola Academic Complex; at Robie St.).* ☎ *902/420-5445. www.smu.ca. Tues–Fri 11am–5pm, Sat & Sun noon–5pm. Closed Mon.*

Backtrack .8km (½ mile) north along Tower Rd. to South St. & turn left. Continue west 4 blocks to Henry St. Turn right & proceed 1 block to University Ave. Park & find the

❼ ★★ Dalhousie Art Gallery.

The oldest public art space in the city, Dal's gallery dates from the mid-1950s and is among the city's top artistic offerings today; there's quite an ongoing program of mod- ernist art presented here, plus excellent traveling exhibitions and the occasional looking-back show, perhaps in conjunction with the fine National Gallery in Ottawa. Groups can take guided tours of the gallery by prior arrangement, and the attached arts center (see "Arts & Entertainment," p 83) always offers plenty of good art-house films. ⏲ *1 hr. 6101 University Ave.* ☎ *902/494- 2403. http://artgallery.dal.ca. Tues– Fri 11am–5pm, Sat & Sun noon–5pm. Closed Mon.*

Halifax Dining & Lodging

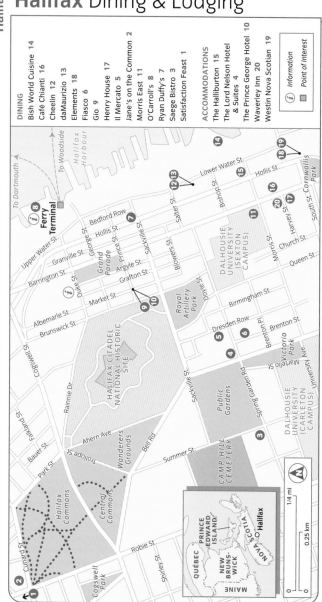

DINING

Bish World Cuisine 14
Café Chianti 16
Cheelin 12
daMaurizio 13
Elements 18
Fiasco 6
Gio 9
Henry House 17
Il Mercato 5
Jane's on the Common 2
Morris East 11
O'Carroll's 8
Ryan Duffy's 7
Saege Bistro 3
Satisfaction Feast 1

ACCOMMODATIONS

The Halliburton 15
The Lord Nelson Hotel & Suites 4
The Prince George Hotel 10
Waverley Inn 20
Westin Nova Scotian 19

ⓘ Information
▪ Point of Interest

Dining & Lodging Best Bets

Best **Use of a Negative Name for a Positive Place**
★★ Fiasco $$$, *1463 Brenton St. (p 76)*

Best Place to **Impress a Foodie**
★★★ Bish World Cuisine $$$, *1475 Lower Water St. (p 76)*

Most **Romantic**
★ Café Chianti $$, *1241 Barrington St. (p 76)*

Best **Hotel Food**
★★ Gio $$, *1725 Market St. (p 77)*

Best Place to **Pretend You're in Europe**
★ Il Mercato $$, *5650 Spring Garden Rd. (p 77)*

Best **Brunch**
★★ Elements $$, *1181 Hollis St. (p 76)*

Best **Pizza Pie**
★ Morris East $$, *5212 Morris St. (p 78)*

Best **Vegetarian**
Satisfaction Feast $, *3559 Robie St. (p 78)*

Best **Palace That Protein Built**
★ Ryan Duffy's $$, *5640 Spring Garden Rd. (p 78)*

Best **Beer & Food Combo**
Henry House $$, *1222 Barrington St. (p 77)*

Best **Waterfront Lodging**
★★★ Westin Nova Scotian $$$, *1181 Hollis St. (p 79)*

Best **Parkside Lodging**
★ Lord Nelson Hotel & Suites $$, *1515 South Park St. (p 78)*

Best **Mix of Old and New**
★★ The Halliburton $$$, *5184 Morris St. (p 79)*

Gio is the best hotel restaurant in town, part of The Prince George Hotel.

Halifax Dining A to Z

★★★ Bish World Cuisine

WATERFRONT *INTERNATIONAL*
World-class cities need world-class
restaurants, and this is Halifax's,
blending Asian and European elements. Japanese-style scallops, Thai
curry, lobster over pasta, steaks,
duck, sugarcane-lacquered pork—
everything's amazing. Finish with a
Bish sundae. *1475 Lower Water St.
(entrance at Bishop St.).* ☎ *902/
425-7993. www.bish.ca. Entrees
C$28–C$39. AE, DC, MC, V. Dinner
Mon–Sat.*

★★ Café Chianti SOUTH END

NORTHERN ITALIAN Romantic Chianti has been a South End favorite
of the university set for 2 decades.
Lamb burgers, lobsters, and veal
dishes are specialties; they also
serve rabbit. *1241 Barrington St.*
☎ *902/423-7471. www.cafechianti.
ca. Entrees lunch C$11–C$18, dinner
C$18–C$24. AE, MC, V. Lunch Mon–
Sat, dinner daily.*

Cheelin WATERFRONT *CHINESE*

The top Chinese restaurant in town
achieves a balance between authen-
ticity and the Haligonian vibe. Good

*Bish World Cuisine blends Asian and
European elements in its creations.*

picks include *mapo* tofu, Szechuan
pork, scallops with mango sauce,
and spring rolls. Prices are reasonable. *1496 Lower Water St. (inside
the Brewery Market).* ☎ *902/422-
2252. www.cheelinrestaurant.com.
Entrees C$10–C$15. AE, MC, V.
Lunch Mon–Sat, dinner Tues–Sun.*

★★★ daMaurizio WATERFRONT

ITALIAN/FUSION Tucked in The
Brewery, this has been the city's
best, most inventive Italian bite
since it opened. Calamari, gnocchi,
penne, ravioli? Check. Seared
salmon, veal scaloppine with lobster, flambéed tenderloin, rack of
lamb? Double-check. Desserts are
outstanding. *1479 Lower Water St.
(in the Brewery Market).* ☎ *902/423-
0859. www.damaurizio.ca. Entrees
C$10–C$34. AE, DC, MC, V. Dinner
Mon–Sat.*

★★ Elements SOUTH END *NEW

CANADIAN* This hotel restaurant
by the water picked a crowded
genre (fusion), but it gets it right—
fancy stuff, but also an upscale
wings-and-ribs platter—and the
candlelit space is undeniably lovely.
1181 Hollis St. (inside the Westin).
☎ *902/496-7960. www.westin.
ns.ca. Entrees lunch C$8–C$19, dinner C$14–C$29. AE, MC, V. Breakfast, lunch & dinner daily.*

★★ Fiasco SPRING GARDEN ROAD

CONTINENTAL Hollywood stars in
town sometimes drop by to try the
seafood at Martin Keyzlar's Fiasco.
Good call; you should follow their
lead, except don't limit yourself to
fish—you can also dine quite nicely
on beef tenderloin, coquilles, and
tortellini here. *1463 Brenton St.*
☎ *902/429-3499. www.fiasco
restaurant.com. Entrees C$29–C$33.
AE, MC, V. Dinner Mon–Sat.*

Visiting Hollywood stars often drop by Fiasco for seafood.

★★ Gio DOWNTOWN *CONTINEN-TAL* Despite the Italian-sounding name, this highly skilled kitchen's cuisine ranges far and wide: jerk chicken, Malaysian beef, and Kobe burgers for lunch, but then anything from swordfish to elk to crispy duck for dinner. Desserts are among the best in town. *1725 Market St. (in Prince George Hotel).* ☎ *902/425-1987. www.giohalifax.com. Entrees lunch C$13–C$15, dinner C$26–C$32. AE, MC, V. Lunch daily, dinner Mon–Sat.*

Henry House SOUTH END *PUB* Said to be Canada's first brewpub, this 1834 stone building features a medium-fancy dining room upstairs (red tablecloths and captains' chairs) and an informal, pleasantly noisy pub downstairs. You can eat fish and chips, and beef stew, but also salmon. *1222 Barrington St.* ☎ *902/423-5660. www.henryhouse. ca. Entrees C$8–C$15. AE, DC, MC, V. Lunch & dinner daily.*

★ Il Mercato SPRING GARDEN ROAD *ITALIAN* It actually looks like you're in Italy when you dine here, from the decor down to the menu of focaccia, pastas, and thin-crust piz-zas. You can also eat rack of lamb or veal scaloppine. Finish with espresso, sambuca, or Campari—and save room for homemade gelati. *5650 Spring Garden Rd.* ☎ *902/422-2866. www.il-mercato. ca. Entrees C$9–C$24. AE, DC, MC, V. Lunch & dinner Mon–Sat.*

Jane's on the Common NORTH END *DINER/FUSION* A fusion diner? It is. Pot pies, lamb burgers with Brie, and fancy grilled cheese sand-wiches at lunch yield to smoked pork chops, veggie curry, and rich stuffed chicken breasts at dinner. Weekend brings a good brunch.

Il Mercato has excellent Italian cuisine and homemade gelati.

2394 Robie St. ☎ *902/431-5683. www.janesonthecommon.com. Entrees C$16–C$20. AE, MC, V. Breakfast Sat & Sun, lunch & dinner Tues–Sun.*

★ **Morris East** SOUTH END *PIZZA* Halifax's numerous students and faculty demand excellent thin-crust pizzas, and Morris East delivers them—cooking in a wood-fired oven, naturally. Top with anything from pepperoni to smoked salmon or pulled pork. Non-pizza specials are excellent, too. *5212 Morris St.* ☎ *902/444-7663. www.morriseast. com. Pizzas C$14–C$18. Lunch & dinner Tues–Sat, dinner Sun. AE, MC, V.*

★ **O'Carroll's** WATERFRONT *SEAFOOD/CONTINENTAL* No longer just another pub. Chef Colin Stone serves inventive entrees (Kobe beef, braised lamb, cedar-planked salmon with whiskey-maple glaze) and there's live music in the pub and beer on tap. *1860 Upper Water St.* ☎ *902/423-4405. Entrees lunch C$8–C$19, dinner C$15–C$22. AE, MC, V. Lunch & dinner daily.*

★ **Ryan Duffy's** SPRING GARDEN ROAD *STEAK* The house specialty here is steak, from corn-fed Hereford to Black Angus and Shorthorn cattle, grilled over natural wood charcoal (no broiling). Compound butters can be added. Some cuts are trimmed tableside and are finished so perfectly you might not need a knife. *5640 Spring Garden Rd.* ☎ *902/421-1116. Entrees lunch C$9–C$15, dinner C$19–C$38. AE, DC, MC, V. Lunch Mon–Fri, dinner daily.*

★ **Saege Bistro** SPRING GARDEN ROAD *INTERNATIONAL* Scandinavia meets Canada (and the rest of the world); taste fireworks result.

Steaks at Ryan Duffy's are grilled over natural wood charcoal.

Asian stir-fries, lobster with pesto cream, Norwegian fish cakes, coconut salmon with chutney, seared Digby scallops—they're all on the menu here. *5883 Spring Garden Rd.* ☎ *902/429-1882. www.saege.ca. Entrees lunch C$9–C$21, dinner C$15–C$26. AE, DC, MC, V. Lunch & dinner Tues–Sun.*

Satisfaction Feast NORTH END *VEGETARIAN* Halifax's vegetarian community congregates here, even if its current location is several long miles north of where it used to be downtown. Still, locals have enjoyed the faux meats, curries, and vegan desserts since 1981. *3559 Robie St.* ☎ *902/422-3540. www.satisfaction feast.com. Entrees C$6–C$12. AE, DC, MC, V. Lunch & dinner daily.*

Halifax Lodging A to Z

★★ The Halliburton SOUTH END
An elegant country inn improbably
situated in the heart of downtown.
Three townhouse-style buildings are
furnished with antiques, but also
flat-screen TVs, iPod players, and
Wi-Fi. Some rooms have skylights,
wet bars, and/or fireplaces. *5184
Morris St.* ☎ *888/512-3344 or
902/420-0658. www.halliburton.
ns.ca. 29 units. Doubles C$145–
C$350. AE, MC, V.*

★ Lord Nelson Hotel & Suites
SPRING GARDEN ROAD Built in 1928,
the Lord Nelson occupies one of the
city's choicest addresses across from
the Public Gardens; pay more for a
room with a view. The lobby pub is
authentic, and the hotel is pet-
friendly. *1515 South Park St.* ☎ *800/
565-2020 or 902/423-6331. www.lord
nelsonhotel.com. 260 units. Doubles
C$139–C$259. AE, DC, DISC, MC, V.*

★ The Prince George Hotel
DOWNTOWN A big, contemporary
business hotel renovated in 2000.
It's one of the closest hotels to the
Citadel and is linked to much of
downtown via underground
passages. The restaurant, Gio

(p 77), is superb. *1725 Market St.*
☎ *800/565-1567 or 902/425-1986.
www.princegeorgehotel.com. 206
units. Doubles C$149–C$299. AE, DC,
DISC, MC, V.*

★ Waverley Inn SOUTH END A
high Victorian style pervades this
built-in-1866 inn. Headboards are
elaborate and Gothic; many rooms
here have private Jacuzzis, and
some have canopy beds. *1266 Barrington St.* ☎ *800/565-9346 or
902/423-9346. www.waverleyinn.
com. 34 units. Mid-May to Oct doubles C$129–C$229; Nov to mid-May
doubles C$109–C$179. AE, MC, V.*

★★★ Westin Nova Scotian
WATERFRONT It's tough to beat
the views from this Westin, a luxurious update of a 1928 Canadian
National Railways hotel by the train
station and harbor. The house restaurant, Elements (p 76), is
excellent, and there's a free downtown shuttle. The AAA auto club
gives it a rare four-diamond rating.
1181 Hollis St. ☎ *888/679-3784 or
902/421-1000. www.westin.ns.ca.
310 units. Doubles C$139–C$299.
AE, MC, V.*

The Waverley Inn exudes Victorian style.

Halifax Shopping, A&E, & Nightlife

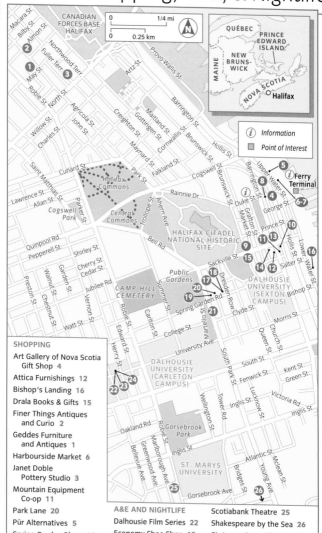

SHOPPING

Art Gallery of Nova Scotia
Gift Shop 4
Attica Furnishings 12
Bishop's Landing 16
Drala Books & Gifts 15
Finer Things Antiques
and Curio 2
Geddes Furniture
and Antiques 1
Harbourside Market 6
Janet Doble
Pottery Studio 3
Mountain Equipment
Co-op 11
Park Lane 20
Pûr Alternatives 5
Spring Garden Place 18
Thornbloom–The Inspired
Home 17
Urban Cottage Antiques
& Collectibles 8

A&E AND NIGHTLIFE

Dalhousie Film Series 22
Economy Shoe Shop 13
The Khyber ICA 9
Lower Deck Pub 7
Neptune Theatre 14
Onyx 19

Scotiabank Theatre 25
Shakespeare by the Sea 26
Sir James Dunn Theatre 24
Symphony Nova Scotia 23
Tribeca 10
Your Father's Moustache 21

Halifax Shopping A to Z

Antiques

★ Finer Things Antiques and Curios
NORTH END   The single best one-stop antiques market in Halifax, this is a huge space collects the merchandise of 15 separate dealers. The owners claim you can find anything, from 18th-century English furniture to modern Scandinavian design and vintage items, and I believe them. *2797 Agricola St.* ☎ *902/456-1412. www.finerthings antiques.com. AE, MC, V.*

★ Geddes Furniture and Antiques
NORTH END   Reproduction Chippendale and Queen Anne pieces, such as dining room chairs and highboys, are the specialty of this shop. You can also order custom-made furniture; the store loads up delivery trucks bound for the northeastern United States regularly. *2739 Agricola St.* ☎ *902/454-7171 or 866/443-3337. www. geddesfurniture.com. AE, MC, V.*

Arts & Crafts

★ Art Gallery of Nova Scotia Gift Shop
DOWNTOWN   The city's best museum maintains an excellent little gift shop selling local crafts, postcards, birdhouses, small sculptures, prints, and the like. There's even some work by native Mi'kmaq artisans. *1723 Hollis St.* ☎ *902/424-4203. www.artgalleryof novascotia.ca. AE, MC, V.*

Janet Doble Pottery Studio
NORTH END   Potter Doble's bright and festive earthenware work is inspired by European majolica techniques; everything here brightens up the kitchen. Note that the studio hours are quirky, since she's a working artist; do her the courtesy of calling ahead, rather than just

Drala Books & Gifts specializes in Asian imports.

showing up. *2641 Fuller Terrace.* ☎ *902/455-6960. www.janetdoble pottery.com. MC, V.*

Books

Drala Books & Gifts
DOWNTOWN   This is the place in town for Asian imports, including raku-style pottery, incense, calligraphy and ikebana (flower-arranging) implements, paper *shoji* screens, chopsticks, tea, teapots, books on Asian design and philosophy, ornate greeting cards—plus a few crystal balls and gongs. *1567 Grafton St.* ☎ *877/422-2504 or 902/422-2504. www.drala.ca. AE, MC, V.*

Edibles

★ Harbourside Market
WATERFRONT   In the Historic Properties, this is a great place to grab a bite on the fly; the options include a deli, a fish market, and a bakery, among others. There's outdoor seating on the docks in summer. *1869 Upper Water St. (in Historic Properties).* ☎ *902/422-3077. Credit cards vary by vendor.*

Attica Furnishings features the work of local designers.

Furniture & Housewares

★★ Attica Furnishings DOWN-TOWN   Appealing, modernist furniture chosen largely from local designers, but also globally; think clean lines, whether it's in a steel table or bed frame by Halifax's Christopher Joyce, a Canadian-made leather couch, or a hardwood dining set. *1566 Barrington St.* ☎ *902/423-2557. www.attica.ca. AE, MC, V.*

Thornbloom—The Inspired Home SPRING GARDEN ROAD   In a small indoor mall along Spring Garden Road, this tiny shop sells housewares, knives by German makers Henckels, good-quality linens, gourmet sweets, and tile "memory blocks" by Vancouver artist Sid Dickens, among other items. *5640 Spring Garden Rd. (in Spring Garden Place).* ☎ *902/425-8005. AE, MC, V.*

Urban Cottage Antiques & Collectibles DOWNTOWN   A consignment store very close to NSCAD, Urban Cottage shows off a big, happily eclectic selection of antiques, furniture, housewares, jewelry, collectible toys, and more. It's all nicely displayed and rather reasonably priced. *1819 Granville St.* ☎ *902/423-3010. AE, MC, V.*

Outdoors

★ Mountain Equipment Co-Op DOWNTOWN   This Vancouver-based Canadian chain is cooperatively owned. They sell good-quality outdoor gear with an environmental philosophy, and also rent kayaks and tents. You must become a member (for a C$5 one-time fee) to shop here. *1550 Granville St.* ☎ *902/421-2667. www.mec.ca. AE, MC, V.*

Personal Care

★ Pür Alternatives DOWNTOWN   Born and raised in Halifax, this is a local producer and purveyor of all-natural cosmetics and baby-care products. Only a few of the items here contain alcohol, and none of them contain preservatives. *1903 Barrington St. (lower level).* ☎ *902/407-3660. www.puralternatives.ca. MC, V.*

Shopping Centers

★ Bishop's Landing WATER-FRONT   A residential complex right on the harbor-front with a sailing theme, Bishop's Landing is chiefly known for the wonderful Bish World Cuisine restaurant (p 76). But you can also buy gourmet chocolates, fancy shoes, vintage wines, or a good cup of espresso from the shops and stalls here. *1475 Lower Water St. (at Bishop St.).* ☎ *902/422-6412. www.bishopslanding.ca.*

Park Lane SPRING GARDEN ROAD   About 85 shops near the Public Gardens, encased in a modernist glass box; inside, it's heaviest on mid-range jewelers and clothing shops, but there's also a Geox shoe store and a tiny food court. *5657 Spring Garden Rd.* ☎ *902/420-0660. www.shopparklane.ca.*

★ Spring Garden Place SPRING GARDEN ROAD   Right on Spring Garden Road, this mall is open daily, has nicely upscale clothing and jewelry shops a cut above those in other city malls, and offers the best mall dining in town, hands-down. *5640 Spring Garden Rd. (btwn. Dresden Row & Brenton St.).* ☎ *902/420-0675. www.springgardenplace.ca.*

Halifax A&E & Nightlife A to Z

Arts Venues

★ The Khyber ICA DOWNTOWN

An artist's collective—the best sort—the Khyber occupies an austere brick building formerly owned by the Church of England. Only in Halifax. Check the website for updated schedules of art shows, live music, CD release parties, lectures, and classes. *1588 Barrington St.* ☎ *902/422-9668. www.khyber.ca.*

Scotiabank Theatre SOUTH

END   St. Mary's University's auditorium hosts a range of thought-provoking talks, readings, and conferences that lean toward the literary and artsy—or even the science-y, when the university's astronomers get into the act. *903 Robie St. (at Gorsebrook Ave.; in the Sobey Building).* ☎ *902/420-5400. www.smu.ca.*

Sir James Dunn Theatre SOUTH

END   Yet another arts-related space in the Dalhousie Arts Centre complex, this theater hosts avant-garde music and dance performances, plus a little bit of theater and classical music, to boot. *6101 University Ave. (Dalhousie Arts Centre).* ☎ *902/494-3820. http://arts centre.dal.ca.Tickets C$20–C$25.*

Bars & Cocktail Lounges

★ Economy Shoe Shop

DOWNTOWN   It's not a shop anymore, but rather a fashionable cafe/bistro/cocktail bar where Halifax's pretty people hang after hours; each of the fun sections has a different theme. The kitchen serves delicious finger foods until 2am, and there's a jukebox. *1663 Argyle St.* ☎ *902/423-8845. www.economy shoeshop.ca.*

Lower Deck Pub WATERFRONT

Locals have been coming to the Lower Deck forever for lively Irish and Maritime music and beer. There's music most nights of the week, and out on a patio in summer. The Beer Market downstairs is equally fine for a drink. *1869 Upper Water St. (in the Historic Properties).* ☎ *902/425-1501. www.lowerdeck.ca.*

★ Onyx SPRING GARDEN ROAD

Wines by the glass, premium martinis, live jazz and piano music, mojitos, champagnes, a fireplace, a sexy vibe—what else do you need? Celebrities visiting town usually pop in here for a drink. The kitchen serves "bar bites" until late. *5426 Portland Place (off Spring Garden Place).* ☎ *902/454-8533. www.onyx dining.com.*

★ Tribeca DOWNTOWN   A two-level bar/club with a sit-down restaurant on the ground level, Tribeca is one of your best choices

Each section of the Economy Shoe Shop has a different theme, and the kitchen is open until 2am.

downtown. There's usually pretty good rock music playing from decades past (but not too far past); a good place to mix, mingle, dance, and listen to tunes. *1588 Granville St.* ☎ *902/492-4036.*

★ Your Father's Moustache

SPRING GARDEN ROAD Not sure where the name came from, but there's no denying this place's popularity; it's practically a Halifax town meeting during the Saturday brunch-time blues jams. The rooftop terrace gets happy and crowded on warm summer nights. *5686 Spring Garden Rd.* ☎ *902/423-6766. www. yourfathersmoustache.ca.*

Film
★★ Dalhousie Film Series

SOUTH END Part of the fine Dalhousie Art Gallery (p 73, ⑦), this series has benefitted from a top-flight curator for 15 years. Screenings might include lesser-known works of director Pedro Almodóvar; a short run of First Nation or PBS-produced films; or shorts by French director Agnès Varda. *6101 University Ave. (Dalhousie Arts Centre).* ☎ *902/494-2403. http://artgallery.dal.ca.*

Symphony
★ Symphony Nova Scotia

SOUTH END Dalhousie's art center includes the home of the city's symphony orchestra, which plays classical concerts in the Rebecca Cohn Auditorium here; the season lasts from September to around May. A few concerts are also performed at a downtown church. *6101 University Ave. (Dalhousie Arts Centre).* ☎ *800/874-1669 or 902/494-3820. www.symphonynovascotia.ca. Tickets C$15–C$49.*

Theater
★★ Neptune Theatre

DOWNTOWN Halifax's most important theater space has done a makeover, adding an intimate, 200-seat theater to augment the more mainstream offerings in the big main house. Neptune's season runs from September through May, but there are also eclectic performances throughout the summer. *1593 Argyle St.* ☎ *800/565-7345 or 902/429-7070 (box office). www.neptunetheatre. com. Tickets C$15–C$60.*

★ Shakespeare by the Sea

SOUTH END Lovely summer performances of the Old Bard in lovely Point Pleasant Park. Park in the upper parking lot and walk about a half-mile in, on the main path; donate 15 bucks before or afterward. *Point Pleasant Dr. (offices in lower parking lot by sea terminal, performances in park at Cambridge Battery).* ☎ *902/422-0295. Free admission (C$15 donation suggested).* ●

The Symphony Nova Scotia performs from September to May.

5 Nova Scotia

The Annapolis Valley

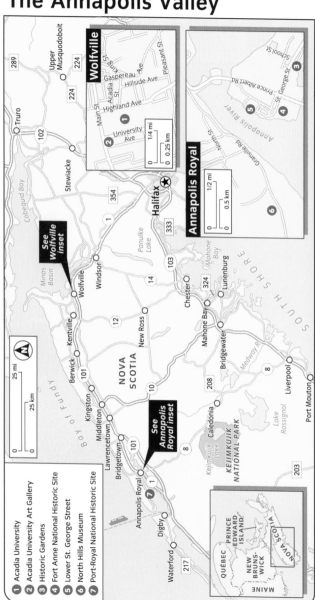

Wolfville

- Pleasant St.
- King St.
- Gaspereau Ave.
- Hillside Ave.
- Acadia St.
- Highland Ave.
- Main St.
- University Ave.

1/4 mi
0 0.25 km

Annapolis Royal

- School St.
- Prince Albert Rd.
- St. George St.
- Granville Rd.
- North St.
- Annapolis River

1/2 mi
0 0.5 km

289
224
224
Upper Musquodoboit
Truro
102
Stewiacke
354
1
Halifax
333
103
Panuke Lake
14
Chester
324
Mahone Bay
Lunenburg
Windsor
See Wolfville inset
Wolfville
Kentville
Berwick
12
New Ross
Minas Basin
Cobequid Bay
101
10
NOVA SCOTIA
Bridgewater
Medway R.
208
8
Liverpool
Port Mouton
Kingston
Middleton
Lawrencetown
Bridgetown
See Annapolis Royal inset
Annapolis Royal
101
1
7
8
Caledonia
Lake Rossignol
KEJIMKUJIK NATIONAL PARK
Kejimkujik Lake
203
Digby
Waterford
217
Bay of Fundy
SOUTH SHORE
Mahone Bay

25 mi
0
25 km
0

① Acadia University
② Acadia University Art Gallery
③ Historic Gardens
④ Fort Anne National Historic Site
⑤ Lower St. George Street
⑥ North Hills Museum
⑦ Port-Royal National Historic Site

QUÉBEC
PRINCE EDWARD ISLAND
NEW BRUNS-WICK
MAINE
NOVA SCOTIA

Previous page: The candy-cane striped lighthouse at Brier Island.

Nova Scotia beyond Halifax is full of wide-open spaces, jaw-dropping views, and quiet bays and coves. A great place to start is the gentle Annapolis Valley, which puts one in mind of England—appropriate, as it was "settled" by Loyalists. Plenty of kicked-out New Englanders found their way here, forced out the original Acadian settlers, and then built elegant, trim towns like Wolfville and Annapolis Royal. START: **Wolfville.**

1 Acadia University. The genteel town of Wolfville is focused around its university, which is nearly as big as the town itself—and was built by locals in 1838. (Men supposedly felled trees for the first buildings, while women knit mittens to raise funds.) Be sure to check out the Georgian-style environmental science center, which was only built in 2002 but looks much older. Its conservatory greenhouses are impressive and open daily year-round, while the fine adjacent botanical gardens can be toured from spring through fall. There's also a mile-long walking trail. 🕐 *30 min. University Ave. (off Rte. 1), Wolfville.* ☎ *902/542-2201 or 902/585-2201. www.acadiau.ca.*

On the campus of the university is the

2 Acadia University Art Gallery. The university's art museum is worth a stop. Open to the public since 1978, it showcases both contemporary and historic Nova Scotian art drawn from the university's collections (it began acquiring pieces in the late 19th century). It's especially notable for showing the work of female provincial artists. There are also faculty and student exhibitions. 🕐 *45 min. 10 Highland Ave. (at Main St.), Wolfville.* ☎ *902/585-1373. http://gallery.acadiau.ca. Free admission. Tues, Wed & Fri–Sun noon–4pm; Thurs noon–8pm.*

Backtrack to Rte. 1 & continue east to Rte. 101 West. Take 101 West 110km (68 miles). Get off at exit 22 (Annapolis Royal). Follow Rte. 8 west 2.5km (1½ miles) to the

3 ★ Historic Gardens. Set on a gentle hill overlooking a diked salt marsh, these attractive gardens offer a mix of formal and informal

The Historic Gardens overlook a diked salt marsh.

Pick Me! The Orchards of the Annapolis Valley

You can't write about the Annapolis Valley without mentioning apples. One of the joys of a fall afternoon in the Valley is picking a bag or basket of fruit in the orchards with the kids. One good place to start is at **Gates U-Pick (☎ 902/542-9340),** less than a 10-minute drive north of Wolfville on Starr's Point Road: They offer free wagon rides, and you can eat in the field as you pick. (Wash 'em off first.) You can also pick pumpkins, pears, or even sunflowers here. To get there, take Route 1 east a short distance to Greenwich, turn right on Route 368, and turn right again. They're open September and October daily from 9am to 6pm.

plantings, including a geometric Victorian garden, a "knot" garden, a rock garden, and a colorful perennial border garden. The place is perhaps best known for its 2,000 rose bushes (of 230 different cultivars) tracking the history of that flower's cultivation. ⏱ *45 min. 441 St. George St., Annapolis Royal.* ☎ *902/532-7018. www.historic gardens.com. Admission C$7.50 adults, C$6.50 seniors & students, C$20 families. July & Aug daily 8am– dusk; May, June, Sept & Oct daily 9am–5pm. Closed Nov–Apr.*

Continue through the Rte. 1 traffic light on St. George St. & turn left into the

4 ★ kids Fort Anne National Historic Site. Grassy earthworks cover this high ground overlooking the river, where the French built a fort around 1643; dozens of fortifications later occupied the same knoll. You can visit a gunpowder magazine or browse through a museum in the old British officers' quarters. But it's almost more fun to laze around on the lawns with the kids; you can even play croquet on the lawns.

The Fort Anne National Historic Site was built by the French in 1643.

1 hr. St. George St., Annapolis Royal. ☎ *902/532-2397. Admission C$3.90 adults, C$3.40 seniors, C$1.90 children, C$9.80 families. Mid-May to mid-Oct daily 9am–6pm; mid-Oct to mid-May buildings by appointment only (grounds open year-round).*

Continue west on foot or by car along

⑤ ★★ Lower St. George Street. Annapolis Royal is arguably Nova Scotia's most historic town—it bills itself as "Canada's birthplace"—and no street is more historic than this one. It's amazing to think, as you stroll the waterfront section (less than half a mile long), that you're walking the *oldest street in Canada.* You'll pass an Anglican church, Canada's oldest courthouse, the oldest wooden house in Canada, and numerous 18th-century wooden homes—each one worthy of contemplation. Continue to the end, where the road hairpins; a walking trail passes the riverfront mud flats, site of a short-lived shipyard that briefly built wooden ships here in 1916. *1 hr.*

Return to Rte. 1 (Prince Albert Rd.) & go north 1.6km (1 mile), past the power station. Turn left off Rte. 1 onto Greenland Rd. Continue 2.8km (1¾ miles) to the

⑥ North Hills Museum. This museum occupies a tidy shingled home built in 1764, filled with top-rate Georgian furniture, ceramics, and glassware. Local banker Robert Patterson accumulated the collection, then donated it to the province in the 1970s. Antiques collectors and history buffs will enjoy it; kids might be frustrated, though, because the opulently furnished rooms are mostly at arm's length, glimpsed through roped-off doorways. *30 min. 5065 Granville Rd., Granville Ferry.* ☎ *902/532-2168. Admission C$3 adults, C$2 seniors & children 6–17, C$7 families. June to mid-Oct Mon–Sat*

9:30am–5:30pm, Sun 1–5:30pm. Closed mid-Oct to May.

Continue 7km (4¼ miles) south-west on Greenland Rd. to the

⑦ ★★ Port-Royal National Historic Site. Now, this is historic: Canada's first permanent settlement was right here, on this attractive point with sweeping views of the basin. French settlers arrived in 1604 and lived pretty comfortably, in handsome little farmhouses designed by explorer Samuel de Champlain (1567–1635) to re-create the French countryside. All signs of that settlement eventually disappeared over the centuries, but this 1939 reproduction is faithful down to the details. Costumed interpreters show off woodworking techniques. *1 hr. Granville Rd., Port Royal.* ☎ *902/532-2898. Admission C$3.90 adults, C$3.40 seniors, C$1.90 children, C$9.80 families. Mid-May to mid-Oct daily 9am–6pm. Closed mid-Oct to mid-May.*

Port-Royal National Historic Site is where you'll find Canada's first permanent settlement by Europeans.

Digby

QUÉBEC PRINCE EDWARD ISLAND

MAINE NEW BRUNS-WICK

Digby○ NOVA SCOTIA

Lighthouse Rd.

303

❹

The Racquette

Raquette Rd.

Victoria St.

Carleton St.

Prince William St.

Sydney St.

Victoria St.

Church St.

West St.

3rd Ave.

King St.

2nd Ave.

Queen St.

1st Ave.

Birch St.

Maiden Ln.

Water St.

Mount St.

❶

❸

❷

0   200 yds
0   200 m

❶ The boardwalk
❷ Trinity Anglican Church
❸ Digby County Courthouse
❹ Point Prim

Digby, a working-class town protected by an encircling cove, is famous for its juicy scallops; huge fleets drag the ocean bottom just offshore. But the town is also full of wooden homes, historic buildings, and great views. (It's also a gateway for cars arriving by ferry from New Brunswick.) Some 1,500 Loyalist New Englanders hurriedly founded the town during the Revolutionary War, including John Edison—grandfather of inventor Thomas.

START: **Water St. at Church St.**

❶ kids **The boardwalk.** You can best see Digby's working harbor by strolling along its boardwalk, which runs below Water Street and takes in shops, tour outfits, views of boats and docks, and the *Lady Vanessa*— a 98-foot scallop dragger dry-docked so kids can walk around it and learn about the fisherman's life through a wheelhouse, shucking house, and videos. 🕐 *1 hr. Foot of Water St. (between Church & Sydney sts.). Lady Vanessa admission C\$2 adults.*

Walk 1 block south along the waterfront to Mountain St. & turn right. After 2 short blocks, turn right on Queen St. to find the

❷ ★★ **Trinity Anglican Church.** Said to be the only church in Canada built by shipwrights, this house of worship is Digby's architectural high point. Designed by Massachusetts architect Stephen Earle (1839–1913) with steeply pitched eaves and a slim bell tower, it was constructed in

The Digby County Courthouse was built in the Richardsonian style.

nearly shoulder-to-shoulder with the church (there's one building between them), and it seems somewhat out of proportion in a small, roistering fishing village. It was built in 1909 after a design by Leslie Fairn (1745–1816) to carry the load not only of Digby but Annapolis Royal, which had lost its own courthouse in a fire. You've got to love those double turrets. ⏲ *15 min. 119 Queen St.* ☎ *902/245-7134. Open to public Mon–Sat 9am–5pm.*

Follow Queen St. 2 blocks to the end; turn left on Racquette Rd. Go .8km (½ mile) & turn right on Shore Rd. After 6km (3¾ miles), turn right on Lighthouse Rd. Continue 1.6km (1 mile) to

1878 to replace an earlier version. The steeple bell dates from the town's founding in the 18th century (it was donated by the same Admiral Digby [1714–1746] who settled the town). Inside, there's abundant and lovely stained-glass window work. ⏲ *45 min. 109 Queen St.* ☎ *902/245-6744. Open to public July & Aug Tues–Sat 9am–5pm.*

Continue a few steps along Queen St. to the

❸ ★ **Digby County Courthouse.** This massive, pointy Richardsonian brick courthouse stands

❹ **Point Prim.** A lighthouse marks Point Prim, where the views are fine; you're certain to see the famous scallop draggers coming and going to Digby Gut (the narrows entering the harbor). This also makes a nice, easy cycling trip from town. Be careful by the cliff edges—it's a long drop down. Note that you can't enter the lighthouse itself—it's sealed off and automated now. But the sunsets are so amazing, you won't care. *30 min. End of Lighthouse Rd. No phone.*

Aw, Shucks! Digby's Scallop Days

When in Digby in summertime, watch for the regionally famous Scallop Days Festival, which brings the town together in early August for a 5-day orgy of shellfish-shucking and eating, music, parades, fireworks, and brawny competitions (woodsmen's competitions, pie-eating, canoe races in the strait, fireman's hose-laying contests, and such). There's also an exhibition of the ancient art of scallop-net knitting, and on the final Sunday, downtown streets close down for vending and merriment. It's all free except for the food. Visit the festival's website at www.digbyscallopdays.com or call ☎ **902/308-9445** for details.

Southern Shores

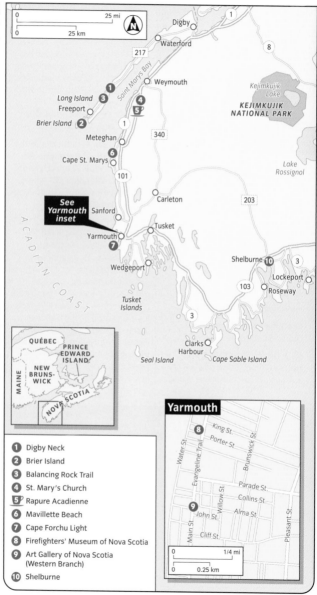

1. Digby Neck
2. Brier Island
3. Balancing Rock Trail
4. St. Mary's Church
5. Rapure Acadienne
6. Mavillette Beach
7. Cape Forchu Light
8. Firefighters' Museum of Nova Scotia
9. Art Gallery of Nova Scotia (Western Branch)
10. Shelburne

The southern tip of Nova Scotia is less drop-dead gorgeous than some other parts of the province, but it compensates with history and culture. This was once an Acadian stronghold, and their influence remains evident. It's also what you're most likely to see first if you're traveling from the United States because all ferries from the U.S. dock here. START: **Digby.**

Day 1
From Digby, drive south 50 km (30 miles) along

1 ★★ **Digby Neck.** Extending southwest from Annapolis Basin, Digby Neck looks like a nondescript, Cape Cod–like sand spit. Wrong. It's actually a 72km-long (45-mile) bony finger of high ridges, low bogs, dense forests, and impressive ocean views. The village of Sandy Cove is a picture-perfect little wide spot in the road, with church steeples poking up from the forest and water views, about 32km (20 miles) into the journey. The final two knuckles of the Neck are islands, connected by quick, 10-minute ferries. 🕐 *1½ hr. Along Rte. 217.*

From East Ferry at the southern tip of the Digby mainland, take the ferry to Tiverton (Long Island). Continue about 24km (15 miles) to Freeport & catch another ferry to

2 ★★ **Brier Island.** One of the most beautiful natural places on the entire Nova Scotian mainland, Brier Island is off the beaten track but well worth it. Here, you can spot rare migrating birds and seasonal whales; the island is laced with hiking trails; and there's a great little hiking trail to and beyond a brightly candy-cane-striped lighthouse. Park near the lighthouse and walk through stunted pines to open meadows on the province's western shore. 🕐 *2 hr.*

Backtrack 16km (10 miles) north to the trail head for the

3 ★ **Balancing Rock Trail.** Most travelers head quickly back to

The candy-cane striped lighthouse at Brier Island.

the mainland after Brier Island, but Long Island has several good hikes with views of St. Mary's Bay and the Bay of Fundy. The Balancing Rock Trail is about 4km (2½ miles) south of the Tiverton ferry on Route 217; look for a parking area. The 2.5km (1.5 mile) trail smoothly crosses through swamp, bog, and forest—until the last 100m (328 ft.), when it abruptly plummets straight down a sheer bluff to ocean's edge via 169 steps. At the bottom, boardwalks carry hikers over the surging sea to a straight-on view of one tall column of basalt balanced on another one. Cool. 🕐 *1 hr. Rte. 217, Long Island.*

Continue 55km (34 miles) north to Digby. Turn right. Take Rte. 101 south 30km (19 miles) to exit 28. Turn left on Rte. 1 & travel 11km (6¾ miles) south to

The Balancing Rock Trail ends at a sheer bluff with a spectacular view.

④ ★★ **St. Mary's Church.** Adjacent to the campus of Université Sainte-Anne, the only French-speaking university in Nova Scotia, this wooden church is awe-inspiring. And tall: 56m (184 ft.) tall, with some 40 tons of rock helping provide stability in the wind. A small museum in the back offers glimpses into its construction and history. ⏲ 1 hr. 1713 Hwy. 1, Church Point. ☎ 902/769-2382. www.baiesainte marie.com/ste-marie. Church free admission (donation requested); museum C$2 adults, C$5 families. Mid-May to mid-Oct daily 9am–5pm.

★ ⑤ **Rapure Acadienne.** Foodies, take note. This extremely unassuming bakery shop on Route 1, less than a mile south of St. Mary's Church, is ground zero for rappie pie. What's that? An Acadian must-try dish, made with beef or chicken, grated potatoes, bacon, and a whole lot of chicken broth. You can pick up a freshly baked pie for a little more than C$5. 1443 Rte. 1, Church Point. ☎ 902/769-2172. $.

Continue another 28km (17 miles) south on Rte. 1. Turn right on St. Mary's Rd. In 1.6km (1 mile), turn left to reach

⑥ ★ **Mavillette Beach.** This beautiful crescent beach has nearly all the ingredients for a pleasant summer afternoon: lots of sand, grassy dunes, changing stalls, a nearby snack bar, and views across the water to scenic Cape St. Mary's. All that's lacking are picnic tables and an ocean warm enough to actually swim in; it's seriously frigid here, though some hardy souls do give it a go. The beach, managed as a provincial park, is 1km (½ mile) off Route 1, and the turnoff is well marked. ⏲ 45 min. John Doucette Rd. (off Rte. 1), Cape St. Mary's. Free admission. Mid-May to mid-Oct dawn–dusk.

Continue about 32km (20 miles) south on Rte. 1 or Rte. 101 to Yarmouth. At Rte. 304 (just past the Lakelawn Motel), turn right onto Vancouver St. (Rte. 304). Continue 14km (8¾ miles) to

⑦ **Cape Forchu Light.** This lighthouse marks, and protects, Yarmouth's harbor. It dates from the early 1960s, when it replaced a much older octagonal version that succumbed to wind and time. There's a tiny photographic exhibit on the cape's history inside the keeper's house. Take time to ramble around the dramatic bluffs and along a short trail out to the point below the light. ⏲ 45 min. End of Rte. 304, Yarmouth. Keeper's house/ museum open June-Sept, daily 11am-7pm; free.

Backtrack to Rte. 1 (Main St.) & turn right; continue 1.6km (1 mile) into Yarmouth. Overnight in Yarmouth.

DAY 2
On Main St. is the

8 kids **Firefighters' Museum of Nova Scotia.** This museum is home to a varied collection of early provincial firefighting equipment. Kids love the 1933 vintage Chev Bickle hand pumper because they can don helmets and take the wheel. ⏱ *45 min. 451 Main St., Yarmouth.* ☎ *902/742-5525. Admission C$3 adults, C$2.50 seniors, C$1.50 children, C$6 families. July & Aug Mon–Sat 9am–9pm, Sun 10am–5pm; June & Sept Mon–Sat 9am–5pm; Oct–May Mon–Fri 9am–4pm, Sat 1–4pm.*

Continue .3km (¼ mile) along Main St. to the

9 ★ **Art Gallery of Nova Scotia (Western Branch).** A satellite of the great art museum in Halifax (p 43, **2**), this gallery is located inside a former bank in the heart of Yarmouth. Exhibits draw from the mothership's permanent collections and might include a rumination on the history of flight or a collection of tall-ship paintings. ⏱ *45 min. 340*

Main St., Yarmouth. ☎ *902/749-2248. Admission C$5 adults, C$4 seniors, C$3.50 students, C$2 children 6–17, C$12 families; free w/ AGNS Halifax receipt. Daily 10am–5pm (Thurs to 8pm in summer).*

From Yarmouth, take the Rte. 103 expressway about 100km (62 miles) north & east to

10 ★★ **Shelburne.** The most historic town in Nova Scotia's southern reaches has got to be Shelburne. A Loyalist town that went mad with wooden shipbuilding, it's host today to a quartet of related historical museums—a single package ticket grants you access to all four. (See "The Best in 3 Days" in Chapter 3 for more details on this historic complex and its museums, including **The Dory Shop** and the **Muir-Cox Shipyard.**) Beyond the history, there are also a few good eateries, such as the **Charlotte Lane Café** (13 Charlotte Lane; ☎ 902/875-3314) and a quiet compact downtown to stroll through. ⏱ *2 hr.*

Kids enjoy playing with the vintage equipment on display at the Firefighter's Museum of Nova Scotia.

Lunenburg to Chester

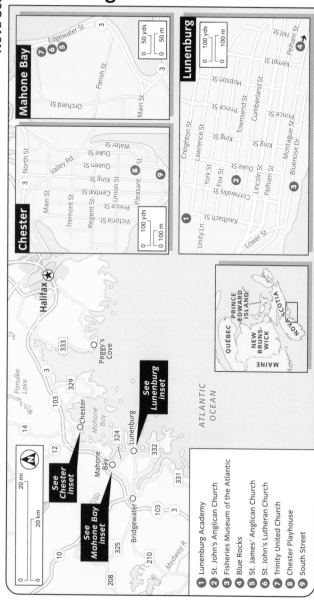

Mahone Bay

Edgewater St.

Parish St.

Orchard St.

Main St.

3

0   50 yds
0   50 m

Lunenburg

0   100 yds
0   100 m

Hill St.

Kempt St.

Pelham St.

Hopson St.

Prince St.

Cumberland St.

Creighton St.

Townsend St.

Lawrence St.

King St.

King St.

Prince St.

York St.

Fox St.

Duke St.

Cornwallis St.

Lincoln St.

Pelham St.

Montague St.

Bluenose Dr.

Kaulbach St.

Unity Ln.

Lower St.

Chester

North St.

Valley Rd.

Main St.

Tremont St.

Water St.

Duke St.

Queen St.

King St.

Central St.

Union St.

Prince St.

Regent St.

Victoria St.

Pleasant St.

0   100 yds
0   100 m

3

Halifax

Peggy's Cove

333

329

103

Panuke Lake

14

Chester

Mahone Bay

Mahone Bay

324

12

Lunenburg

332

ATLANTIC OCEAN

331

Bridgewater

103

3

325

210

208

10

Medway R.

N

0   20 mi
0   20 km

See Chester inset

See Mahone Bay inset

See Lunenburg inset

MAINE

QUÉBEC

NEW BRUNS-WICK

PRINCE EDWARD ISLAND

NOVA SCOTIA

1 Lunenburg Academy
2 St. John's Anglican Church
3 Fisheries Museum of the Atlantic
4 Blue Rocks
5 St. James' Anglican Church
6 St. John's Lutheran Church
7 Trinity United Church
8 Chester Playhouse
9 South Street

If I had just one or two days to spend in Nova Scotia, I'd make a beeline for the South Shore trifecta of Lunenburg, Mahone Bay, and Chester. All three of these attractive towns are within an easy half-hour drive of each other, and each of them looks great in its own unique way. START: **Lunenburg, at the top of Kaulbach St.**

1 Lunenburg Academy. Looming over the town from a ridge-top perch, this architecturally unique, red-and-white school is easy to spot as you enter Lunenburg; it sets a tone for the town, the same way the Citadel does in Halifax. The exaggerated mansard roof, pointy towers, and extravagant use of ornamental brackets sets it apart from anything else in Lunenburg, and the bottom two floors are *still* used as a public school. So the interior is only open to the public on special occasions, but it's worth a quick look. ⏱ 15 min. 97 Kaulbach St. No admission.

Travel 2 blocks downhill on Kaulbach St. to Townsend St. & turn left. In 1½ blocks, you reach

2 ★★ St. John's Anglican Church. This church is one of the most impressive architectural sights in Eastern Canada, even if it is a reconstruction. The original, built in 1754 of oak timbers shipped up from Boston, burned in 2001; the interior was nearly a total loss. Four years later, the church reopened using almost exactly the same design, thanks to the help of master restorers. It was built in a simple New England–meetinghouse style, but in several subsequent waves was overlaid by ornamentation and shingling in classic Carpenter Gothic style. Many local residents can say they were baptized here. It's a must-see. ⏱ 1 hr. Townsend St. (btwn. Duke & Cornwallis sts.). Free admission.

Continue to Duke St. Turn right & go 5 blocks down to the waterfront, site of the

3 ★★ kids Fisheries Museum of the Atlantic. Lunenberg's big Fisheries Museum is professionally designed and curated. You'll find aquariums on the first floor,

The picturesque cove of Blue Rocks.

including a touch-tank, and answers to burning questions like "Do fish sleep?" Dioramas depict various Canadian fishing vessels. There's also an exhibit on (hypothetical) sea monsters, and you can tour a trawler, salt-bank schooner, boat shop, and scallop-shucking house. 🕐 1¼ hr. ☎ 866/579-4909 or 902/634-4794. http://museum.gov. ns.ca/fma. Admission mid-May to mid-Oct C$10 adults, C$7 seniors, C$3 children 6–17, C$22 families; mid-Oct to mid-May C$4 adults & seniors, free for children. Mid- to end of May, June, Sept & early to mid Oct daily 9:30am–5:30pm; July & Aug daily 9:30am–7pm; Nov–Apr Mon–Fri 9:30am–4pm.

Follow the waterfront east along Montague St. (which becomes Pelham St. & then Blue Rocks Rd.) for 6.4km (4 miles) to

④ ★ **Blue Rocks.** East of the working harbor, Blue Rocks isn't so much a fishing village as it is a tiny, picturesque cove (sans tour buses). The winding roadway gets narrower as the homes become more and

more humble. Eventually, you reach the tip of the point, where there are just rocks, fishing shacks, nets, buoys, boats, and views of spruce- and heath-covered islands offshore. (The rocks are said to glow in a blue hue in certain light, hence the name.) Bring a camera. 🕐 45 min. Blue Rocks Rd., Lunenburg.

Return to town & follow Pelham St. west out of town, turning left on Lincoln St. (which becomes Dufferin St.). Follow Rte. 3 north 10km (6¼ miles) to Mahone Bay. Turn right (stay on Rte. 3); in a few blocks, you reach the

⑤ ★★ **St. James' Anglican Church.** If forced to choose a "best" of Mahone Bay's three lovely churches, this 1887 Gothic Revival stunner takes the prize. It was actually the third and final addition to the tableau, but Halifax architect William Critchlow Harris (1854–1913) did the town proud. His lovely, swirling Victorian spire, triangular main hall, and cream-and-maroon color scheme are striking. 🕐 45 min. Edgewater St. ☎ 902/624-8614. Free admission.

Mahone Bay's three churches.

Tours July & Aug Mon–Sat 9am–noon (occasionally closed to tours).

Two buildings to the right of St. James' make up

6 ★ St. John's Lutheran Church. The town's "middle" church was built on the harbor in 1869 by Lutherans, making it the *first* one sited on the waterfront. But that version was much simpler than what you see today; the church was greatly expanded in 1903, with the additions of the big wings and some stained-glass windows. Inside, the church ceiling closely resembles a ship's hull—and that was on purpose. ⏱ *15 min. 89 Edgewater St.* ☎ *902/624-9660. www.stjohns mahonebay.ca. Free admission. Free tours July & Aug Tues–Sat 9am–noon (occasionally closed to tours).*

Just the right of St. John's is

7 Trinity United Church. Originally located at the top of the hill overlooking the harbor, this church (Presbyterian at the time) was jacked up and literally rolled downhill—slowly, pulled by oxen along a set of thick rollers—over 10 nail-biting days in 1885. The church survived the trip and took its place second in the harbor lineup, but was later truncated of its steeple. It features plenty of narrow arches. ⏱ *15 min. 101 Edgewater St.* ☎ *902/624-8255. Free admission. Tours July & Aug Mon–Fri 11am–3pm (occasionally open other days as well).*

Travel north on Rte. 3 for 23km (14 miles) to Chester. Turn right on King St. & continue 4 blocks to Pleasant St. & the

8 ★ Chester Playhouse. Chester's intimate blue playhouse was actually a movie house when it was built in 1938, but it eventually morphed into a live performance venue. Today, it hosts a full program

The Chester Playhouse is now both a live performance venue and the town's de facto community center.

of plays, concerts, theater festivals, puppet shows, films, and other events nearly year-round; essentially, it functions as the town's social center. ⏱ *1 hr. 22 Pleasant St.* ☎ *800/363-7529 or 902/275-3933. www.chesterplayhouse.ca. Tickets C$12–C$25.*

From the playhouse, walk a block south to

9 South Street. Chester's humble harbor road is simply known as South Street, and there's nothing pretentious to mark it: no inflatable lobsters, no fish houses, no bars, no cruise ships docked up. Instead, the star attraction is the beautiful view of Back Harbour—this could be a tiny, forgotten harbor or summer-cottage town somewhere in Maine. Sit on the plain wooden benches, stroll past the docks and a yacht club, or admire a few summer homes and small mansions. ⏱ *30 min.*

Cape Breton Highlands

1 Mabou

2 Glenora Distillery

3 Margaree Salmon Museum

4 Cape Breton Highlands National Park information center

5 Cabot Trail (Chéticamp to Pleasant Bay section)

6 Whale Interpretive Centre

7 Lone Shieling Trail

8 North Highlands Community Museum

9 Cabot Landing Provincial Park

10 Bay St. Lawrence

11 Meat Cove

12 White Point

13 Neil's Harbour

14 Cabot Trail (Cape Smokey section)

Cape Breton Island is Atlantic Canada writ large. The scenery doesn't get any better than this east of Alberta unless you count Newfoundland, and lots of folks think it's *still* better here. The only way to do the Cape is by car, circling slowly—west to east is traditional, and that's how I've laid out this tour. You can also do it the opposite way. START: **Port Hastings, on the western shore of Cape Breton Island.**

Day 1
From the bridge at Port Hastings, drive 58km (36 miles) north on Rte. 19 (the Ceilidh Trail) to

1 ★ Mabou. For getting the flavor of this island, there's perhaps no better first stop than the tiny village of Mabou. Once a coal-mining town, Mabou remade itself into a lobster-fishing town, though there are few seafood restaurants in the town; instead, come for the lovely scenery and amazing Celtic music scene. The town basically consists of a main street, a few eateries and services, and a scenic little beach or two—but go inside any pub or arts center, almost any time of year, and you can hear live fiddles, dance at a *ceilidh*, or hear Celtic-style singing. The Rankin Family, a famous Canadian band, hailed from here. ⏲ *2 hr. Rte. 19.*

Continue 9km (5½ miles) north on Rte. 19 to the

2 ★ Glenora Distillery. This modern distillery, tucked into a valley between Mabou and Inverness, is said to be North America's only single-malt whisky (i.e., scotch) producer. It began producing spirits from the pure local waters in 1990 but waited 10 years to age them properly before making them available for sale. Production runs take place in the fall, but tours are offered year-round; helpful guides explain why the owner sited the factory here—seemingly in the middle of nowhere—and why the distillery uses Kentucky bourbon casks to age its whisky. The tours culminate, of course, in free samples of the good stuff. ⏲ *1½ hr. Rte. 19, Glenville.* ☎ *800/839-0491 or 902/258-2662. www.glenoradistillery.com. Tours C$7 adults. Tours year-round daily 9am–5pm; pub mid-June to mid Oct, daily 11am–11pm.*

The Glenora Distillery is said to be North America's only single-malt whisky producer.

The Margaree Salmon Museum explains Canada's most famous fly-fishing river.

Continue 40km (25 miles) north on Rte. 19 to Margaree Forks. Turn right onto the Cabot Trail. In .4km (¼ mile), turn left on East Margaree Rd. Cross the river & turn right to find the

❸ ★ kids Margaree Salmon Museum. The Margaree is arguably Canada's most famous fly-fishing river, and this handsome little museum explains why. You learn about the river's history and the life cycles of salmon, but the highlight is the fishing ephemera: antique rods down through history and an eye-catching collection of skillfully hand-tied flies. If you want to fish, museum docents can even help you find a local guide—late spring and early fall are the best times to try. 🕐 45 min. 60 West Big Intervale Rd. (just off Cabot Trail), Margaree Forks. ☎ 902/248-2848. Admission C$2 adults, C$1 children. Mid-June to mid-Oct daily 9am–5pm.

Backtrack to the Cabot Trail & turn right (north). Continue 45km (28 miles) through the town of

Chéticamp (p 40, ❺). A few miles beyond, park at the

❹ Cape Breton Highlands National Park information center. The first of two info centers bracketing either end of the most spectacular sections of the park, Chéticamp's is bigger and better than its Ingonish counterpart. There's extensive information here, including a slide presentation, exhibits on geology and natural history, a cool large-scale relief map of the stunning hills and cliffs, and a good bookstore. The center's also stocked with lots of maps. 🕐 30 min. 16650 Cabot Trail (3km/1¾ miles north of town), Chéticamp. ☎ 902/224-2306. www. pc.gc.ca. Park entry C$7.80 adults, C$6.80 seniors, C$3.90 children, C$19.60 families. July & Aug daily 8am–8pm; mid-May to June & Sept to mid-Oct daily 9am–5pm; mid-Oct to mid-May park offices Mon–Fri 8am–4pm, info center closed.

Overnight in Chéticamp.

Day 2
Continue about 35km (22 miles) north along the

❺ ★★★ Cabot Trail (Chéticamp to Pleasant Bay section). As soon as you leave Chéticamp, things get *really* interesting. The island's northwestern coast quickly becomes visually stunning as you ascend high, high above the water you just walked right beside. Budget lots of extra time for driving this 35km (20-mile) section because you'll want to stop often at the pull-outs to gawk at the views, read signs, and snap photos for your trip blog. The last few miles into Pleasant Bay are the stuff of calendar and postcard legend. 🕐 2 hr.

In Pleasant Bay, turn left on Pleasant Bay Rd. at the sign for

Red River & immediately left onto Harbour Rd. to find the

6 kids **Whale Interpretive Centre.** Built on a rise overlooking the harbor, Pleasant Bay's small whale museum opened in 2000 and features exhibits that explain why the waters offshore are so rich with marine life. The hanging, life-sized model of a local whale (named "Hook") is both awe-inspiring and a bit frightening. 🕐 *30 min. Harbour Rd., Pleasant Bay.* ☎ *902/224-1411. Admission C$4.50 adults, C$3.50 seniors & children, C$14 families. Mid-May to mid-June, Sept & Oct daily 9am–6pm; Mid-June to Aug daily 9am–8pm. Closed Nov to mid-May.*

Backtrack to the Cabot Trail, turn left & continue 6.4km (4 miles) to the parking lot for the

7 **Lone Shieling Trail.** There are plenty of spectacular hikes in the park, and then there are a few which are just nice for a quick break from all the driving. This easy, .8km (.5-mile) loop through lush hardwood forest is one of them. There are no ocean views, but you can gaze upon a stand of 350-year-old sugar maple trees. There's also a re-created hut of a

Scottish crofter (shepherd), another cool feature of this trail. 🕐 *30 min.*

Continue 26km (16 miles) to Cape North. At the intersection with Bay St. Lawrence Rd., on the left, is the

8 kids **North Highlands Community Museum.** This is a small local museum of highland life, with things you'd expect, such as items from early village schoolrooms, treasures salvaged from local shipwrecks, and fishing gear. But what makes it more interesting than usual is a working blacksmith's forge and a carefully designed series of gardens. Special exhibits highlight aspects of local culture, such as the gypsum quarry trade, histories of churches, and shipwreck tales. 🕐 *30 min. 29263 Cabot Trail, Cape North.* ☎ *902/383-2579. www. northhighlandsmuseum.ca. Free admission (donations requested). Mid-June to Oct daily 10am–5pm. Closed Nov to mid-June.*

Turn left onto Bay St. Lawrence Rd. & go 9.7km (6 miles) to

10 **Cabot Landing Provincial Park.** Local lore claims that the Italian explorer John Cabot first made

"Hook", the life-sized model at the Whale Interpretive Centre.

A recreated Scottish crofter hut on the Lone Shieling Trail.

landfall in North America on this spot in 1497. Debate the issue with fellow travelers near the statue of Cabot or take a long walk along the lovely 3.2km (2-mile) red-sand beach fronting the bay. The views of the remote coastline are camera-worthy, and you can swim in the bay. 🕐 *1 hr. Bay St. Lawrence Rd.,*

Cabot Landing Provincial Park marks the spot where the Italian explorer is said to have first set foot in North America in 1497.

Sugarloaf. No phone. Free admission. Daily dawn–dusk.

Continue north on Bay St. Lawrence Rd. 7km (4¼ miles), bearing right at the fork, to reach

⑪ ★ **Bay St. Lawrence.** This tiny fishing village is hard to find, lightly visited, and barely populated. But there's actually quite a bit to do once you make it here: a wharf; a takeout seafood hut called simply **The Hut** (☎ 902/383-2513); and several good whale-watching outfits, the premier of which is **Oshan** (3384 Bay St. Lawrence Rd.; ☎ 877/383-2883 or 902/383-2883; www.oshan.ca). There's even a motel with a view, **Burton's Sunset Oasis** (105 Money Point Rd.; ☎ 902/383-2666; www.burtons oasismotel.ca). And the town's **community center** (3160 Bay St. Lawrence Rd.; ☎ 902/383-2334), is a one-stop place to read a book, check your e-mail, or eat lunch in its **Bay Café**—which also opens weekends, with live music, for breakfast and lunch in July and August. *End of Bay St. Lawrence Rd.* 🕐 *1 hr.*

Backtrack 3km (1¾ miles) to the fork in the road & turn right. Go 13km (8 miles) to

⑫ ★ Meat Cove. The journey to Meat Cove *is* the destination. You drive a stunning cliff-side road, the last 4.8km (3 miles) along a dirt track high on the shoulders of coastal mountains. Do not try this with a new car or if you're nervy about heights. The road ends at a rough-hewn settlement that's always been home to a few hardy fishermen—and a few shady ravines, brooks, and rivers. For sheer end-of-the-worldness, it can't be beat. ⌚ *30 min.*

Backtrack 30km (19 miles) to Cape North. Turn left onto the Cabot Trail & go 5km (3 miles) to White Point Rd. Turn left (off Cabot Trail) & go 11km (6¾ miles), bearing left at the fork, to

⑬ ★ White Point. This village makes a nice detour from the Cabot Trail. The road climbs upward amidst jagged cliffs with sweeping views of Aspy Bay, then descends to a smattering of fishing boats, a resort hotel, and a nice beach. From the harbor, be sure to go 2km (1¼ miles) out to the tip of the land for even *more* dramatic views. ⌚ *15 min.*

Backtrack 1.6km (1 mile) & turn left onto New Haven Rd. Follow it 8km (5 miles) to

⑭ ★ Neil's Harbour. Yet another fishing village on Cape Breton—and another one that's postcardworthy—Neil's Harbour is just moments off the Cabot Trail, even if it feels far away from it. On a rocky knob across the bay is a square, red-and-white lighthouse—far from the most attractive one on the coast, but the only one I know of in the province that doubles as a summertime ice cream shop. ⌚ *15 min.*

Continue .8km (½ mile) to the Cabot Trail. Turn left & travel 32km (20 miles) through all the Ingonish towns. Stock up on food, drink, or gas before retackling the

⑮ ★★ Cabot Trail (Cape Smokey section). How much more scenery can a person take? A few miles beyond South Ingonish Harbour, the Trail begins a final ascent as it crawls up and across the face of 330m (1,082-ft.) Cape Smokey. As you round the headland, the ocean explodes into panoramic views. This 16km (10-mile) ride is your last shot at jaw-dropping photos before leaving the park region. Sure, the rest of Cape Breton is nice—but you've just finished driving the *very* best of it. ⌚ *45 min. Cabot Trail, South Ingonish Harbour to Wreck Cove.*

The Cabot Trail near Cape Smokey.

Sydney

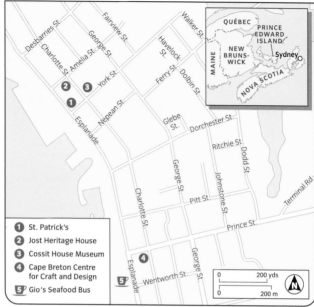

1 St. Patrick's
2 Jost Heritage House
3 Cossit House Museum
4 Cape Breton Centre for Craft and Design
5 Gio's Seafood Bus

The city of Sydney isn't exactly a charmer—it's the gritty, working-class hub of Cape Breton—but it does hold a few historic attractions in its pleasing North End. Founded as a Loyalist port, Sydney later morphed into a steel and coal powerhouse before fading out. (It's still the jumping-off point for ferries to Newfoundland.) These stops are all within 2 blocks of each other. **START: North end of Sydney's waterfront, on Esplanade Rd.**

1 **St. Patrick's.** Known locally simply as "St. Pat's," this is Cape Breton Island's oldest Roman Catholic house of worship, dating from around 1828, and it looks it. It's smallish and made of rugged stone. During summer, a small museum in the church opens daily. ⏱ *30 min. 87 Esplanade Rd.* ☎ *902/539-1572. Free admission. Museum June to early Sept Mon–Sat 9:30am–5:30pm, Sun 1:30–5:30pm; early Sept to May by appointment only.*

Walk 1 block north to Amelia St. At the corner of Charlotte St. is the

2 ★ **Jost Heritage House.** One of the oldest homes in the city, this one was built around the same time as Cossit House (see below). It had a number of incarnations in the intervening years, including time as both a store and pharmacy; many of the display items, though, are from a century later, when a Halifax merchant filled it with Victoriana.

30 min. 54 Charlotte St. ☎ *902/539-0366. Admission C$2 adults. June–Aug Mon–Sat 9:30am–5:30pm, Sun 1:30–5:30pm; Sept–May call for hours.*

Continue ½ block on Charlotte St. to the

❸ **Cossit House Museum.** Built in 1787 by an Anglican minister, this is likely Sydney's oldest standing home, now carefully restored and furnished with a fine collection of 18th-century antiques. *15 min. 75 Charlotte St.* ☎ *902/539-7973. Admission C$2 adults, C$1 seniors & children 6–17. June to mid-Oct Mon–Sat 9am–5pm, Sun 1–5pm.*

Continue downtown .7km (½ mile) south along Charlotte St. Just past Prince St. is the

❹ ★ **Cape Breton Centre for Craft and Design.** An outgrowth of a regional arts alliance, this downtown Sydney museum/gallery is first-rate. Its exhibitions have highlighted everything from local rug art to quilting, flower art, the work of Cape Breton's musical instrument-makers, and multimedia ruminations on time by regional artists. *1 hr. 322 Charlotte St.* ☎ *902/270-7491. www.capebretoncraft.com. Free*

They take their fiddling seriously in Sydney.

admission. Mon–Fri 10am–4pm, Sat noon–4pm.

☕ ❺ **Gio's Seafood Bus.** Not the first bus I've ever seen converted into a seafood hut. It's not even the first one in Nova Scotia I've seen. But it seems to be the most enduring. It offers chowder, plus lobsters and a few meal options. Yes, you sit on the bus and eat. *Corner of Esplanade Rd. & Wentworth St.* ☎ *902/561-0809. $$.*

The Celtic Colours Festival

Each fall, a huge, island-wide music festival—timed to coincide with the peak of the lovely highland foliage—takes place (in early to mid-Oct), and Sydney is its center. The mix of local musicians getting together to jam beneath the beautiful backdrop is breathtaking. The festival (☎ **877/285-2321** or 902/562-6700; www.celtic-colours. com) usually lasts for about 10 days of foot-stomping, penny-whistling, and fiddle-playing. Performers include both the leading lights of Celtic music and newer acts. Book well ahead if you want to see a particular act; tickets, which cost C$20 to C$60, sell out fast.

Bras D'Or Lake

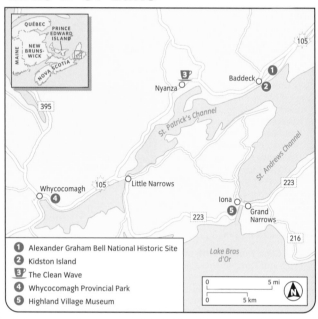

1 Alexander Graham Bell National Historic Site
2 Kidston Island
3 The Clean Wave
4 Whycocomagh Provincial Park
5 Highland Village Museum

This driving tour touches on some of the best parts of Bras D'Or Lake, the huge lake at the heart of Cape Breton Island. It's worth visiting for the views, quiet, and wildlife. The lake's "capital" is Baddeck, a trim village offering boat tours of the lake, plus a clutch of inns, restaurants, and services. START: **North end of Chebucto St. (Rte. 205) in Baddeck.**

1 ★★ kids Alexander Graham Bell National Historic Site. For much of his life, Bell (1847–1922) summered at this hillside mansion, which is now part tribute and part science center. Exhibits cover the telephone, but also Bell's kites, hydrofoils, airplanes, and metal detector. There's a cool section where kids can apply their own creativity to real-life science problems. ⏱ 1½ hr. 559 Chebucto St. (Rte. 205), Baddeck. ☎ 902/295-2069. www.pc.gc.ca/lhn-nhs/ns/graham bell/index.aspx. Admission C$7.80

adults, C$6.55 seniors, C$3.90 children 6–16, C$20 families. May & mid-Oct to late Oct daily 8:30am–5pm; June daily 9am–6pm; July to mid-Oct daily 8:30am–6pm. Closed Nov–Apr.

Return to town & turn left on Cameron St. In 1 block is Water St. & the town wharf, from which you can take a boat to

2 ★ Kidston Island. About 183m (600 ft.) offshore from Baddeck in the lake is this quiet little island, owned by the town. It has a wonderful sand beach with lifeguards and a

The Black House, one of the Highland Village Museum's replica structures.

quite striking old lighthouse to explore (.8km/½ mile from the dock). The local Lion's Club offers frequent pontoon boat shuttles across St. Patrick's Channel, when the weather's warm and clear enough. The crossing is free, but donations are encouraged. ⏱ 1¼ hr. Dock at Water St. Free crossing (donations recommended). Crossings daily July & Aug, depending on weather and demand.

3 **The Clean Wave.** There's a First Nation (Native Canadian) reserve right on Route 105, about midway between Baddeck and Whycocomagh, and it's worth stopping in for a look. There's drumming and crafts, but if you're in a hurry, stop by the reserve's diner/ restaurant, the Clean Wave: they serve bowls of chowder and daily specials. 10765 Rte. 105, Wagmatcook; ☎ 866/295-2999 or 902/295-2999. www.wagmatcook.com. $$.

From Baddeck, follow Rte. 205 3km (1¾ miles) south to Rte. 105; turn left & go 35km (22 miles) west to

4 ★★ kids **Whycocomagh Provincial Park.** From this park at lake's edge, three short but steep

trails (none longer than 2km/1.2 miles) ascend a plateau and the Salt Mountain look-off. You'll not only see splendid views of Bras D'Or; you may very well see bald eagles. There's also a campground, playground, and good fall foliage here. ⏱ 1 hr. 960 Hampton Mountain Rd., Whycocomagh. ☎ 902/756-2248. Free admission. Mid-June to mid-Oct dawn–dusk.

Backtrack 8km (5 miles) to Rte. 223 (Bras D'Or Lakes Rd.). Turn right & continue 24km (15 miles) to the

5 ★ kids **Highland Village Museum.** On a grassy lakeside hill just before Iona, this is a beautiful spot for a history museum. The 16-hectare (40-acre) "village" consists of buildings reflecting the region's Gaelic heritage—some historic structures, others good replicas. Poke through Black House (a Scottish stone-and-sod hut), a schoolhouse, and a 1920s-era general store. ⏱ 1 hr. 4119 Rte. 223, Iona. ☎ 866/442-3542 or 902/725-2272. http://museum.gov.ns.ca/hv. Admission C$9 adults, C$7 seniors, C$4 children 6–17, C$22 families. June to mid-Oct daily 9:30am–5:30pm. Closed mid-Oct to May.

Nova Scotia Dining

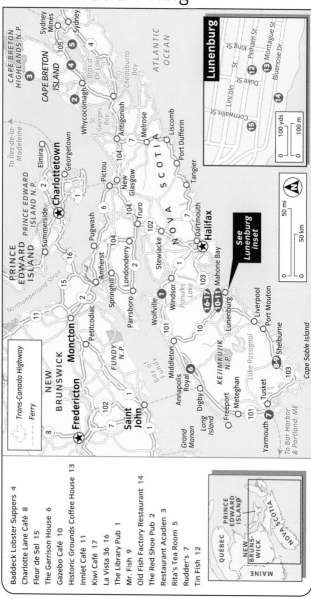

Baddeck Lobster Suppers 4
Charlotte Lane Café 8
Fleur de Sel 15
The Garrison House 6
Gazebo Café 10
Historic Grounds Coffee House 13
Innlet Café 11
Kiwi Café 17
La Vista 36 16
The Library Pub 1
Mr. Fish 9
Old Fish Factory Restaurant 14
The Red Shoe Pub 2
Restaurant Acadien 3
Rita's Tea Room 5
Rudder's 7
Tin Fish 12

Dining A to Z

kids Baddeck Lobster Suppers
BADDECK *SEAFOOD* This no-frills
restaurant has the charm of a
Legion Hall and charges a lot, but
you can chow down on lobster, plus
all-you-can-eat mussels, chowder,
biscuits, dessert, and soda. (Beer
and wine cost extra.) There's also
cedar-planked fish and a kids' menu.
20 Ross St. ☎ *902/295-3307.
Entrees C$28–C$30. MC, V. June–Oct
dinner daily. Closed Nov–May.*

★ **Charlotte Lane Café** SHEL-
BURNE *INTERNATIONAL* On a tiny
lane between Shelburne's waterfront and its tiny main street, this
kitchen's eclectic menu ranges from
pasta dishes to Thai-spiced tofu,
rack of lamb, seared scallops, and a
filet mignon–lobster combo. There's
a wine list, too. *13 Charlotte Lane
(btwn. Water & Dock sts.).* ☎ *902/
875-3314. Lunch items C$10, dinner
entrees C$16–C$21. MC, V. Lunch &
dinner daily.*

★★ **Fleur de Sel** LUNENBURG
FRENCH Some say this is the best
French food in the Maritimes. Not
sure about that, but it's awfully
good—and modernized and made
healthier with touches like potato
crème brûlée, olive oil hollandaise
sauce, and unusual spicing. *53 Montague St.* ☎ *902/640-2121. www.fleur
desel.net. Brunch entrees C$12–C$18,
dinner entrees C$28–C$36. AE, MC, V.
Late May to mid-Oct dinner Mon–Sat,
brunch Sun; mid-Oct to late Oct dinner
Thurs–Sat, brunch Sun. Closed Nov to
late May.*

★★ **The Garrison House** ANNAP-
OLIS ROYAL *INTERNATIONAL* The
Garrison House Inn's restaurant is
arguably the most intimate, attractive, and innovative of Annapolis
Royal's eating choices. Three cozy
dining rooms each have a different

*Fleur de Sel in Lunenburg has some of
the Maritimes' most notable French food.*

feel, and chef Patrick Redgrave's
menu ranges all over the world
without ever losing its Canadian
footing. *350 St. George St.* ☎ *866/
532-5750 or 902/532-5750. Entrees
C$14–C$27. AE, MC, V. May–Oct
dinner daily. Closed Nov–Apr.*

★ **Gazebo Café** MAHONE BAY
CAFE My favorite place to eat in
Mahone Bay is this refreshingly simple, affable, and affordable cafe
right on the bay. Sandwiches, thick
bowls of seafood chowder, smooth-
ies, and good coffee. Check here for
news about local art shows and
musical performances. *567 Main St.*
☎ *902/624-6484. Entrees C$6–C$15.
AE, MC, V. May–Oct lunch & dinner
daily. Closed Nov–Apr.*

★ **Historic Grounds Coffee
House** LUNENBURG *CAFE* More
than just great coffee, Historic
Grounds also serves hearty breakfasts, chowder, sandwiches, salads,
and fish cakes throughout most of
the day. Wash your meal down with
espresso or a frappé (a sort of

frozen espresso). Get a table on the small balcony, if you can. *100 Montague St.* ☎ *902/634-9995. Entrees C$3.95–C$8.95. AE, DISC, MC, V. Mon–Fri breakfast, lunch & dinner (no dinner entrees).*

★ **Innlet Café** MAHONE BAY *SEAFOOD* The Bavarian owners of the Innlet serve a mix of seafood, steaks, stir-fries, pastas, and the like. The best seats in the house are on the stone patio, with its fine view of the harbor and famous churches. There's a wine list and cocktails. *249 Edgewater St.* ☎ *902/624-6363. www.innletcafe.com. Entrees C$12–C$21. MC, V. Lunch & dinner daily.*

kids **Kiwi Café** CHESTER *CAFE* A little enclave of New Zealand on the southern coast of Nova Scotia. Proprietress Lynda Flynn serves up eggs and bagels (try the lobster scramble) for breakfast, plus sandwiches, wraps, soups, fish cakes, and gourmet salads for lunch. On the go? Get a "Dinner in a Box" (Flynn also runs a catering business). *19 Pleasant St.* ☎ *902/275-1492. www.kiwicafe chester.com. Entrees C$4.50–C$8.50. V. Breakfast & lunch daily.*

★ **La Vista** WESTERN SHORE *CONTINENTAL* The dining room of the Oak Island Resort spa and convention center north of Chester offers great sunset views and an excellent Canadian-European fusion menu. *36 Treasure Dr. (at Oak Island Resort).* ☎ *800/565-5075 or 902/627-2600. Entrees C$18–C$23. MC, V. Breakfast, lunch & dinner daily.*

★ **The Library Pub** WOLFVILLE *CANADIAN* Once a coffee shop, this Wolfville mainstay (with a downstairs section known as the Wine Tavern) has morphed into a slightly fancier place, serving burgers, salads, lamb, and—in the tavern—a good range of wines by the glass and bottle. Local wines are a specialty here. *472 Main St.* ☎ *902/542-4315. Entrees C$9–C$14. MC, V. Lunch & dinner daily.*

kids **Mr. Fish** SHELBURNE *SEAFOOD* You can't miss this fried-fish stand on the side of busy Route 3; what it lacks in location, it more than makes up for in character and good, simple fried seafood. *104 King St. (Rte. 3, north of town).*

The affable and affordable Gazebo Café in Mahone Bay.

☎ *902/875-3474. Entrees C$3–C$13. V. Lunch & dinner daily.*

★ **Old Fish Factory Restaurant**
LUNENBURG *SEAFOOD* In a former old fish-processing plant (which it shares with Lunenburg's museum), this place swallows whole bus tours; try for the patio. They serve fish cakes, sandwiches, filets, and stew—but also lobster, crab, scallops, and even seafood pasta. *68 Bluenose Dr.* ☎ *800/533-9336 or 902/634-3333. www.oldfishfactory. com. Entrees lunch C$9–C$18, dinner C$17–C$29. AE, DC, DISC, MC, V. Mid May–mid Oct lunch & dinner daily. Closed mid Oct to mid May.*

★ **The Red Shoe Pub** MABOU
CANADIAN The "Shoe," owned by the famous Rankin family of musicians, is much different from what it used to be: Now you *can* get a goat-cheese panini and you *can't* smoke a cigarette. A skillful, upscale menu, lots of good beer, and great music daily. *11573 Hwy. 19 (Main St.).* ☎ *902/945-2996. Entrees C$9–C$19. MC, V. June to mid-Oct lunch & dinner daily.*

Restaurant Acadien CHÉTICAMP
FRENCH This local restaurant is attached to a crafts shop on the south side of Chéticamp. Servers wear costumes, and the food is absolutely authentic, down to the baked beans and blood pudding. *15067 Main St.* ☎ *902/224-3207. Breakfast items C$3.50–C$5, lunch & dinner entrees C$4–C$17. AE, MC, V. Mid-May to Oct breakfast, lunch & dinner daily. Closed Nov to mid-May.*

Rita's Tea Room BIG POND
CAFE Celtic singer/songwriter Rita MacNeil (1944–) grew up in Big Pond, and she never forgot her roots. This converted 1939 school-house that she now owns serves

Rita's Tea Room, a British-styled café in Big Pond.

and sells typically British tearoom fare. *8077 Hwy. 4 (40km/25 miles SW of Sydney).* ☎ *902/828-2667. Entrees & afternoon tea C$7–C$14. V. Late June to mid-Oct breakfast, lunch & afternoon tea daily. Closed mid-Oct to late June.*

Rudder's YARMOUTH *BREWPUB*
Yarmouth's first brewpub opened in 1997 on the waterfront in an old warehouse. It serves pub fare and steak, plus Acadian and Cajun specialties like rappie pie and jambalaya. And beer, of course. *96 Water St.* ☎ *902/742-7311. Sandwiches C$4– C$11, entrees C$10–C$24. AE, DC, MC, V. Mid-Apr to mid-Oct lunch & dinner daily. Closed mid-Oct to mid-Apr.*

★★ **Tin Fish** LUNENBURG *CANA-DIAN* The house restaurant of the Lunenburg Arms features Canadian food, done fusion-style—scallops on the half-shell in Béchamel sauce, *panko*-fried fish, haddock maple-curry pasta. *94 Pelham St.* ☎ *800/679-4950 or 902/640-4040. Entrees breakfast C$3-C$12, lunch C$10–C$15, dinner C$18–C$28. AE, MC, V. Breakfast, lunch & dinner daily.*

Nova Scotia Lodging

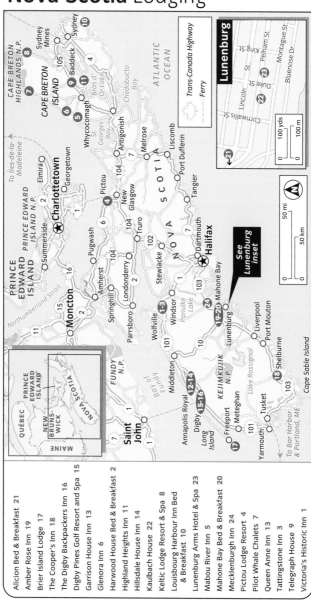

Alicion Bed & Breakfast 21
Amber Rose Inn 19
Brier Island Lodge 17
The Cooper's Inn 18
The Digby Backpackers Inn 16
Digby Pines Golf Resort and Spa 15
Garrison House Inn 13
Glenora Inn 6
Harwood House Bed & Breakfast 2
Highland Heights Inn 11
Hillsdale House Inn 14
Kaulbach House 22
Keltic Lodge Resort & Spa 8
Louisbourg Harbour Inn Bed & Breakfast 10
Lunenburg Arms Hotel & Spa 23
Mabou River Inn 5
Mahone Bay Bed & Breakfast 20
Mecklenburgh Inn 24
Pictou Lodge Resort 4
Pilot Whale Chalets 7
Queen Anne Inn 13
Tattingstone Inn 3
Telegraph House 9
Victoria's Historic Inn 1

Lodging A to Z

Shelburne's best lodging: the elegant Cooper's Inn on the waterfront.

★ Alicion Bed & Breakfast

LUNENBURG   A big, ship-shape home in a serene neighborhood within walking distance of Lunenburg's Old Town, Alicion has passed into new ownership and is still terrific. Two of the three rooms have jetted tubs, while fabrics and foods are organic. *66 McDonald St. ☎ 877/ 634-9358 or 902/634-9358. www. alicionbb.com. 3 units. Doubles C$135–C$155 w/breakfast. MC, V.*

★ Amber Rose Inn MAHONE

BAY   A small, upscale B&B carved out of a blue heritage home on Mahone Bay's main street. All three units are spacious suites with whirlpools, a steal for the price. *319 W. Main St. ☎ 902/624-1060. www. amberroseinn.com. 3 units. Doubles C$95–C$135 w/breakfast. MC, V. Closed Jan–Apr.*

★ Brier Island Lodge BRIER

ISLAND   Basic, log cabin–style accommodations for nature-lovers, with plenty of windows overlooking the ocean and a lighthouse. Some

rooms are motel-style, while some have Jacuzzis. The on-site roosters might wake you early. *557 Water St., Westport. ☎ 800/662-8355 or 902/ 839-2300. www.brierisland.com. 40 units. Doubles C$79–C$149. MC, V.*

★ The Cooper's Inn SHELBURNE

Facing the harbor in Shelburne's historic district, this is the best lodging in town, with elegant suites and nice touches from the friendly owners. It dates from 1785, but the courtyard, pond, and fountain are recent additions. *36 Dock St. ☎ 800/688-2011 or 902/875-4656. www.thecoopers inn.com. 8 units. Doubles C$100– C$185 w/breakfast. MC, V.*

The Digby Backpackers Inn

DIGBY   On Digby's most historic street, this newish inn/hostel is perfectly located and well run by an international couple. All bathrooms are shared. *168 Queen St. ☎ 902/ 245-4573. Single beds C$25, doubles C$60 w/breakfast. Cash only. Closed Nov–Apr.*

★★ kids **Digby Pines Golf Resort and Spa** DIGBY Red-roofed Digby Pines is situated on 121 hectares (300 acres) with marvelous views. It's built in a château style, with a spa, good 18-hole golf course, and gourmet dining room. Ask for a water view (no extra charge). *103 Shore Rd.* ☎ *800/667-4637 or 902/245-2511. www.digbypines.ca. 147 units. Doubles C$159–C$225, suites & cottages C$225–C$325. AE, DC, DISC, MC, V. Closed mid-Oct to mid-May.*

★ **Garrison House Inn** ANNAPOLIS ROYAL Across from Fort Anne, this has been an inn since 1854. Rooms are nicely appointed with antiques, pine floors, braided rugs, wing-back chairs, skylights, and the like. The restaurant (p 111) is very good. *350 St. George St.* ☎ *866/532-5750 or 902/532-5750. www.garrisonhouse.ca. 7 units. Doubles C$69–C$149. AE, MC, V. Closed Dec–Apr.*

★ **Glenora Inn** GLENVILLE Attached to a whisky distillery (p 101), Glenora offers nine modern hotel rooms over a courtyard, but the real draw is a half-dozen log chalets of one to three bedrooms each on the hillside overlooking the distillery. Each chalet has a Jacuzzi, satellite TV, and wonderful view of the mist-covered valley. *Rte. 19.* ☎ *800/839-0491. www.glenoradistillery.com. 15 units. Doubles C$125–C$175, chalets C$175–C$295. AE, MC, V. Closed mid-Oct to mid-May.*

Harwood House Bed & Breakfast WOLFVILLE Downtown, right beside Acadia University—in fact, it was built for the university provost—this home was converted to an inn in 1999. The owners are warm and helpful, and speak French and German. *34 Highland Ave.* ☎ *877/897-0156 or 902/542-5707. www.harwoodhouse.com. 3 units.*

One of the many nicely appointed rooms in Annapolis Royal's Garrison House Inn.

Doubles C$100–C$160 w/breakfast. MC, V.

Highland Heights Inn IONA This is a simple motel on Bras D'Or Lake, but one with terrific views. Every room has a great vista of the lake bordering on the spectacular. Second-floor rooms are best. *Hwy. 223.* ☎ *800/660-8122 or 902/725-2360. www.highlandheightsinn.ca. 32 units. Doubles C$80–C$109. DISC, MC, V. Closed mid-Oct to mid-May.*

★ **Hillsdale House Inn** ANNAPOLIS ROYAL This Italianate home features a sitting room with lovely furniture that's nice to look at and comfortable to sit on. Guest rooms are handsome, furnished with antique writing desks, new linens, claw-foot tubs, and poster beds. All units have flat-screen televisions and CD players, too. *519 St. George St.* ☎ *877/839-2821 or 902/532-2345. www.hillsdalehouse.ns.ca. 15 units. Doubles C$79–C$149 w/breakfast. MC, V.*

★ **Kaulbach House** LUNENBURG This inn has changed with the times, unlike many small-town inns in the province: flat-screen TVs, robes, fresh flowers, and Wi-Fi complement the classic Victorian styling. *75 Pelham St.* ☎ *800/568-8818 or 902/634-8818. www.kaulbachhouse.com. 6 units. Doubles C$99–C$169 w/ breakfast. MC, V. Closed Nov–May.*

★★ kids Keltic Lodge Resort & Spa INGONISH BEACH
Great views of one of Cape Breton's most impressive headlands, from log cabin–like cottages set among birches. There's a great golf course (see p 36, ❷), newish spa, and heated outdoor swimming pool. *313 Keltic In Rd.* ☎ *800/565-0444 or 902/285-2880. www.kelticlodge.ca. 105 units. Doubles C$179–C$339 w/ breakfast, suites & cottages C$449–C$749 w/breakfast. AE, DC, DISC, MC, V. Closed late Oct to late May.*

★★ Louisbourg Harbour Inn Bed & Breakfast LOUISBOURG
This yellow clapboard inn sits off Louisbourg's main street, overlooking the famous French fortress in town (see p. 40, ❹). Many units face the ocean and have Jacuzzis. *9 Lower Warren St.* ☎ *888/888-8466 or 902/733-3222. 8 units. Doubles C$110–C$180 w/breakfast. MC, V. Closed mid-Oct to mid-June.*

★★ Lunenburg Arms Hotel & Spa LUNENBURG
Once a tavern, this hillside hotel is Lunenburg's most "boutique" hotel, with upscale furnishings, a stuffed teddy bear or two in each room, Jacuzzis and harbor views, and a spa. *94 Pelham St.* ☎ *800/679-4950 or 902/640-4040. www.lunenburgarms.com. 26 units. Doubles & suites C$89–C$269. AE, MC, V.*

kids Mabou River Inn MABOU
This former boarding school was originally a hostel, now a very friendly inn. It's walking distance from the music in town. Pizza and beer are served at night for an extra charge. *19 Southwest Ridge Rd.* ☎ *888/627-9744 or 902/945-2356.*

The Keltic Lodge Resort & Spa is nestled in the Cape Breton headlands.

www.mabouriverinn.com. 12 units. Doubles & suites C$89–C$145. AE, MC, V.

Mahone Bay Bed & Breakfast

MAHONE BAY   This bright yellow house in the center of Mahone Bay was built in the 1860s by a ship-wright. There's a widow's walk (rooftop porch) and good wood-working details. *558 Main St.* ☎ *866/239-6252 or 902/624-6388. 4 units. Doubles C$95–C$135 w/breakfast. MC, V.*

★ Mecklenburgh Inn CHESTER

This brightly painted inn has a motto: "the door is always open." Two broad porches (one on each floor) are a big draw, as are touches like French truffles, Frette linens, and robes. *78 Queen St.* ☎ *866/ 838-4638 or 902/275-4638. www. mecklenburghinn.ca. 4 units. Doubles C$95–C$155 w/breakfast. AE, V. Closed Jan–Apr.*

★ kids Pictou Lodge Resort

PICTOU   This property has been renovated in recent years to create family suites and luxe "chalets" that depart from the log cabin–like feel of the rest of the place. Ocean views are splendid. *172 Lodge Rd.* ☎ *800/495-6343 or 902/485-4322. www.pictoulodge.com. 61 units. Doubles C$139–C$229, cottages C$165–C$425. AE, DC, DISC, MC, V. Closed mid-Oct to mid-May.*

Pilot Whale Chalets CHÉTICAMP

These spare, modern cottages near the national park entrance have kitchens, TVs, and grills; some even have Jacuzzis and fireplaces. They're plain but attractive, with great views of the coastal mountains. *15775 Cabot Trail (Rte. 19).* ☎ *902/224-1040. www.pilotwhalechalets.com. 13 units. Doubles C$95–C$115, cab-ins C$159–C$249. AE, MC, V.*

★★ Queen Anne Inn ANNAPOLIS

ROYAL   You can't miss this Second Empire mansion, built in 1865, on your way into Annapolis Royal. Guest rooms are elegant and fur-nished in Victoriana—plus Jacuzzis, featherbeds, and handmade soaps. The park-like grounds are very nice. *494 St. George St.* ☎ *877/536-0403 or 902/532-7850. www.queenanne inn.ns.ca. 12 units. Doubles & suites C$99–C$209 w/breakfast. MC, V. Closed Nov–Apr.*

★★ Tattingstone Inn WOLF-

VILLE   This handsome Wolfville mansion overlooks the village's main street. The inn is decorated with informal country antiques and regal Empire pieces; rooms in the carriage house are smaller but showcase modern Canadian art-work. The dining room is refined, and a heated outdoor pool and sun porch are lovely. *620 Main St.* ☎ *800/565-7696 or 902/542-7696. www.tattingstone.ns.ca. 10 units. Doubles C$98–C$178 w/breakfast. AE, MC, V.*

Telegraph House BADDECK

This lodging on Baddeck's main street is divided among an 1861 home, an annex of motel units, and a set of cabins; Alexander Graham Bell slept here, but the rooms still don't have phones. Ironic. The new-est rooms in the main lodge now have whirlpool baths, as do some cottages. *479 Chebucto St.* ☎ *888/ 263-9840 or 902/295-1100. www. baddeck.com/telegraph. 41 units. Doubles C$75–C$125, cottages C$100–C$225. AE, MC, V.*

★★ Victoria's Historic Inn

WOLFVILLE   Built by an apple mogul (really), this inn feels like a Victorian parlor inside. Most rooms are themed and adorned with fine wood-work, fireplaces, and Jacuzzis. *600 Main St.* ☎ *800/556-5744 or 902/542-5744. www.victoriashistoricinn.com. 15 units. Doubles & suites C$108–C$245 w/breakfast. AE, MC, V.* ●

Charlottetown

1. Confederation Landing Park
2. Peake's Wharf
3. Great George Street
4. St. Dunstan's Basilica
5. Province House National Historic Site
6. Victoria Row
7. Confederation Centre of the Arts
8. Confederation Centre Art Gallery
9. Trinity United Church
10. St. Paul's Church
11. COWS
12. All Souls' Chapel
13. St. James Presbyterian Church
14. Beaconsfield
15. Government House
16. Victoria Park

Previous page: Prince Edward Island's famous red-sand beaches.

There's only one place on Prince Edward Island that qualifies as a city—Charlottetown, the provincial capital—and even it counts just 32,000 people. But this is one of my favorite cities in Atlantic Canada, precisely because it *is* so compact, friendly, and richly historic. This quick tour takes you past more historic homes and churches than you thought one city could have. START: **Charlottetown's waterfront (at the foot of Great George St.).**

❶ ★ Confederation Landing Park. Charlottetown's waterfront park is the ideal place to start a city tour. The park is not only home to the city's tourist information office (inside Founder's Hall; the attraction itself can be skipped)—it also is the start of a lovely boardwalk along the edge of the harbor and green lawns. And there's plenty of parking. Hang out on the benches watching yachts pull into the marina and cruise ships docking. ⏱ *30 min. Foot of Prince & Great George sts. (below Water St.). Always open. Free admission.*

Inside the park, you'll find

❷ Peake's Wharf. This collection of boutiques and restaurants across several waterfront docks attracts plenty of tourists in summer. It's *not* the real PEI, but the free summer concert series often features local musicians strumming, riffing, and singing—and that's a good thing, right? There's also a seafood market, lobster restaurant, the aforementioned marina, and public restrooms inside the Peake's Quay building. ⏱ *15 min. Foot of Queen, Great George & Prince sts. www.walkandseacharlottetown.com/content/view/130/237. Hours vary by merchant.*

From the wharf, stroll north along

❸ ★★ Great George Street. It's only 4½ blocks long, yet this is one of the best-looking streets in all of the Maritimes. Stroll beneath big shady trees, alongside handsome Georgian townhouses, and past churches such as St. Dunstan's (see

Great George Street is one of the best-looking streets in all of the Maritimes.

below) and galleries like the **Pilar Shephard Gallery** (82 Great George St.; ☎ 902/892-1953), specializing in native Canadian art. One of the city's premier inns, the **Great George** (58 Great George St.; see p 144), is also here. ⏱ *15 min. From Confederation Landing Park north to Richmond St.*

Walk 3 blocks north on Great George St. to

❹ ★★ St. Dunstan's Basilica. There have been cathedrals on this spot since the early 19th century, but several of them burned down. The current version, which is doubled-spired and dripping Gothic style, was built of New Brunswick stone and it too burned in 1916—but the cathedral wasn't a total loss, and the church was restored and reopened in 1919. While the exterior is nice, the arched and vaulted interior is truly

The doubled-spired and dripping Gothic styled St. Dunstan's Basilica on George Street.

this impressive sandstone capitol, built in 1847 when the neighborhood was still empty lots and mud flats. It's the place where the details of Confederation were hammered out in 1864, the idea that led to Canada becoming a nation. After a short film, peek at the small Legislative Assembly (PEI's legislators hash out provincial laws here when they're in session). Then head for the attractive Confederation Chamber; the original furniture's still here. ⏱ *45 min. 165 Richmond St. (at Great George St.).* ☎ *902/566-7626. www.gov.pe.ca. Free admission (donation requested). June–Oct daily 8:30am–5pm; Nov–May Mon–Fri 8:30am–5pm.*

In summer, the block of Richmond St. immediately to the left of Province House is transformed into

stunning. ⏱ *30 min. 45 Great George St.* ☎ *902/894-3486. Free guided tours Mon–Fri 8am–5pm.*

Continue to the top of Great George St. Across the intersection is the

⑤ ★★ Province House National Historic Site. PEI's government business is done inside

⑥ ★ Victoria Row. The block of Richmond Street between Great George and Queen streets is cordoned off to car traffic in summertime, resulting in an instant pedestrian mall; the eateries and bars here set out chairs and tables to create a fun al fresco dining space. Expect live tunes, beer, and a summery vibe. Architecture buffs: Note the Italianate detailing on the stone and brick Cameron (nos. 138–142 Richmond) and Newson (160–164 Richmond) blocks. ⏱ *30 min. Richmond St. (from Queen St. to Great George St.).*

Built in 1847, the Province House National Historic Site is where the initial details of Confederation were hammered out.

The Confederation Centre of the Arts hosts year-round dance and dramatic performances.

Walk along Victoria Row & turn right on Queen St. Partway down the block, on the right, is the box office of the

7 ★★ kids Confederation Centre of the Arts.

PEI's most significant arts center isn't too architecturally appealing (the words "concrete slab" quickly come to mind), but artistically, it's a home run. Inside the complex, you'll find three separate theater spaces, hosting year-round dance and dramatic performances, live folk and classical music concerts and shows, and the long-running *Anne of Green Gables* musical. ⏱ *2 hr. (for performances). 145 Richmond St. (box office on Queen St., btwn. Richmond & Grafton sts.).* ☎ *800/565-0278 or 902/566-1267. www.confederation centre.com. Tickets for Anne of Green Gables musical C$55–C$75 adults; less for seniors & children. Box office June–Aug, Mon–Sat 9am–10:30pm, Sept–May Mon–Sat 10am–5pm. Anne of Green Gables musical, mid-June to late Sept 7 times per week.*

Inside the arts center, you'll also find the

8 ★★ Confederation Centre Art Gallery.

This is the biggest art gallery in all of Atlantic Canada; too bad it's housed inside an unfortunate modernist complex. Yet the gallery itself—spread out across two levels—is spacious and well designed, with plenty of exposed wood, bright walls, and natural lighting. Curators and artists sometimes give talks; there are also kids' programs and art classes. ⏱ *1 hr. 145 Richmond St. (inside Confederation Centre of the Arts).* ☎ *902/628-6142. www.confederationcentre.com. Free admission (donation requested). May–Oct, daily 9am–5pm, Nov–Apr Wed–Sat 11am–5pm, Sun 1–5pm (closed Mon–Tues).*

Backtrack to Richmond St. & walk east to Prince St. Past the intersection on the right is the

9 ★ Trinity United Church.

This immense, turreted brick church—finished in 1864, now the oldest surviving church in the city—was originally a testament to the long intellectual reach of English theologian John Wesley (1703–1791), who had founded the Methodist movement with his brother Charles roughly a century earlier. It's positively huge, with a large dome roof and newer stained glass work on the big arched windows framing the organ. Who designed this massive edifice? Two of its parishioners, furniture maker Mark Butcher (1814–1883) and architect Thomas Alley (1840–1869). ⏱ *30 min. 220 Richmond St.* ☎ *902/892-4114. Interior not open to public touring; Sunday services public.*

Backtrack to Prince St. Turn right & walk north. On your left is

One of Canada's National Historic Sites, the All Soul's Chapel.

10 St. Paul's Church. One of the city's Anglican churches, St. Paul's opened in 1896—the third church built on this spot. It was designed by noted local architect William Critchlow Harris (1854–1913), who also designed the lovely All Souls' Chapel (see below), and built using huge rough blocks of local sandstone that feel a bit much, even for a Gothic structure. But some wonderful stained-glass paneling lightens the mood and saves the day. ⏱ *15 min. 101 Prince St. (between Richmond & Grafton sts.).* ☎ *902/892-1691. Interior not open to public touring; Sunday services public.*

kids 11 COWS. You're going to end up here sooner or later— whether it's because one of your kids spotted the iconic cow-on-a-sign, or you just got a sudden craving for ice cream, it doesn't much matter. COWS is PEI's version of Ben & Jerry's: a locally produced, premium all-natural ice cream that keeps loyal customers coming back for more. (Local island strawberries are used in season, for instance.) This is the most central branch in the city, around the back of the Confederation Centre. *150 Queen St.* ☎ *902/ 892-6969. www.cows.ca. $.*

Continue to Grafton St. Turn left & walk 3 blocks west to Pownal St. Turn right & walk 2 blocks north to Fitzroy St. On your left, you will pass Rochford Sq. &

12 ★★ All Souls' Chapel. Built less than 20 years after the St. Peter's cathedral it serves, this sandstone chapel was intended as a tribute to the congregation's original priest. But it stands on its own today as one of the city's loveliest examples of High Gothic architecture—so beautiful it's a National Historic Site. William Critchlow Harris' interior is spectacular, marked by a huge stone arch framing a gorgeous altar. The lovely round mural paintings on and above the altar, of various scenes from the Bible, were made by the architect's brother Robert; the chapel itself was constructed and detailed by local builders and woodworkers. One of my favorite buildings in the city. ⏱ *45 min. 7 All Souls Lane (behind St. Peter's, in Rochford Sq.).* ☎ *902/566-2102. Interior not open to public touring; Sunday services public.*

Continue past the cathedral along Pownal St. 1 block; turn left onto Fitzroy St. to find the

13 ★ St. James Presbyterian Church. Also calling itself "the Kirk," this stone church at Pownal and Fitzroy streets bears a passing resemblance to St. Paul's. But it feels lighter and airier, thanks to better proportions and its graceful, slender spire. The Kirk was erected in 1878, replacing a wooden Presbyterian church that had stood on the same site. ⏱ *15 min. 35 Fitzroy St.* ☎ *902/892-2839. Interior not open to public touring; Sunday services public.*

Continue 1 block on Fitzroy St. to Rochford St. Turn left. Walk 2 blocks to Kent St. & turn right. In 1 block, on the left, is

⓮ ★ **Beaconsfield.** This distinctive, mansard-roofed mansion was designed in 1877 by a local architect for a wealthy local shipbuilder; its architecture mixes several styles, but Victorian takes the lead. The property is now owned and operated by PEI's Museum and Heritage Foundation, which also hosts various talks and other events here during the year. 🕐 *1 hr. 2 Kent St.* ☎ *902/368-6603. Admission C$4.25 adults, C$3.25 students, C$11.75 families; free for children under 12. July & Aug daily 10am–4:45pm, Sept Sun–Fri noon–4pm. Closed Oct–June.*

Continue walking along the boardwalk that runs along the harbor. In 150m (492 ft.), across the roadway on your right, you pass

⓯ ★★ **Government House.** In a town of grand buildings, this handsome park-side mansion might take the cake. A whitewashed structure built in 1834, it announces itself with eight stout Doric columns, yet never looks foreboding. This is still the official residence of the island's

Lieutenant Governor, the Queen of England's personal representative to PEI. It's also often called Fanning-bank around town—the original, official name, as it was built on river-bank land owned by a former island governor named Edmund Fanning (1739–1818). (At the time, PEI was called St. John's Island and was still part of Nova Scotia.) 🕐 *45 min. 1 Government Dr. (at Park Roadway).* ☎ *902/368-5480. Free admission. Free tours (required for entry) July & Aug Mon–Fri 10am–4pm every 30 min.; grounds open daily year-round dawn–dusk.*

Continue on the boardwalk another .3km (¼ mile) to reach

⓰ **Victoria Park.** This little loop tour of the city ends at Victoria Park, a quiet place of trees, grass, and picnicking areas (plus the ruins of a wartime battery and magazine). The park has been here since 1873. From here, you can walk unencumbered back to the tour's starting point at Confederation Landing Park, with clear views of the city's harbor and the Northumberland Strait beyond. 🕐 *30 min. 50 Park Roadway (from Brighton Rd. to Kent St.).*

Beaconsfield mansion is notable for its blend of architectural styles.

PEI National Park & Anne's Land

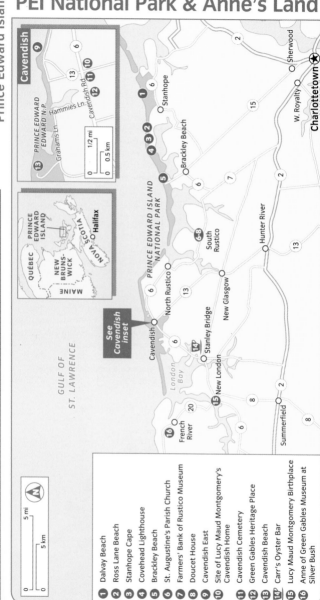

Cavendish

PRINCE EDWARD EDWARD N.P.

Grahams Ln.

Hammies Ln.

Cavendish Rd.

0   1/2 mi
0   0.5 km

QUÉBEC

MAINE

NEW BRUNS- WICK

PRINCE EDWARD ISLAND

NOVA SCOTIA

Halifax

GULF OF
ST. LAWRENCE

See
Cavendish
inset

London
Bay

Cavendish

North Rustico

Stanley Bridge

New Glasgow

Hunter River

South Rustico

Brackley Beach

Stanhope

PRINCE EDWARD ISLAND NATIONAL PARK

Charlottetown ✪

Sherwood

W. Royalty

French River

New London

Summerfield

0   5 mi
0   5 km

① Dalvay Beach
② Ross Lane Beach
③ Stanhope Cape
④ Covehead Lighthouse
⑤ Brackley Beach
⑥ St. Augustine's Parish Church
⑦ Farmers' Bank of Rustico Museum
⑧ Doucet House
⑨ Cavendish East
⑩ Site of Lucy Maud Montgomery's Cavendish Home
⑪ Cavendish Cemetery
⑫ Green Gables Heritage Place
⑬ Cavendish Beach
⑭ Carr's Oyster Bar
⑮ Lucy Maud Montgomery Birthplace
⑯ Anne of Green Gables Museum at Silver Bush

Most travelers come to Prince Edward Island to see one of two things: *Anne of Green Gables* memorabilia, or else the island's famous red-sand beaches. This driving tour through the north-central section of the island shows you a little of each—from hokey tourist attractions to stately mansions; soothing, quiet shores; and even a little Acadian history thrown in for good measure. START: **Gulf Shore Pkwy. to Dalvay by the Sea parking area.**

Day 1

1 ★★ Dalvay Beach. Low, wind-scoured sand dunes and small, easy sets of steps leading down to the beach tell you you're at Dalvay, where sunlight falls right over the water and onto the wet sand. It's one of the best spots on the island for taking photographs; stand on top of the green knoll for the best perspective. ⏲ *1 hr. Gulf Shore Pkwy., Grand Tracadie (across the road from the Dalvay by the Sea Resort). Daily dawn to dusk. Park pass required for entry. (See "Passing into PEI National Park," below.)*

Travel 3km (1¾ miles) west along Gulf Shore Pkwy. to the turnoff for

2 ★ kids Ross Lane Beach. This nearly hidden beach is a wonderful detour, with an especially cute approach (down a boardwalk through bracketing dunes on either side). It's also staffed by lifeguards

Dalvay Beach is one of the best places in PEI for taking pictures.

in summer, which many of the island's beaches aren't. ⏲ *45 min. Gulf Shore Pkwy., Stanhope. Park pass required for entry. (See "Passing into PEI National Park," below.)*

Continue 1.6km (1 mile) west to the parking area for

3 Stanhope Cape. It's marked by scrubby deadwood, shrubs, a screen of evergreen trees, and a campground; no, Stanhope isn't the PEI beach of your dreams, calendars, and coffee mugs. It's a lot rougher and more weather-beaten than that, yet it has its own lonesome charm as a walking spot. ⏲ *15 min. Gulf Shore Pkwy., Stanhope. Park pass required for entry. (See "Passing into PEI National Park," below.)*

Continue about 1.2km (¾ mile) west. Just before the small bridge is the

4 ★ Covehead Lighthouse. This blockish, squat lighthouse keeps ships from drifting too close to the shallow, sandy bay here while marking the harbor and narrow entrance to protected Covehead Bay. It's also something of a local landmark. Only 8m (26 ft.) high, it was erected in 1975 and is equipped with both a century-old Fresnel lens (shipped here from New Brunswick) and a foghorn that's occasionally called into duty. Take a picture (the lighthouse itself can't be entered). ⏲ *30 min. Gulfshore Pkwy. (at Covehead Beach), Stanhope by the Sea. Parking at marina across street.*

Continue about 3km (1¾ miles) farther west on the Pkwy. to reach

⑤ ★★ **Brackley Beach.** Now the sandy cliffs begin to rise higher and become genuinely tall—as high as 15m (49 ft.) above sea level in some places. Wooden walkways traverse the dunes safely and touch down on the beach. This is the prettiest, most western part of the string of beaches along the eastern Parkway. Great for snapping photos. ⏱ 1½ hr. Gulf Shore Pkwy., Stanhope by the Sea. Park pass required for entry. (See "Passing into PEI National Park," below.)

Turn south on Rte. 15. Drive 5km (3 miles), then turn west onto Rte. 6. Continue 7km (4¼ miles), bearing right at Oyster Bed Bridge to South Rustico. Turn right onto Church Rd. (Rte. 243) & drive .5km (¼ mile) to

⑥ ★★ **St. Augustine's Parish Church.** You can't miss this church: It stands right in the middle of Church Road, which curves around it. This big white country church was built in 1838, and it's now the oldest standing Catholic church on the island. A classic, boxy Gothic

Revival structure that almost looks stenciled in black and white against the lush landscape, St. Augustine holds three bells in its tower that were cast in London. There are plenty of arched windows and several prominent rows of quatrefoils. ⏱ 15 min. 2190 Church Rd. (Rte. 243), South Rustico. ☎ 902/963-2245. Free tours by appointment.

To the right of the church is the

⑦ ★ **Farmers' Bank of Rustico Museum.** Made of sandstone, this bank is a blocky, rugged structure that looks more like a fort than a lending institution. Yet this bank was a historic one, founded by a local churchman in 1864 to assist his farmer parishioners who had fallen on hard times; the reverend and his churchgoers built the bank themselves. It didn't last long—only 3 decades—but it sparked ideas (cooperative banking, credit unions) that endure today. A museum explains the history; the original vault and fireplaces remain. ⏱ 45 min. Church Rd. (Rte. 143), South Rustico. ☎ 902/963-3168. Admission C$4 adults, C$3 seniors, C$2 children, C$8 families (ticket also

Farmer's Bank of Rustico Museum looks more like a fort than a lending institution.

Doucet House is thought to be the oldest home on the island.

gains entry to Doucet House). *Tours June–Sept Mon–Sat 9:30am–5:30pm, Sun 1–5:30pm; Oct–May call.*

Walk around behind the museum (toward the water) to find the

8 ★ **kids** **Doucet House.** This simple log-and-wood building dates from around 1770, though what you see is mostly restored (and also relocated from its former location down by the harbor). It's believed to be the oldest home on the whole island, and period furnishings have also been added to spruce it up; the wooden shakes on the roof and so-called "dovetail" log-work (whereby log ends are joined in interlocking fashion) were typical of Acadian dwellings at the time. ⏱ *45 min. Church Rd., South Rustico. Admission C$4 adults, C$3 seniors, C$2 children, C$8 families (ticket also gains entry to Farmers' Bank*

Museum).Tours June–Sept Mon–Sat 9:30am–5:30pm, Sun 1–5:30pm; Oct–May call.

Backtrack to Rte. 6 & continue 6km (3¾ miles) north to North Rustico. Bear right onto Churchill Ave. & follow it to the water (it becomes Gulf Shore Pkwy. West). Continue 5km (3 miles) along the Pkwy. to the parking area for

9 ★ **Cavendish East.** Yes, you're back in the national park again. There are genuine sandstone cliffs (as in rocks) here at Cavendish East, and this is one of very few places on the island where you can actually see exposed bedrock this way. Pull into the parking area and check out the views across to Cavendish Beach. ⏱ *30 min. Gulf Shore Pkwy. West, Cavendish. Park pass required for entry. (See "Passing into PEI National Park," below.)*

Passing into PEI National Park

From June through September, you'll need a pass to visit the beaches of **PEI National Park** (www.pc.gc.ca). There are two toll-houses where you pay the fee, which from July through September is C$7.80 adults, C$6.80 seniors, C$3.90 children 6 to 16, and C$20 families; all rates are discounted by half in June. Ask about a multi-day pass if you'll visit for more than 3 days, because it works out more cheaply over your entire visit.

Turn south on Cawnpore Lane & return to Rte. 6; at the intersection with Rte. 13, turn left. In a few hundred meters, on the right, is the

⑩ ★ Site of Lucy Maud Montgomery's Cavendish Home. Now we're into the "Anne" portion of our tour. Author Montgomery (1874–1942) lived in a house on this spot with her grandparents from 1876 (when she was still a few months shy of 2 years old) through 1911, and wrote nearly all her famous *Anne of Green Gables* novels here. The home is gone, but you can walk the fields and read descriptions of what Montgomery's life here was like. ⏱ *1 hr. Rte. 6, Cavendish (just east of Rte. 13).* ☎ *902/ 963-2231. Free admission (C$3 donation suggested). Mid-May to June, Sept & Oct daily 9am–5pm; July & Aug daily 9am–6pm. Closed Nov to mid-May.*

Overnight in Cavendish.

Day 2
Backtrack to the major intersection of rtes. 6 & 13. On your left, at the southwest corner, is the

⑪ ★ Cavendish Cemetery. This cemetery opened in 1835, and droves of summer tourists pass beneath its arched entrance with a single quarry in mind: the gravestone of author Lucy Maud Montgomery. The path is clearly marked by stone, but you might not realize until you get there that Montgomery was married to a reverend—they're buried together, so her stone is marked "MacDonald." There's another reason to visit here, as well. An anchor and plaque in the cemetery's lower section memorialize hundreds of local seamen killed in a freak storm just off this coast in 1851. ⏱ *30 min. Intersection of rtes. 13 & 6, Cavendish. Free admission. Daily dawn–dusk.*

Cavendish Cemetery is the home of author Lucy Maude Montgomery's gravestone.

Continue west through the intersection on Rte. 6 .8km (½ mile) to

⑫ Green Gables Heritage Place. This is the place everyone comes to see, though it's frankly less than it's cracked up to be. This is not the author's birthplace nor her home, but rather a farmhouse that belonged to relatives of hers. It *may* have inspired the farm in the novels. Who knows? There are a few exhibits, a video, some rustic trails, locations that may relate to those in the book—but also a golf course and endless crowds. Be prepared. Still, nearly every *Anne* enthusiast makes a stop here anyway. ⏱ *1 hr. Rte. 6, Cavendish.* ☎ *902/963-7874. Mid-June to Aug C$7.80 adults, C$6.55 seniors, C$3.90 children, C$20 families; Sept to mid June, 25–50% discount. May–Oct daily 9am–5pm; Apr & Nov Sun–Thurs 10am–4pm; Dec–Mar by appointment.*

Continue about 2.4km (1½ miles) west on Rte. 6. to Grahams Lane; turn right & drive 1.6km (1 mile) to the entrance to

⑬ ★ Cavendish Beach. There's a massive campground here and some other accouterments of the national park complex. But there's also a curving, floating boardwalk across an inlet; plenty of dunes; a bike path; and a long, 8km (5-mile) beach that stretches east toward the stony cliffs of Cavendish East. Walk away from the crowds and find a quiet spot, and you'll enjoy it. ⏱ 1½ hr. Off Grahams Lane, Cavendish. Park pass required for entry. (See "Passing into PEI National Park," below.)

Carr's Oyster Bar. It's not very fancy, but the view from this bayside seafood bar—where hard-working shuckers unveil some of the world's best oysters in a flash—is just right: boats, houses, and a little working harbor at a bend in the road. They serve lobster, but you want raw oysters, and maybe some quahogs (raw or baked) as a chaser. *32 Campbellton Rd. (at Rte. 6), Stanley Bridge.* ☎ *902/886-3355. $$.*

Backtrack to Rte. 6 & continue west 10km (6¼ miles) to the intersection with Rte. 20. At the crossroads is the

⑮ ★★ Lucy Maud Montgomery Birthplace. This simple white home with green trim is where the famous author was born in 1874. It

has been restored in period style, and some interesting items are actually kept here—including Montgomery's wedding dress and, more relevantly, scrapbooks of some of her fiction and poetry. ⏱ 1¼ hr. Rte. 6 (at Rte. 20), New London. ☎ 902/886-2099 or 902/836-5502. Admission C$3 adults, C50¢ children 6–12. Mid-May to mid-Oct daily 9am–5pm. Closed mid-Oct to mid-May.

Turn onto Rte. 20 & drive 10km (6¼ miles) north to the

⑯ ★★ Anne of Green Gables Museum at Silver Bush. Plain on the outside, this white clapboard home was Anne's favorite place to visit during her lifetime. (Her aunt and uncle lived here, and her wedding ceremony was held inside.) Some of Montgomery's furniture, photos, and other personal items are on display. You can even take a carriage ride through the pretty grounds. This is among the best of the Montgomery attractions on the island, to my mind, and makes a good final stop for any tour. ⏱ 1¼ hr. Rte. 20, Park Corner. ☎ 800/665-2663 or 902/886-2884 (weekends only). Admission C$3 adults, C$1 children 6–16. May & Oct daily 11am–4pm; June & Sept daily 10am–4pm; July & Aug daily 9am–5pm. Closed Nov–Apr.

Lucy Maude Montgomery's birthplace, where scrapbooks of some of her fiction and poetry are kept.

Eastern Prince Edward Island

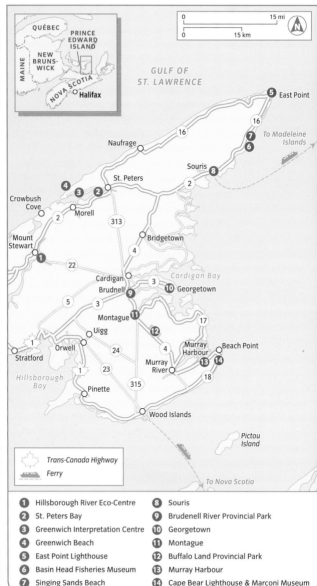

1. Hillsborough River Eco-Centre
2. St. Peters Bay
3. Greenwich Interpretation Centre
4. Greenwich Beach
5. East Point Lighthouse
6. Basin Head Fisheries Museum
7. Singing Sands Beach
8. Souris
9. Brudenell River Provincial Park
10. Georgetown
11. Montague
12. Buffalo Land Provincial Park
13. Murray Harbour
14. Cape Bear Lighthouse & Marconi Museum

Eastern PEI is usually neglected by travelers hurrying to tick off "Anne" destinations or walk the national park's boardwalks and beaches. Yet this is actually one of the most family-friendly parts of the island, with a mix of quiet riverside towns and villages, tranquil beaches, and grown-up golf courses and resort hotels. And it feels much more like the "real" PEI than either Charlottetown or Anne's Land. START: **Mt. Stewart. From Charlottetown, drive east on Rte. 2 22km (14 miles).**

Day 1

① kids Hillsborough River Eco-Centre.

Right beside the Confederation Trail, on Mount Stewart's Main Street, is this good nature center full of videos about area history and ecology. You'll learn how the local river—the biggest river system on the island—was one of the original British settlements on PEI and about its important ecological functions. There's also a gift shop and tourist information kiosk. Be sure to stroll one of several trails that depart from the center, too. 🕐 *30 min. 104 Main St. (Rte. 22, just off Rte. 2), Mount Stewart. ☎ 902/676-2050. Free admission; small fee for special exhibits. July & Aug daily 10am–6pm; Sept–June call.*

Return to Rte. 22 & drive east 26km (16 miles) to St. Peters, where you can see the length of

② ★ St. Peters Bay.

This tidal inlet—gouged out of farmlands from the coast—is attractive, and it's surrounded by the relaxing, thrown-back-in-time PEI you expected when you got here: full-service gas station, fishermen, purple fields of lupines. (If you've brought a bicycle, the Confederation Trail runs right alongside the bay here—its most beautiful stretch.) 🕐 *30 min. Rte. 22 (at Rte. 2), St. Peters.*

Drive north on Rte. 16 a few hundred meters & bear left onto Rte. 313. Follow the road 8km (5 miles) to the

③ ★ Greenwich Interpretation Centre.

Once again, you're in PEI National Park—it's the park that won't quit—and this section is distinct for its lovely, high dunes (with rare bird life) and this modern nature center. These dunes were supposed to be carved up for housing in the 1990s, but the Canadian government stepped up and bought the land. The seasonally open center teaches about dunes and history, and rangers lead tours through them. (The good, boardwalked trails west of the center stay open year-round.) 🕐 *30 min. Rte. 313, Greenwich. ☎ 902/961-2514 or 902/672-6350. www.pc.gc.ca. Park pass required for entry. (See "Passing into PEI National Park," above.) July & Aug daily 10am–6pm; June & Sept daily 10am–5pm. Closed Oct–May.*

You can learn about local history and the dunes at the Greenwich Interpretation Centre.

From the center, turn right & drive .8km (½ mile) north to the parking area for

④ ★★ Greenwich Beach. This is one of the island's best beaches, with lifeguards in summer to oversee swimmers—the water's not as cold as in other places on the island, despite the northerly location. It's also a good spot for just a walk or for taking pictures of those dunes, which actually shift somewhat each year with the incessant winds. There are bathrooms, an observation tower, and boardwalked trails.
🕐 *1 hr. Wild Rose Rd. (off Rte. 313), Greenwich.* ☎ *902/961-2514 or 902/672-6350. Park pass required for entry. (See "Passing into PEI National Park," p 129.) Open year-round.*

Return to St. Peters & turn left onto Rte. 16. Drive east along the north shore of PEI for 53km (33 miles), about a 45 min. drive, to East Point. Turn left onto Lighthouse Rd. & follow it 1.6km (1 mile) to the

⑤ ★★ East Point Lighthouse. This stone-and-wood, octagonal light (built in 1867) is one of PEI's most famous. It's a dramatic spot for a photo as it guards both the St. Lawrence River *and* the Northumberland Strait. Wander around inside, noting the red steel lantern, gabled windows, and simple "porch" on a lower level. (It's now fully automated.) You even get a ribbon indicating to the world you reached this spot. 🕐 *45 min.*
☎ *902/357-2106. Lighthouse Rd. (off Rte. 16), East Point. Grounds free admission; lighthouse admission C$3 adults, C$2 seniors, C$1 children, C$8 families. Grounds open year-round dawn–dusk; lighthouse mid-June to early Sept daily 10am–7pm, closed early Sept to mid-June.*

Return to the main road (Rte. 16) & turn left. Drive 12km (7½ miles) southwest to Kingsboro. At Basin Head Rd., turn left & follow the road (bearing left en route) 1.6km (1 mile) to Basin Head Park & the

⑥ ★ 𝗸𝗶𝗱𝘀 Basin Head Fisheries Museum. This government-operated museum tells the brawny story of the local fisheries, of course, but as a side note, there are also twice-weekly kids' programs held here in summer—classes in art, sand casting, and the making of crafts using naturally beach-combed materials like driftwood and seashells, for example. There's a boardwalk, too.
🕐 *30 min. Basin Head Rd. (in Basin Head Provincial Park), Basin Head.* ☎ *902/357-7233. Park entry C$4 adults, C$3.50 children 12 & over, C$12 families. June to mid-Sept daily 9am–5pm.*

East Point Lighthouse guards both the St. Lawrence River and the Northumberland Strait.

Basin Head Fisheries Museum has summer programs for kids and the story of the local fisheries.

From the park, walk down stairs to

❼ ★★ Singing Sands Beach.
The beach here at Basin Head is said to "sing" when you walk on it, though I've found that it sounds more like a squeaked melody than a classical or pop one. Still, a unique experience if you've never tried it before. As a bonus, the dunes here are attractive, and the beach is often thinly populated or outright deserted. You can take a long, long walk and be undisturbed. ⏱ *30 min. Basin Head Rd., Basin Head.* ☎ *902/357-7233. Park entry C$4 adults, C$3.50 children 12 & over, C$12 families. June to mid-Sept daily 9am–5pm.*

Return to Rte. 16 & continue 13km (8 miles) west to

❽ ★ Souris. The name of this village (SOO-ree) means "mice" or "rats" in French, but don't worry—you won't be eaten alive. This town is the unofficial capital of northeastern PEI, with the most eateries and services in this corner of the island, as well as the best visitor information center (the McLean Building, at 95 Main St.). Acadians squatted here in the 18th and 19th centuries, and built ships or farmed; today, it's still a strongly Franco place. There's

a busy fishing harbor, plus the dock for the Iles-de-la-Madeleine ferry; both the approach to and departure from town feature bright lupine fields, red-dirt farms, and sparkling bay views. ⏱ *30 min. Rte. 16.*

Follow Main St. (Rte. 2) west out of town for 18km (11 miles) to Rte. 4 (for more scenery, detour onto the Rte. 310 loop at Fortune Bridge). Turn left onto Rte. 4 & travel 18km (11 miles), then turn left onto Rte. 321. Travel 4km (2½ miles) to Rte. 3. Turn left again; in 1.6km (1 mile), you reach

❾ ★★ kids Brudenell River Provincial Park. One of the province's best parks, Brudenell River is locally and nationally famous as the home to two of PEI's best golf courses (p 37), a big resort hotel (p 146), and a golf academy. It's not *all* about the little white ball, though; you can also rent canoes and other outdoors equipment, play Frisbee golf, walk a riverfront pathway, bring your kids to one of the children's programs, or camp at a big campground. ⏱ *1 hr. 283 Brudenell Island Blvd. (off Rte 3), Georgetown Royalty.* ☎ *902/652-8966. Park free admission; fees for equipment rentals & camping. Mid-May to early Oct daily.*

Brudenell River Provincial Park is the home of two of PEI's best golf courses.

Overnight in the park resort or in Georgetown (see below).

Day 2
Backtrack to Rte. 3 & continue east 5km (3 miles) to

⑩ ★ Georgetown. Set in a protected harbor where the Brudenell River meets the open Northumberland Strait, Georgetown may be a tiny town, but it carries a lot of cultural weight for its size. The French landed here first; the British later displaced them (hence the name). Today, the stone courthouse (this is the capital of Kings County), brick post office, and central grid of streets are undeniably attractive, and there's an active theater, the **King's Playhouse** (65 Grafton St.; ☎ 888/346-5666 or 902/652-2053). Meanwhile, fishing and lobster boats tie up in a small, attractive harbor that's also home to the last remaining shipyard on PEI. ⏲ *1½ hr. End of Georgetown Rd. (Rte. 3).*

Backtrack 11km (6¾ miles) west along Rte. 3 to Rte. 4; turn left & drive 5km (3 miles) south to

⑪ Montague. The biggest town for miles (population: 2,000), Montague is a supply depot of sorts for local farmers and fishermen. The old, spooky-looking brick customs house on the hill has been converted into the **Garden of the Gulf Museum** (564 Main St.; ☎ 902/838-2467), open June through September weekdays 9am to 5pm (also Sat from July to Aug) for a nominal fee; it holds tools, documents, and other items from the town's and island's history. The waterfront features a lawn, several gazebos, and the pleasing sight of sailboats, yachts, and fishing boats at anchor. ⏲ *45 min. Rte. 4 (at Rte. 17).*

Continue south 8km (5 miles) to reach, on the left, the turnoff for

⑫ kids Buffalo Land Provincial Park. You read that correctly: This 40-hectare (100-acre) park is haven to a clutch of about 25 buffalo, a gift to the province from some friendly Albertans. Walk the boardwalk to a raised observation area with info and views out over the gentle animals. Bring binoculars if you've got some. ⏲ *30 min. Rte. 4, Milltown*

Cross. ☎ 902/652-8950. Free admission. Open year-round.

Return to Rte. 4. Continue south 11km (6¾ miles) to Murray River. Cross the river & turn left on Rte. 18 (Cape Bear Rd.). Drive east 6.5km (4 miles) to reach

⑬ ★ **Murray Harbour.** This cute little river village is notable for its boats—fishing boats, lobster boats, excursion boats, rowboats—as well as its seals. (Yes, the Murray River is full of harbor seals, believe it or not, but you need to know where to look.) Browsing through the general store, grabbing a lobster dinner, or photographing the local harbor and fields might be worth up to an hour of your time. ⏱ 1 hr. Cape Bear Rd. to Main St. (Rte. 18).

Continue east on Rte. 18 (Cape Bear Rd.) about 7km (4¼ miles) around the headland to the

⑭ ★★ kids **Cape Bear Lighthouse & Marconi Museum.** Walking distance from a beach, this 1881 lighthouse sits on a slowly disintegrating cliff. There was once a wireless station here—the one that took the *Titanic's* distress call. That

The slowly disintegrating cliff at Cape Bear Lighthouse.

station is gone now, but inside the lighthouse, a museum documents its rich history. Climb the stairs for an overlook view of the beaches and cliffs of Cape Bear. ⏱ 1½ hr. Cape Bear Rd., Murray Harbour. ☎ 902/962-2917. Admission C$3.50 adults, C$2.50 seniors, C$1.50 children, C$7.50 families. Mid-June to mid-Sept, daily 10am–6pm.

At the Buffalo Land Provincial Park you can view some of the 25 buffalo who roam here.

Prince Edward Island Dining

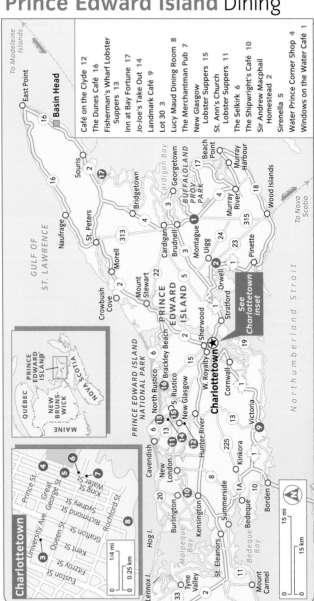

Café on the Clyde 12
The Dunes Café 16
Fisherman's Wharf Lobster Suppers 13
Inn at Bay Fortune 17
Jo-Joe's Take Out 14
Landmark Café 9
Lot 30 3
Lucy Maud Dining Room 8
The Merchantman Pub 7
New Glasgow Lobster Suppers 15
St. Ann's Church Lobster Suppers 11
The Selkirk 6
The Shipwright's Café 10
Sir Andrew Macphail Homestead 19
Sirenella 5
Water Prince Corner Shop 4
Windows on the Water Café 1

PEI Dining A to Z

★ kids **Café on the Clyde** NEW GLASGOW *CANADIAN* Part of the Prince Edward Island Preserve Company, this is a place for breakfasts, country lunches, and gourmet dinners. Sweets are a highlight, and there's live jazz on weekends. *Rte. 224 (at Rte. 258).* ☎ *902/964-4301. Entrees C$7–C$17. AE, DC, MC, V. July & Aug breakfast, lunch & dinner daily; June & Sept variable hours. Closed Oct–May.*

★★ **The Dunes Café** BRACKLEY BEACH *ECLECTIC* Originally a coffeehouse in a gallery, The Dunes is now one of the island's best fusion menus. Foodies are taking notice of the fish chowder, Pad Thai, curries, kids' menu, and great cocktails. *Rte. 15.* ☎ *902/672-1883. www.dunes gallery.com. Entrees lunch C$8– C$14, dinner C$17–C$32. MC, V. June–Sept lunch & dinner daily. Closed Nov–Apr.*

kids **Fisherman's Wharf Lobster Suppers** NORTH RUSTICO *LOBSTER* The 18m (60-ft.) salad bar is the claim to fame here; get some veggies with your steamed crustacean. There's a kids' menu, and unusually, they serve lunch in the summer, as well as dinner. *7230 Rustico Rd. (Rte 6).* ☎ *877/289-1010 or 902/963-2669. Lobster meals C$31–$40. AE, MC, V. July & Aug lunch & dinner daily; May, June, Sept & Oct dinner daily.*

★★★ **Inn at Bay Fortune** BAY FORTUNE *CONTEMPORARY* Herbs and edible flowers from the gardens fill the wonderful menu at this inn. Chef Warren Barr dazzles with chicken-liver crème brûlée, scallop *tartare*, smoked duck, grilled lobster, and the like. The chef's table is a booth right in the kitchen. *758 Rte. 310 (off Rte. 2).* ☎ *902/687-3745. Entrees C$25–C$35. AE, MC, V. June to mid-Oct dinner daily. Closed mid-Oct to May.*

kids **Jo-Joe's Take Out** RUSTICO-VILLE *SEAFOOD* It's just a shack overlooking Rustico Bay at a bend in the road, serving fried seafood. But you can't beat the portion sizes nor the views. Deep-sea fishing tours are offered by the same folks. *Rte. 6.* ☎ *902/963-2295. Entrees C$3–C$15. No credit cards. Mid-June to Aug lunch & dinner daily. Closed Sept to mid-June.*

The Dune's Café has one of the island's best fusion menus.

Landmark Café VICTORIA

CAFE Across from the Victoria Playhouse, this used to be the local general store-slash-post office. The menu is simple: sandwiches and lobster rolls for lunch, steamed PEI mussels, salads, fish, and steak for dinner. *12 Main St.* ☎ *902/658-2286. Entrees C$6–C$16. MC, V. July to mid-Sept lunch & dinner daily. Closed mid-Sept to June.*

★★★ Lot 30 CHARLOTTETOWN

FUSION Legendary former Day-boat chef Gordon Bailey reappears in Charlottetown with his one-of-a-kind cuisine: cheddar-steamed mussels, butter-poached lobster, pan-roasted salmon with Thai black rice, grilled duck breast with Yukon gnocchi, and so on. He's still at the top of his game. *151 Kent St.* ☎ *902/629-3030. www.lot30restaurant.ca. Entrees $20–$35. MC, V Feb–Dec dinner Tues–Sun. Closed Jan.*

★★ Lucy Maud Dining Room

CHARLOTTETOWN *REGIONAL* Part of a culinary school in Charlotte-town, this dining room is a local secret. Before a lovely view of the bay and park, student chefs whip up duck, venison, steaks, seafood, and more; side dishes and flavorings utilize Eastern Canadian harvests. There's always salmon on the menu. *4 Sydney St.* ☎ *902/894-6868. Entrees C$8–C$28. AE, MC, V. June–Sept lunch Tues–Fri, dinner*

Former Dayboat chef Gordon Bailey's one-of-a-kind fusion restaurant, Lot 30.

Tues–Sat. Closed Oct–May & holiday weekends.

★★ The Merchantman Pub

CHARLOTTETOWN *FUSION* The first "gastropub" on PEI; even the nachos are gourmet. Seafood rules, often cooked with Thai or Cajun sauces. There are plenty of thick sandwiches, burgers, and gourmet choices, too—beef medallions in whiskey butter sauce; seared trout; lobster linguine; rack of lamb in a rhubarb-wine sauce. *23 Queen St.* ☎ *902/892-9150. Entrees C$8–C$25. Lunch & dinner daily. MC, V.*

★ kids New Glasgow Lobster Suppers

NEW GLASGOW *LOBSTER* One of PEI's iconic lobster suppers, this one features all-you-can-eat mussels and chowder. The pies are good, and the kids' menu is substantial. There's roast beef for non-shellfish eaters. *604 Rte 258 (off Rte. 13).* ☎ *902/964-2870. Lobster meals $31–$41. AE, MC, V. June to mid-Oct dinner daily. Closed mid-Oct to May.*

St. Ann's Church Lobster Suppers

ST. ANN *LOBSTER* St. Ann's says it created the PEI lobster supper concept in 1963; who am I to argue? It's housed in a church hall (which it helps to fund), yet has a full liquor license. Service is by wait-staff, rather than the usual self-serve buffet. *Rte. 224 (off Rte. 6/13).* ☎ *902/621-0635. Entrees $31–$40. MC, V. Mid-June to Sept dinner Mon–Sat. Closed Oct to mid-June.*

★★ The Selkirk CHARLOTTE-TOWN

CANADIAN/FUSION Charlottetown's most stylish restaurant, in the lobby of the Delta Prince Edward hotel (see p 144). This is resort fare—chicken brochettes, beef tenderloin, pan-seared scallops. The pianist is a nice touch. *18 Queen St.* ☎ *902/566-2222. Entrees C$18–C$25. AE, DC, DISC, MC, V. Breakfast, lunch & dinner daily.*

Water Prince Corner Shop serves great lobster dinners, chowder, and other seafood.

roast lamb—plus a version of haggis (minus the sheep stomach). *Rte. 1.* ☎ *902/651-2789. Entrees C$3–C$16. V. July–Sept lunch & dinner daily. Closed Oct to June.*

kids **Sirenella** CHARLOTTETOWN *ITALIAN* Another Italian family restaurant in Charlottetown, serving veal, calamari, Pernod-steamed mussels, ravioli, and fancy treatments of lobster. It's a tiny, romantic space down a side alley. Children are welcome. *83 Water St.* ☎ *902/628-2271. Entrees C$14–C$27. AE, MC, V. Mon–Sat lunch & dinner.*

★ **Water Prince Corner Shop** CHARLOTTETOWN *SEAFOOD* A lobster pound in the heart of the city? Yes; this Charlottetown gem is a skip from the water and serves great lobster dinners, chowder, and other seafood to a mix of locals and tourists. *141 Water St.* ☎ *902/368-3212. Entrees C$5–C$25. AE, DISC, DC, MC, V. May–Oct breakfast, lunch & dinner daily. Closed Nov–Apr.*

★★ **The Shipwright's Café** MARGATE *REGIONAL* This friendly local family restaurant is elegant yet informal, with a more upscale menu than expected: organic greens, lamb wraps, chili tostadas, curried mussels, and lobster sandwiches alongside the fish cakes, salmon, pot pies, and mussel chowder. *1869 Rte. 6 (at Rte. 233).* ☎ *902/836-3403. Entrees C$9–C$20 (more for lobster). MC, V. June–Sept lunch & dinner daily. Closed Oct–May.*

★ **Windows on the Water Café** MONTAGUE *SEAFOOD* PEI's renowned mussels are center stage at this cafe, which prepares them in interesting ways to support main dishes of sole stuffed with crab, fish cakes, and sandwiches. The covered deck has a nice view of the river. *106 Sackville St. (at Main St.).* ☎ *902/838-2080. Entrees lunch & dinner C$7–C$21. AE, DC, MC, V. June–Sept lunch & dinner daily. Closed Oct–May.*

Sir Andrew Macphail Homestead ORWELL *TRADITIONAL* This simple restaurant is located within the historic Macphail homestead in Orwell Corner, and serves inexpensive heavy regional cuisine—fish,

PEI's renowned mussels anchor the menu at Windows on the Water Café.

Prince Edward Island Lodging

Barachois Inn 3
Best Western
  Charlottetown 15
Caernarvon Cottages
  and Gardens 21
Cavendish Beach Cottages 1
Dalvay by the Sea 5
Delta Prince Edward 17
The Doctor's Inn B&B 22
Forest and Stream Cottages 12
Fox River Cottages 11
The Great George 16
Green Gables
  Bungalow Court 2
Hillhurst Inn 14
Inn at Bay Fortune 8
Inn at Spry Point 9
Matthew House Inn 7
Orient Hotel 20
Rodd Brudenell River Resort 10
Rodd Charlottetown 18
Rodd Crowbush Golf
  & Beach Resort 6
Shaw's Hotel 4
Shipwright Inn 19
Trailside Inn Café
  & Adventures 13

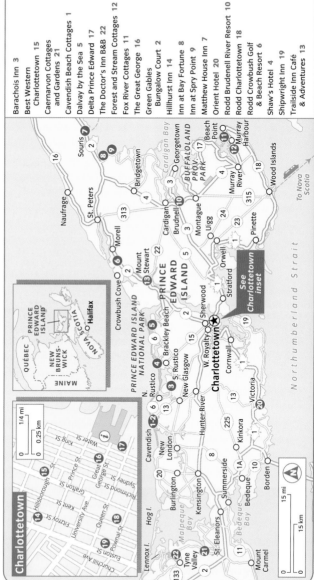

PEI Lodging A to Z

A room in the proudly Victorian Barachois Inn overlooking the bay in North Rustico.

★ **Barachois Inn** SOUTH RUS-TICO   The proudly Victorian Barachois is amongst the impressive clump of historic buildings overlooking the bay in North Rustico. Innkeepers Judy and Gary MacDonald have upgraded the inn, which features canopy beds and claw-foot tubs; the annex has a sauna. *2193 Church Rd.* ☎ *800/963-2194. http:// barachoisinn.com. 8 units. Doubles C$125–C$235 w/breakfast. AE, MC, V. Closed Nov–Mar.*

Best Western Charlottetown CHARLOTTETOWN   In two buildings across the street from each other a few blocks east of the Confederation Court Mall, this is the most central chain hotel in PEI's capital. You pay for the walk-to-it-all location, but parking is free. *238 Grafton St.* ☎ *800/528-1234 or 902/892-2461. www.bestwestern. com. 146 units. Doubles C$100– C$235. AE, DISC, MC, V.*

kids Caernarvon Cottages and Gardens BAYSIDE   A quiet cottage-and-inn complex overlooking a bay near Tyne Valley. Four cottages are plain yet well furnished; three simple inn rooms include breakfast. *4697 Rte. 12 (13km/8 miles south of Tyne Valley).* ☎ *800/514-9170 or 902/854-3418. www.cottagelink.com/cottlink/pei/ pe10018.html. 7 units. Doubles C$125 w/breakfast; cottages C$700– C$750 per week. V. Cottages closed mid-Sept to mid-June.*

★ **kids Cavendish Beach Cottages** CAVENDISH   These 13 pine-paneled cottages sit on a grassy knoll in PEI's beachy national park, right above the sand. All have direct ocean views, kitchens with dishwashers, and barbecue grills. *1445 Gulf Shore Dr.* ☎ *902/963-2025. www.cavendishbeachcottages.com. 13 units. C$95–C$215. MC, V. Closed Oct to mid-May.*

★★ **Dalvay by the Sea** GRAND TRACADIE   This Tudor inn was built across the road from the beach in 1895. There's great woodwork, a big

You'll find great woodwork in the rooms at Dalvay by the Sea, located across the road from the beach.

stone fireplace, and 26 elegant rooms without TVs or phones; a set of luxe three-bedroom cottages have wet bars and propane stoves. Dining and afternoon tea are highlights here. *Rte. 6.* ☎ *888/368-2955 or 902/672-2048. www.dalvaybythesea.com. 34 units. Doubles and cottages C$284–C$525 w/breakfast & dinner; extra charge for children. AE, DC, MC, V. Closed late Sept to May.*

★ 🚸 **Delta Prince Edward** CHARLOTTETOWN This towering business hotel by Charlottetown's harbor features swimming pools, a fitness center, and one of the city's best gourmet restaurants. The hotel added apartment-like suites in 2009. *18 Queen St.* ☎ *888/890-3222 or 902/566-2222. www.deltaprince edward.com. 211 units. Doubles & suites C$169–C$345. AE, DC, DISC, MC, V.*

The Doctor's Inn B&B TYNE VALLEY Great food is the highlight of this tiny B&B. It's basically just a farmhouse with three plain rooms, but dinner is memorable, cooked on the inn's woodstove. *Rte. 167 (at Rte. 12).* ☎ *902/831-3057. www. peisland.com/doctorsinn. 3 units. Doubles C$60 w/breakfast. MC, V.*

🚸 **Forest and Stream Cottages** MURRAY HARBOUR Six decent cottages, run by a friendly local couple. The property's lake is ever-popular, and rowboats, canoes,

and pedal boats are supplied for free. *446 Fox River Rd. (off Rte. 18).* ☎ *800/227-9943 or 902/962-3537. www. forestandstreamcottages.com. 6 units. Doubles C$75–C$125, weekly rates C$475–C$790. MC, V. Closed Nov–Apr.*

Fox River Cottages MURRAY HARBOUR These four two-bedroom cottages overlook a scenic bay; all of them are modernized with decks, Wi-Fi access, and barbecues. There's a long, swimmable beach on the river below. *239 Machon Point Rd. (off Rte. 18).* ☎ *902/962-2881. www.foxriver. ca. 4 units. Doubles C$80–C$140, weekly rates C$500–C$925. MC, V. Closed Nov–May.*

★★★ **The Great George** CHAR-LOTTETOWN This Charlottetown complex, a hotel plus nearby town-houses, manages to be both historic and luxurious. Rooms feature antiques, down duvets, and black-and-white prints; some have gas fire-places, double Jacuzzis, or claw-foot tubs. *58 Great George St.* ☎ *800/361-1118 or 902/892-0606. www.thegreat george.com. 54 units. Doubles C$179–C$349 w/breakfast, suites C$219–C$899 w/breakfast. AE, DC, MC, V.*

★ **Green Gables Bungalow Court** CAVENDISH Next to the "official" Green Gables house, these cottages are attractively trimmed with painted window boxes, decks, and trees. All units have kitchens with refrigerators, utensils, and gas grills; a few have TVs. There's a nice heated outdoor pool, too. *8663 Cavendish Rd. (Rte. 6).* ☎ *800/965-3334 or 902/963-2722. www.greengables bungalowcourt.com. 40 cottages. Cottages C$70–C$149, weekly rates C$699–C$999. AE, MC, V. Closed Oct–June.*

★ **Hillhurst Inn** CHARLOTTE-TOWN A handsome mansion 3 blocks north of Province House, Hill-hurst features extraordinary wood-work by local shipbuilders. Rooms are basic but finally have phones, air-conditioning, and TVs, and some even have Jacuzzis. *181 Fitzroy St.* ☎ *877/994-8004 or 902/894-8004. www.hillhurst.com. 9 units. Doubles C$99–C$235 w/breakfast. AE, DISC, MC, V. Closed Dec–Apr.*

★★ **Inn at Bay Fortune** BAY FORTUNE David Wilmer's attractive brick-and-shingle compound near the bay features some of PEI's best dinners, plus intriguing tower rooms with great views; the Green Room even has a rooftop deck. *758 Rte. 310 (off Rte. 2).* ☎ *902/687-3745 or 902/687-3745. www.innat bayfortune.com. 17 units. Doubles C$135–C$335 w/breakfast. DC, MC, V. Closed mid-Oct to mid-May.*

★★ **Inn at Spry Point** LITTLE POND This rambling house on a point of land was once an alternative social experiment; today, it's an inn of spacious, cleanly furnished suites. The dining room is outstanding. *Spry Pt. Rd. (off Rte. 310).* ☎ *888/687-3745 or 902/583-2400. www.innatsprypoint. com. 15 units. Doubles C$159–C$299 w/breakfast. DC, MC, V. Closed mid-Sept to late June.*

Matthew House Inn SOURIS Italian émigrés own this B&B just off Souris' main street. Overlooking the harbor and ferries, it's full of flowery prints, odd angles, and simple wood furniture. *15 Breakwater St.* ☎ *902/687-3461. www.matthew houseinn.com. 8 units. Doubles C$105–C$170 w/breakfast. AE, MC, V. Closed early Sept to mid-June. Children over 10 welcome.*

Orient Hotel VICTORIA The only hotel in Victoria, near the big bridge onto PEI; you can't miss the century-old building's bright yellow shingles. Rooms are painted in pastel tones and furnished basically; this place defines "old fashioned". There are folk dances at night and afternoon teas in a tea room. *34 Main St.* ☎ *800/565-6743 or 902/658-2503. 8 units.*

The Inn at Spry Point is spacious with cleanly furnished suites.

Doubles C$80–C$150 w/breakfast. MC, V. Closed mid-Oct to mid-May. Not suitable for children under 12.

★★ kids Rodd Brudenell River Resort CARDIGAN
This seasonal resort opened in 1991 beside several upscale golf courses. The "gold" cottages each have two bedrooms, Jacuzzis, kitchens, and wet bars; cabins down by the river are much simpler and showing their age. *Dewars Lane (at Rte. 3).* ☎ *800/565-7633 or 902/652-2332. www.rodd-hotels.ca. 181 units. Doubles and cabins C$139–C$568. AE, DC, MC, V. Closed mid-Oct to early May.*

Rodd Charlottetown CHARLOTTETOWN
Built of brick in 1931 by CN Railways, the Rodd features Georgian flourishes and some modern touches. There are several newer suites, a rooftop patio, and a lobby bar. *75 Kent St. (at Pownal St.).* ☎ *800/565-7633 or 902/894-7371. www.rodd-hotels.ca. 115 units. Doubles C$109–C$350. AE, DC, DISC, MC, V.*

★★★ Rodd Crowbush Golf & Beach Resort MORELL
Anchored by the island's best golf course, this resort's rooms include king-bedded suites (some with balconies) and plenty of cottages with luxe touches like Jacuzzis, dishwashers, porches, and grills. You can swim in an indoor pool, soak in an outdoor hot tub, or play on the tennis courts if you don't golf. *Rte. 350.* ☎ *800/565-7633 or 902/961-5600. www.rodd vacations.com. 81 units. Doubles and cottages C$151–C$656. MC, V. Closed late Sept to mid-June.*

★ kids Shaw's Hotel BRACKLEY BEACH
You can't miss the red, red roof of Shaw's, a Brackley Beach fixture for more than a century. More than two-thirds of the beds are actually in adjacent cottages. A sandy lane leads to the beach; kids'

Shipwright Inn is in the heart of downtown Charlottetown but has a surprisingly rural feel.

programs are excellent. *Rte. 15.* ☎ *902/672-2022. www.shawshotel. ca. 38 units. Doubles C$75–C$710 w/breakfast. AE, MC, V. Closed Nov to late May.*

★★ Shipwright Inn CHARLOTTETOWN
Even though it's located downtown in PEI's biggest city, this inn almost feels rural. It's decorated in period furniture, yet surprisingly modern and luxurious; the wood floors are gorgeous. And the rates are very reasonable. *51 Fitzroy St.* ☎ *888/306-9966 or 902/368-1905. www.shipwrightinn.com. 9 units. Doubles $99–C$299 w/breakfast. AE, DC, MC, V.*

★ Trailside Inn Café & Adventures MOUNT STEWART
In a former grocery store, the Trailside is a combination adventure center/ supply depot/inn. Rooms are simple; clients are largely bicyclists (the Confederation Trail bike route runs right past the door). Local musicians sometimes play sets. *109 Main St.* ☎ *888/704-6595 or 902/676-3130. www.trailside.ca. 4 units. Doubles C$80. MC, V. Closed late Sept to mid-June.* ●

New Brunswick

Saint John

Carleton St.

Hazen Ave.

Peel St.

Wellington Row

Dorchester St.

Coburg St.

Waterloo St.

Union St. **6**

Smythe St.

St. Patrick St.

Chipman Hill

Charlotte St.

7 ⓘ

Loyalist Plaza

King St.

5

King's Square **1**

2

3

4

Grannan St.

Water St.

Prince William St.

Canterbury St.

Germain St.

Princess St.

Saint John Harbour

Duke St.

Germain Street Baptist Church †

Queen St.

Sydney St.

Queen Square

9

QUÉBEC

PRINCE EDWARD ISLAND

MAINE

NEW BRUNSWICK

Saint John ○

NOVA SCOTIA

"The Inside Connection"

0 ——— 1/4 mi
0 ——— 0.25 km

1 King's Square
2 Old Burial Ground
3 Imperial Theatre
4 Trinity Church
5 Saint John City Market
6 Loyalist House
7 New Brunswick Museum
8 Rockwood Park
9 Irving Nature Park

Previous page: Tourists explore Hopewell Rocks at low tide.

Saint John—the oldest incorporated city in Canada—is the "capital" of the Bay of Fundy. As one of the largest cities in the Maritimes, it wields economic clout: There's plenty of heavy industry (shipping, oil, paper, pulp) in the port. Yet first-time visitors are often surprised by the city's lovely surroundings, which include bays, islands, gardens, and forests. START: **Downtown in King's Sq.**

1 ★ King's Square. The physical and spiritual heart of Saint John resides in King's Square, which has been present since the town's founding in 1785. But it was originally used as a sort of town "common" and only formally laid out as a park in the mid-19th century. If you were a bird, you'd see that its paths are designed in the shape of the Union Jack (the British flag). The bandstand, flower beds, war memorial, and Loyalist cross were all added during the 20th century. ⏱ *45 min. Sydney & Charlotte sts.*

From the northeast corner of the square, cross Sydney St. to the

2 Old Burial Ground. This soothing, park-like cemetery dates from at least 1784. Yet, despite its central position, the grounds had fallen into serious disrepair until they were cleaned up and renovated in the mid-1990s by the Irving family—they added the bronze,

four-beavered fountain, meant to be symbolic of Canada and its hard-working citizens. Pathways branch throughout the grounds from Sydney Street; the right-hand gate leads to most of the gravestones, while the middle gate takes you to the fountain. ⏱ *30 min. Sydney St. (at King's Sq.). Free admission. Daily dawn–dusk.*

On the south side of King's Square is the

3 ★ Imperial Theatre. Canada's leading newspaper, the *Globe and Mail*, called the Imperial the "most beautifully restored theatre in Canada." It opened in 1913 and hosted such performers as Edgar Bergen (1903–1978), Al Jolson (1886–1950), and Walter Pidgeon (1897–1984; a Saint John native). Later driven out of business by movie houses, it was nearly demolished. But locals stepped in, and the theater reopened in 1994; now, it hosts

The bronze, four-beavered fountain at Old Burial Ground is meant to be symbolic of Canada and its hardworking citizens.

traveling Broadway shows, local theater, and concerts. If nothing's scheduled during your visit, take the half-hour tour anyway. ⏱ *30 min. 24 King's Sq. South.* ☎ *506/674-4100. www.imperialtheatre.nb.ca. Tours C$2 adults. Mon–Sat 9am–5pm (reservation required).*

From around the corner from the theater, on Charlotte St., is the

④ **Trinity Church.** The city's stony, arched Anglican church is hard to miss: Its steeple rises 70m (230 ft.) high. It was built of limestone in 1880 to replace a wooden church on the site that burned. Look way up to the top: Is that a wooden, gold-leafed fish serving as a weathervane? There's a royal coat of arms from the early 18th century hanging inside, too. ⏱ *30 min. 115 Charlotte St.* ☎ *506/693-8558. www.trinitysj.com. Free admission. Mon–Fri 8:30am–12:30pm.*

From the church, walk 2 blocks north on Charlotte St. to the

⑤ ★★ **Saint John City Market.** This spacious, bustling marketplace is crammed with vendors hawking meat, fresh seafood, cheeses, flowers, baked goods, and bountiful fresh produce. The market was built in 1876 and has exerted a magnetic pull on local residents ever since. Look for small, enduring traces of the market's history: The handsome iron gates have been in place since 1880, and a loud bell is still rung daily by a clerk to signal the opening and closing. ⏱ *1¼ hr. 47 Charlotte St. (off King's Sq.).* ☎ *506/658-2820. Mon–Fri 7:30am–6pm, Sat 7:30am–5pm. Closed Sun & holidays.*

Continue 1 block on Charlotte St. to Union St. Turn left & continue 2 blocks to

⑥ ★ **Loyalist House.** This stately mansion was built in 1817 for a family of Loyalists from New York.

Inside, there's an extraordinary collection of furniture; most pieces were original to the home, including extensive holdings of Duncan Phyfe Sheraton furniture and a rare piano-organ combination. The house still has its original brass knocker and doors that were steamed and bent to fit into the curve of the stairway. ⏱ *45 min. 120 Union St.* ☎ *506/652-3590. Admission C$3 adults, C$1 children, C$7 families. July to mid-Sept daily 10am–5pm; mid-May to June Mon–Fri 10am–5pm.*

Walk 2 blocks south on Germain St.; turn right on King St. & continue 3 blocks to the

⑦ ★ **kids New Brunswick Museum.** This imposing-looking museum is a primer on the province's natural and cultural history. You can see the complete interior of a bar where city longshoremen once drank, a massive section of a ship's frame, geological exhibits, and even a sports car from a failed try at auto-manufacturing during the 1970s. There's a gallery of

Inside the New Brunswick Museum is a Hall of Whales where you can see leviathon skeletons and scale models.

The excellent golf course at Rockwood Park.

19th-century shipbuilding, too, and a Hall of Great Whales with skeletons and scale models. ⏱ *45 min. 1 Market Sq.* ☎ *506/643-2300. Admission C$6 adults, C$4.75 seniors, C$3.25 students & children 4–18, C$13 families. Mon–Wed & Fri 9am–5pm, Thurs 9am–9pm, Sat 10am–5pm, Sun noon–5pm. Closed Mon Nov to mid-May.*

Harbour Passage

You might also want to get a glimpse of Saint John's working waterfront while you're in town, and that's easy to do thanks to the bright red waterfront walking path known as the Harbour Passage. (It's only 1.6km/1 mile now, but one day, it will reach all the way to Reversing Falls for a 5km/3-mile stroll.) Interpretive signs point out historical and environmental features of the harbor as you walk, or you can use the path for your morning jog. Find the path by walking behind the waterfront Hilton hotel (1 Market Sq.) at the foot of Smythe St., 1 block west of the New Brunswick Museum (see p 150, **7**).

Follow St. Patrick St. north to Main St. Take the ramp onto Rte. 100 (Station St.) & travel 1.6km (1 mile); exit onto Mt. Pleasant Ave. In .8km (½ mile), bear right on Lake Drive South to

8 ★ kids **Rockwood Park.** This huge, 890-hectare (2,200-acre) urban park is filled with lakes, woods, rocky hills, beaches, picnic areas, a small but good zoo, and an excellent little golf course. You can even rent canoes and kayaks, or hit golf balls at an eco-friendly aquatic driving range: You hit *floating* golf balls into a lake, which are later scooped up by a trolling boat. ⏱ *1 hr. Lake Dr. South (off Rte. 1).* ☎ *506/658-2883. Park free admission; zoo C$7–C$9 adults, C$4.50–C$6 children. Interpretation Centre late May to early Sept daily 8am–dusk.*

Backtrack along Mount Pleasant Ave. to the Rte. 1 West ramp; turn left & merge onto Rte. 1. Drive 6km (3¾ miles) to exit 119A; exit & turn right on Bleury St. Travel .5km (¼ mile) to Sand Cove Rd., turn right & continue 1.2km (¾ mile) to

9 ★★ kids **Irving Nature Park.** This gem of a park consists of 243 dramatic hectares (600 acres) on a coastal peninsula. Trails and boardwalks provide access to forest, shoreline, marshes, and bird life; seals throng the park in late spring and late fall. Call ahead to ask about tours and events, such as moonlight snowshoeing, meteor-shower watches, and kids' camps. ⏱ *1½ hr. Sand Cove Rd.* ☎ *506/653-7367. Free admission. Daily dawn–dusk; auto road & visitor's booth daily dawn–dusk May to mid-Nov.*

Bay of Fundy

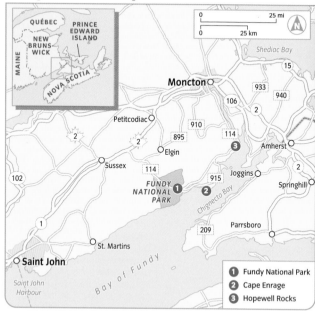

1 Fundy National Park
2 Cape Enrage
3 Hopewell Rocks

Nowhere in the world do tides rise and drop as dramatically as they do here in the Bay of Fundy. That's one reason to come: to see this awesome spectacle repeat itself twice a day, every day. But there are also stunning headlands, weird rocks, gentle bike rides, and plenty of unusual birds. **START: Alma, 130 km/80 miles northeast of Saint John via Rte. 1 north & Rte. 114 east.**

1 ★★★ Fundy National Park. The coastal sections of this park are a must-see, and not only for the tides; the hikes, vistas, and woods are also wonderful. There are plenty of local outdoor activities (such as kayaking; also consider camping at one of the park's three campgrounds from June through September. (Of the three, **Headquarters Campground** is the most family-friendly and sophisticated, but also the least serene and outdoorsy; it's a short walk from an outdoor theater, pool, and downtown Alma.) The main visitor center is just inside the Alma (eastern) entrance to the park—the exit if you're coming from Saint John—where you can orient yourself, pick up maps, and look over exhibits on wildlife and tides. 🕐 *4 hr. Rte. 114, Alma.* ☎ *506/887-6000. www.pc.gc. ca/eng/pn-np/nb/fundy/index.aspx. Admission C$7.80 adults, C$6.80 seniors, C$3.90 children, C$20 families. Campsites C$23–C$35/night. Alma info center July & Aug daily 8am– 10pm, Sept–June daily 8am–4:30pm; Wolf Lake info center June to Aug daily 10am–6pm, closed Sept–May.*

Rocks and Rolls

One of Eastern Canada's best hiking trails and driving experiences, the Fundy Trail is rarely crowded, and scenically, it's close to spectacular; the Trail also connects directly to the Fundy Footpath, a longer-distance wilderness hike for hardcore outdoors enthusiasts. I detail a few of the best stops along the Trail in chapter 8 (see p 170).

From the Alma (eastern) park entrance, turn onto Rte. 915 & travel 15km (9¼ miles) north to the turnoff for

② ★ **Cape Enrage.** This privately owned cape of rock juts boldly out into Chignecto Bay and is chiefly worth a visit if you're pumped up about outdoor adventures. The outdoors center here offers a great selection of rock-climbing workshops and also arranges custom adventure vacations. Too tired for that? Take pictures of the bay and lighthouse from the top of the cliffs—or from *inside* the lighthouse. You can also rent a bike or descend to Samurai Beach and walk the ocean floor at low tide. ⏱ *1 hr. Cape Enrage Rd. (off Rte. 114), Cape*

It's not only tides; the hikes, vistas, and woods at Fundy National Park are also wonderful.

Enrage. ☎ *888/280-7273 or 506/887-2273. www.capenrage.com. Admission C$4 adults, C$3.50 seniors, C$2.50 children, C$13 families (tours & activities extra; bike rentals C$8/hr.). Mid June–early Sept, daily 8am–8pm; mid May to mid June and early Sept–mid Oct, daily 9am–5pm. Closed mid Oct–mid May.*

Return to Rte. 915 & continue 16km (10 miles) to Rte. 114. Turn right & travel 16km (10 miles) to Rocks Rd. Turn right to reach the

③ ★★ **Hopewell Rocks.** One of New Brunswick's most amazing scenes is the sight of the eroded, 15m (50-ft.) columns of red rock on the ocean floor at Hopewell Rocks. Time your visit carefully (the attraction's website lists tidal charts for May–Oct, with expected sizes of the drops); during low tide, you can descend stairs to the sea floor and touch those rocks. Bring comfortable shoes and snap away before the waters rush back in to cover them. While (or after) the rocks are submerged, the visitor center is a pleasant spot to pass the time. ⏱ *2 hr. Rocks Rd., Hopewell Cape.* ☎ *877/734-3429. www.thehopewell rocks.ca. Admission C$8.50 adults, C$7.25 seniors, C$6.25 children 5–18, C$23 families. Mid-June to mid-Aug daily 8am–8pm; mid-May to mid-June & mid-Aug to mid-Oct daily 9am–5pm. Closed mid-Oct to mid-May.*

Fredericton

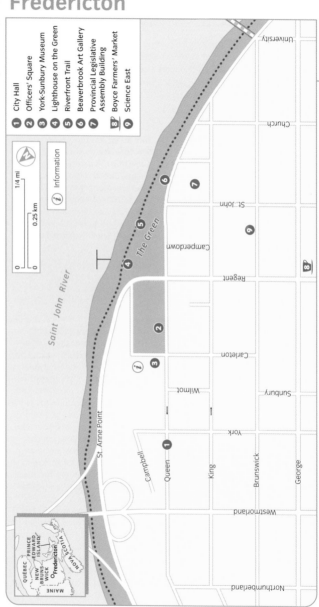

1 City Hall
2 Officers' Square
3 York-Sunbury Museum
4 Lighthouse on the Green
5 Riverfront Trail
6 Beaverbrook Art Gallery
7 Provincial Legislative Assembly Building
8 Boyce Farmers' Market
9 Science East

ⓘ Information

0 ____ 1/4 mi
0 ____ 0.25 km

Saint John River

The Green

St. Anne Point

University
Church
St. John
Camperdown
Regent
Carleton
Wilmot
York
Sunbury
Campbell
Queen
King
Brunswick
George
Westmorland
Northumberland

QUEBEC
MAINE
NEW BRUNSWICK
Fredericton
PRINCE EDWARD ISLAND
NOVA SCOTIA

ew Brunswick's capital city doesn't always get the respect it deserves from through-going travelers, simply due to its geography: It's a little off the beaten path from the Fundy–Saint John–PEI coastal axis. But if you enjoy historic buildings, take time to make that detour—Fredericton has the best concentration of them in the province. START: **Queen St. at York St., Fredericton.**

Free tours are offered twice daily at Fredericton's City Hall.

1 ★ City Hall. Fredericton's city hall is an elaborate Victorian building with a prominent brick tower and a big, 2.6m (8½-ft.) clock dial. The second-floor City Council chamber occupies what used to be Fredericton's opera house until the 1940s. Small, folksy tapestries adorn the visitor's gallery. You can learn about them and the rest of the building during free tours offered twice daily. From May through October, this is also home to the city's main tourist information office, making it the logical first stop. ⏲ 30 min. 397 Queen St. ☎ 506/460-2129. Free tours mid-May to mid-Oct, daily 9:30am and 3:30pm (English) and daily 9pm (French).

Walk 2 blocks east on Queen St. to

2 ★ Officers' Square. It's a handsome city park with cannons and river views now, but in 1785, this was the center of the city's military activity; it was chiefly used for drills, first by a British garrison, and then, until World War I, by Canada's armed forces. Today, the only soldiers are local actors who put on a little show for the tourists. Free concerts and dramatic events are staged on the square during summer. Note the prominent statue of a robed Lord Beaverbrook in the middle of the square. ⏲ 15 min. Queen St. (btwn. Carleton & Regent sts.).

On the west side of the square is the handsome

3 kids York-Sunbury Museum. That arched, colonnaded stone building facing the parade grounds once held British officers' quarters, and it looks like it. Now, though, it's home to a small museum touting a stuffed 19kg (42-lb.) frog (a big disappointment when you finally see it), plus some other historical artifacts and information about the local Loyalist settlers. Kids might like the claustrophobic, faithfully re-created World War II trench on the second floor; if you're in a hurry, you could skip this stop, but don't miss the exterior. ⏲ 30 min. 571 Queen St. ☎ 506/455-6041. www.yorksunburymuseum.com. Admission C$3 adults, C$1 children, C$6 families. July & Aug Mon–Sat 10am–5pm, Sun noon–5pm; Apr–June & Sept–Oct Tues–Sat 1–4pm. Closed Nov–May.

The Riverfront Trail is a lovely walk and passes by many of Fredericton's key sight-seeing points.

Turn left & follow Regent St. downhill to the water and the

④ Lighthouse on the Green.

You can get active by visiting this attractive red-and-white lighthouse, which has been converted into a sort of activities center; staff here rent bikes and sell tickets for good city walking tours. From here, walk along the river's banks in the lush park known as The Green: The riverfront park is a great place to hang out in summer watching boats go by. 🕐 *15 min. Foot of Regent St.* ☎ *506/460-2939. Walking tours free; bike rentals C$7/hr. or C$25/ day. July & Aug daily 10:30am– 9:30pm; June & early to mid-Sept daily 10:30am–6pm.Closed mid-Sept to May.*

The Green also intersects with the

⑤ ★ Riverfront Trail. The cen-
terpiece of Fredericton's excellent trail system is its riverfront trail, a 5km (3.1-mile) pathway that follows the riverbank from the Delta hotel to the Princess Margaret Bridge. It's a lovely walk and passes by many of the city's key sightseeing points: the Old Government House (which we'll visit at the end of this tour), the downtown area, and open park-lands near Waterloo Row. 🕐 *45 min. Entrances at Regent St. & Queen St. (near Brunswick St.).*

Between the riverside park & Queen St., just west of Officers' Sq., is the

⑥ ★★ Beaverbrook Art Gal-
lery. This excellent museum over-looks the city's waterfront and holds an extensive collection of British art, including works by Reynolds (1723–1792), Gainsborough (1727–1788), Constable (1727–1788), and Turner (1774–1851); other rooms hold fur-nishings and decorative art. Dali's (1904–1989) massive *Santiago El Grande* and studies for a portrait of Churchill are also here, and the

Lord Beaverbrook, I Presume?

You see the name "Beaverbrook" a lot in Fredericton. Who was this fellow? Born Max Aitken (1879–1964), he grew up in New Brunswick's quiet Miramichi area before amassing a fortune in Hali-fax, Montréal, and London. Aitken was made a lord in 1917, taking the name of a stream he'd fished as a boy. He died in 1964, but the *faux* name lives on.

holdings of modern art are growing. Traveling shows are high-quality, and the gallery's also strong in First Nations (native Canadian) art. ⏱ 1½ hr. 703 Queen St. ☎ 506/458-2028. www.beaverbrookartgallery.org. Admission C$8 adults, C$6 seniors, C$3 children, C$18 families; no fee Thurs after 5:30pm. Tues–Sat 9am–5:30pm (Thurs to 9pm), Sun noon–5:30pm; also Mon 9am–5:30pm June–Dec (closed Mon Jan–May).

Directly across Queen St. from the museum is the regal

⑦ ★★ Provincial Legislative Assembly Building. New Brunswick's official legislative building, built in 1880, boasts an exterior in extravagant Second Empire style. Inside, in the small rotunda, look for Audubon prints in a display case, then proceed to the assembly chamber itself—it nearly takes one's breath away, especially when viewed from the visitor gallery (reached via a spiral stairway). This chamber is ornate all out of proportion to the legislative humdrum within. The regal trimmings also include a portrait of a young Queen Elizabeth (1926–). ⏱ 45 min. 706 Queen St. ☎ 506/453-2506. www.gnb.ca/legis. Free admission. Tours June to mid-Aug daily 9am–5pm; mid-Aug to May 9am–4pm.

⑧ ★★ Boyce Farmers' Market. If you're in town on a Saturday, don't miss the city farmer's market held beside Science East (see below). This award-winning market has been here, in one form or another, since the late 18th century. Today about 200 vendors—butchers, bakers, even candlestick makers—hawk everything from fresh produce to crafts, croissants, and artisanal smoked meats, from early morning until 1pm. 665 George St. (at Regent St.). ☎ 506/451-1815. $.

Walk half a block back toward town; turn left on St. John St. & go 2 blocks. Turn right onto Brunswick St. On the left is

⑨ ★★ kids Science East. Kids old enough to like science uniformly enjoy this excellent science center, housed inside a blocky, plain-looking jail. Inside, it's much better than it looks. The exhibits tend toward the hands-on. (Create a tornado? Sign me up.) ⏱ 1¼ hr. 668 Brunswick St. ☎ 506/457-2340. www.scienceeast.nb.ca. Admission C$8 adults, C$7 seniors, C$5 children 15 & under, C$22 families. June–Aug Mon–Sat 10am–5pm, Sun noon–4pm; Sept–May Mon–Fri noon–5pm, Sat 10am–5pm, closed Sun.

A portion of the Beaverbrook Art Gallery's extensive British art collection.

St. Andrews

1 Kingsbrae Garden
2 All Saints Anglican Church
3 Charlotte County Courthouse
4 St. Andrews Blockhouse
5 Ministers Island Historic Site

Compact, handsome St. Andrews spills down its hillside right to the Bay of Fundy. You'll find good architecture and salt air here, plus an appealing friendliness in the locals. Water Street, the long commercial street paralleling the bay, is the main hub of the whale-watching, strolling, and shopping in town. There's also a classic resort with a superb golf course (see p 37). START: **Fairmont Algonquin hotel (Adolphus St. at Prince of Wales St.). Walk or drive 3 blocks east along Prince of Wales St. to King St.**

1 ★★ kids Kingsbrae Garden. This big public garden opened in 1998, on the former grounds of a long-gone estate. There are nearly 2,000 varieties of trees (including old-growth forest), shrubs, and plants here; a day lily collection, extensive rose gardens, and a maze; a Dutch windmill and duck ponds; and a children's garden with a Victorian mansion–like playhouse. 🕐 *1 hr. 220 King St.* ☎ *866/566-8687 or 506/529-3335. Admission C$9.75*

adults, C$8.25 seniors, C$24 families; free for children 5 & under. Mid-May to mid-Oct daily 9am–6pm. Closed mid-Oct to mid-May.

Travel 3 blocks down King St. to Montague St. Turn left. On the corner is the

2 All Saints Anglican Church. Dating from 1867, this town's tallest church features lovely stained-glass work within, plus a great old pipe organ. This church also administers the Loyalist cemetery running along King Street to Kingsbrae Garden; it's likely the town's oldest burying ground. 🕐 *15 min. 77 King St. (at Montague St.).* ☎ *506/529-8662. July–Aug, free tours Mon–Fri 9am–5pm (call ahead); rest of the year, by appointment only.*

Continue 1 block to Frederick St. Turn left & go 1 block uphill. On the right is the

❸ Charlotte County Courthouse.

This simple-looking, columned courthouse dates from the mid-18th century, but it holds all the town's copious archives—invaluable if you're a history or genealogy buff. And there's a scarifying little jail in the basement you can tour for free. 🕐 *15 min. 123 Frederick St.* ☎ *506/529-4248. www.ccarchives. ca. Free admission. Apr, May, Oct & Nov daily 1–4pm; June–Sept daily 9am–5pm. Closed Dec–Mar.*

Descend 2 blocks to Water St. Turn right & continue 5 blocks (Water St. becomes Mowat Dr.). Bear left (toward the water) on Joe's Point Rd. to find the

❹ ★ kids St. Andrews Blockhouse.

This stout wooden blockhouse sits behind low, grass-covered earthworks. It was built by townspeople during the War of 1812, bracing for a U.S. attack that never came. The remarkably well-preserved structure is all that remains of the old fort (save a few cannons). But come for the great bay views and sunsets. 🕐 *45 min. Joe's Point Rd.* ☎ *506/529-4270. www.pc.gc.ca. Admission C90¢ adults, C40¢ children, C$2.40 families. June–Aug daily 10am–6pm. Closed Sept–May.*

Return to Mowat Dr. & bear left. Follow the road out of town 2km (1¼ miles) to Crestwood Rd. Turn right & continue to the parking lot for

❺ ★ Ministers Island Historic Site.

This 202-hectare (500-acre) island is linked to the mainland by a sandbar at low tide only. Visitors drive in a convoy across the sea floor to a once-magical estate built here in 1890 by railroad president William Van Horne (1843–1915); the mansion has 50 rooms (including 17 bedrooms), a circular bathhouse, and one of Canada's largest barns. It's falling apart with age, but it's still a fascinating visit. 🕐 *2½ hr. 199 Carriage Rd. (off Rte. 127), Chamcook.* ☎ *506/529-5081. Admission C$14 adults, C$11 seniors, C$45 families; free for children 6 & under. Tours (required for entry) mid-May to mid-Oct.*

Built by townspeople during the War of 1812, the St. Andrews Blockhouse is all that remains of the old fort.

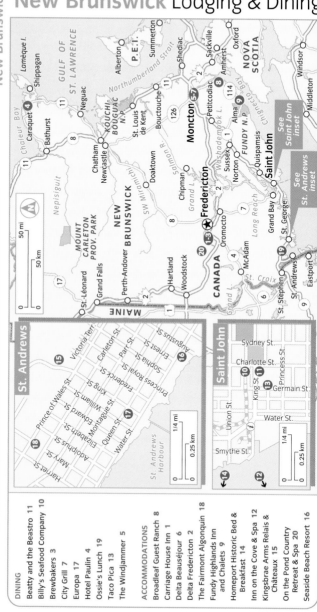

New Brunswick Dining A to Z

★ Beatty and the Beastro

SAINT JOHN *CONTINENTAL*   A big-windowed, modern bistro fronting Saint John's King's Square, serving good food: soups, salads, omelets, and gourmet sandwiches for lunch; lamb, curries, chicken *parmigiana*, schnitzel, and steaks for dinner. *60 Charlotte St. (on King's Sq.).* ☎ *506/652-3888. Entrees lunch C$7–C$10, dinner C$20–C$21. AE, DC, MC, V. Mon–Fri lunch & dinner; Sat dinner. Closed Sun.*

kids Billy's Seafood Company

SAINT JOHN *SEAFOOD*   Fresh-off-the-boat seafood, affordable pricing, and a welcome way with kids: This is a family place. Specialties include cedar-planked salmon, bouillabaisse, lobster rolls, and oysters-and-chips. *49–51 Charlotte St. (at City Market).* ☎ *888/933-3474 or 506/672-3474. www.billysseafood. com. Entrees C$6–C$29. AE, DC, MC, V. Mon–Sat lunch & dinner daily, year-round; Apr–Dec Sun dinner, Jan–Mar closed Sun.*

Brewbakers

FREDERICTON *CONTEMPORARY CANADIAN*   A pub, cafe, and restaurant all in one, on three levels in a cleverly adapted downtown building. The cafe section is quietest, as is a mezzanine dining room above the cafe; lunch features fancy sandwiches, while gourmet pastas and pizzas star at dinner. *546 King St.* ☎ *506/459-0067. Entrees lunch C$8–C$16, dinner C$18–C$28. AE, DC, MC, V. Mon–Fri lunch & dinner, Sat-Sun dinner.*

City Grill

MONCTON *CANADIAN*   A popular downtown Fredericton eatery with prints of city skylines, a modern vibe, and a chic black-on-white color scheme. The kitchen integrates some of its old menu (steaks) with healthier choices such as salads, pizzas, and food cooked over one of Atlantic Canada's only working charcoal grills. Fun place. *130 Westmoreland St.* ☎ *506/857-8325. Entrees lunch C$9–C$15, dinner C$17–C$28. AE, DC, DISC, MC, V. Mon–Fri lunch & dinner, Sat dinner. Closed Sun.*

★ Europa

ST. ANDREWS *CONTINENTAL*   Bavarian transplants

Beatty and the Bistro has great food and looks out on Saint John's King's Square.

Taco Pica is a bright Latin American eatery in the heart of Saint John.

Markus and Simone Ritter whip up French-, Swiss-, and Austrian-accented cuisine for the St. Andrews crowd. Starters could run to French onion soup, smoked salmon with *rösti* and capers, or scallops in Mornay sauce. There's also schnitzel, steak Béarnaise, duck, and lamb. *48 King St.* ☎ *506/529-3818. Entrees C$18–C$27. MC, V. Dinner mid-May to Sept daily, Oct Tues–Sat, Nov to mid-Feb Thurs–Sat. Closed mid-Feb to mid-May.*

★ **Hotel Paulin** CARAQUET *FRENCH* When in Caraquet, you're probably going to be staying at the Hotel Paulin. Good; the restaurant here is the best in town, if small (only about a half-dozen tables). You'll need to reserve in advance. The food is French, the wine list compact yet compelling. *143 Blvd. St-Pierre Ouest.* ☎ *866/727-9981 or 506/727-9981. www.hotelpaulin. com. Entrees C$23–C$36. MC, V. Breakfast daily, dinner Tues–Sun.*

Ossie's Lunch BETHEL *SEAFOOD* Locals on the south coast of New Brunswick swear nobody in the province does Canadian comfort food better than Ossie's. This is a diner, plain and simple, serving local lobster and fish, seasonal caloric

fare, and sweet pies made from New Brunswick berries to locals and tourists alike. *3222 Hwy. 1, (west of St. George).* ☎ *506/755-2758. Apr to mid-Oct breakfast, lunch & dinner daily. Closed Nov–Mar.*

Taco Pica SAINT JOHN *LATIN AMERICAN* A bright Latin American eatery in the heart of Saint John. The menu is a cut above the usual local North American attempts at Mexican and Latin fare: authentic *pepian* (spicy beef stew with chayote) or shrimp tacos (with potatoes, peppers, and cheese), for instance. Fresh juices and fruity margaritas are also on the menu. *96 Germain St.* ☎ *506/633-8492. Entrees C$8–C$17. AE, MC, V. Lunch & dinner Mon–Sat. Closed Sun.*

★★ **The Windjammer** MONCTON *SEAFOOD/CONTINENTAL* Off the lobby of Moncton's Delta hotel, this is no fish-and-chips joint, despite the nautical decor. Chef Stefan Müller's menu serves smoked lobster tails, a cold seafood "martini," mussels steamed in apple wine, and the like. Non-fish-eaters can order bison steak, veal, lamb, and duck. *750 Main St. (inside the Delta Beauséjour).* ☎ *506/877-7137. Entrees C$20–C$42. AE, DC, MC, V. Dinner Mon–Sat.*

New Brunswick Lodging A to Z

kids Broadleaf Guest Ranch
HOPEWELL HILL Near Cape Enrage
and the Hopewell Rocks, these
two-bedroom cottages are family-
oriented. The cottages sport full
kitchens and lovely sweeping views,
but this is simple bunking, not luxury. *5526 Rte. 114.* ☎ *800/226-5405
or 506/882-2349. www.broadleaf
ranch.com. 7 units. Doubles C$60;
cottages C$150–C$200. MC, V.*

Carriage House Inn FREDERIC-
TON Fredericton's premier bed-
and-breakfast is a short stroll from
the riverfront pathway, in a quiet
residential neighborhood. A local
lumber baron built the three-story
Victorian home in 1875; inside, it's
all dark wood, floral prints, and lots
of period art and antiques. *230 University Ave.* ☎ *800/267-6068 or
506/452-9924. www.carriagehouse
inn.net. 10 units. Doubles C$99–
C$129 w/breakfast. AE, MC, V.*

★ Delta Beauséjour MONCTON
This hotel is more inviting once you
get inside. Rooms are business-hotel
nice; a third-floor indoor pool offers
year-round swimming, and a pleasant
deck overlooks the marshes of the
Petitcodiac River. The **Windjammer**
restaurant (see p 162) is excellent.

750 Main St. ☎ *888/351-7666 or
506/854-4344. www.deltahotels.com.
310 units. Doubles C$129–C$199
w/breakfast. AE, MC, V.*

★ Delta Fredericton FREDERIC-
TON A resort-style business hotel,
right on the St. John River and about
a 10-minute stroll from downtown
Fredericton's attractions via the
city's riverfront pathway. The outdoor pool sits on a deck overlooking
the river. *225 Woodstock Rd.*
☎ *888/462-8800 or 506/457-7000.
www.deltafredericton.com. 222
units. Doubles C$119–C$219; suites
C$249–C$800. AE, DC, MC, V.*

★★★ The Fairmont Algonquin
ST. ANDREWS Commanding the
hill in St. Andrews, the Algonquin is
a classic resort dating from 1889,
though the original structure burned
in 1914. The surviving annexes were
rebuilt in Tudor style. Many rooms
have bay views, and there's a spa, a
dining room, two pubs, and a top-
notch golf course (p 37). *184 Adolphus St. (at Prince Wales St.).*
☎ *800/441-1414 or 506/529-8823.
www.fairmont.com. 234 units. Doubles C$99–C$459; suites C$299–
C$1,169. AE, DC, MC, V.*

The Fairmont Algonquin is a classic resort dating from 1889.

kids Fundy Highlands Inn and Chalets ALMA   Two dozen simple cottages with televisions and kitchenettes; some have built-in bunk beds. Good views of the bay and coastline from many of the cottages' windows. *8714 Rte. 114, Fundy National Park.* ☎ *877/883-8639 or 506/887-2930. www.fundy highlandchalets.com. 24 units. Cottages C$79–C$105. MC, V.*

★ **kids Homeport Historic Bed & Breakfast** SAINT JOHN   This impressive 1858 home is furnished in sleigh beds, (nonworking) marble fireplaces, and antique furniture. *80 Douglas Ave. (via exit 121 or 123 to Main St.).* ☎ *888/678-7678 or 506/672-7255. www.homeport. nb.ca. 10 units. Doubles C$109–C$175 w/breakfast. AE, MC, V.*

★★ **Inn on the Cove & Spa** SAINT JOHN   A lovely inn in a pretty seaside setting, about a 15-minute drive from Saint John. Some rooms have decks, Jacuzzis, and great bathtub views; the Irving Nature Park (p 151) is within walking distance. *1371 Sand Cove Rd.* ☎ *877/257-8080 or 506/672-7799. www.innonthecove.com. 9 units. Late June to mid-Oct doubles C$175–C$225 w/breakfast; mid-Oct to May doubles w/light breakfast C$135–C$195. MC, V. Children 12 & over welcome.*

★★★ **Kingsbrae Arms Relais & Châteaux** ST. ANDREWS   A luxe, five-star inn with a European feel beside Kingsbrae Garden, this property occupies an 1897 manor house built by jade merchants. There's a heated pool amid rose gardens, and the five-course meals are outstanding. *219 King St.* ☎ *506/529-1897. www.kingsbrae.com. 8 units. Doubles C$395–C$995 w/breakfast (2-night minimum). AE, MC, V. Closed Nov–Apr.*

★ **On the Pond Country Retreat & Spa** MACTAQUAC   About 15 minutes west of Fredericton, this is a comfortable retreat with spa treatments. The lodge is lovely, with dark wood trim, and fieldstone fireplaces. *20 Scotch Settlement Rd. (Rte. 615).* ☎ *800/984-2555 or 506/363-3420. www. onthepond.com. 8 units. Doubles C$125–C$145. MC, V. No children.*

★ **kids Seaside Beach Resort** ST. ANDREWS   This complex of cabins, cottages, and apartment units clusters by the St. Andrews docks and boardwalk. All units are equipped with up-to-date kitchens, and there's a beachy feeling throughout. *339 Water St.* ☎ *800/ 506-8677. www.seaside.nb.ca. 24 units. Mid-June to Aug doubles C$120–C$200; Sept to mid-June doubles C$65–C$135. MC, V.* ●

Kingsbrae Arms Relais and Châteaux is a luxe, 1897 manor house.

The Best **Ocean Adventures**

Puffin-watching on Cape Breton Island **3**
Sea kayaking the Bay of Fundy **5**
Seal-watching on PEI **1**
Sighting whales off Digby Neck **4**
Whale-watching off Cape Breton Bay **2**

Canada's eastern provinces are surrounded by the sea—
which means they're surrounded by sea *life.* Many of my favorite
outdoor adventures in this region involve boats, birds, and marine
life. Fortunately, nearly every significant destination in this book has
some form of cruise or sail option. Here are a few of the best.

★★ Puffin-watching on Cape Breton Island.
Between Sydney and Baddeck, Bird Island Boat Tours' 3-hour cruises take guests a few miles out to the Bird Islands, home to a colony of 300 puffins. The boat comes within 18m (60 ft.) of the birds without disturbing them; you might also see razorbills, seals, guillemots, or an eagle. *Old Rte. 5, New Campbellton, NS.* ☎ *800/661-6680. www.birdisland.net. Tours C$37 adults, C$15 children 7–12.*

Previous page: Visit PEI's biggest seal colony with Cruise Manada.

Mid-May to Aug, 1–2 tours per day. No tours Sept to mid-May.

★★ Sea kayaking the Bay of Fundy.
Sea kayaking is a great way to get an up-close look at the marine environment in one of the continent's most dramatic bays—but you need expert help when kayaking amongst the world's highest tides. **FreshAir Adventure** in Alma supplies it, with tours that range from 2 hours to several days. Half-day tours explore marshes and the nearby beaches; a full-day adventure includes a hot meal and some 6 hours of time along a wild shoreline. You might see

A view of a whale tail during a whale-watching expedition off the coast of Nova Scotia.

whales, puffins, and dolphins, too. *16 Fundy View Dr., Alma.* ☎ *800/ 545-0020 or 506/887-2249. www. freshairadventure.com. Half-day tours C$48–C$60 adults, full-day tours C$90–C$110 adults.*

kids Seal-watching on PEI. Visit the island's biggest seal colony with Cruise Manada; its two fully enclosed boats depart from Murray River and Montague (the Montague season is longer). Along both rivers are seals, woodlots, farmland, mussel-farming operations, herons, and (with luck) maybe even bald eagles. Kids sometimes get a turn at the wheel. *Cruises depart from Montague Marina (Station St., off Main St.), Montague & Murray River Marina (Main St. South, south end of town bridge), Murray River.* ☎ *800/986-3444 or 902/838-3444. www.sealwatching.com. Tours C$28 adults, C$26 seniors, C$14 children 5–13. Mid-May to Sept 1–3 tours/day.*

★ Sighting whales off Digby Neck. A cottage industry of whale-watching tours has sprung up in Digby Neck, using the simple local fishing and lobster boats (don't expect cushy seats). Right, sperm, blue, and pilot whales have been spotted. Each tour outfitter offers

something different: **Ocean Explorations** has a staff biologist on board and uses Zodiac-type boats, for instance, while **Mariner, Pirate's Cove,** and **Petit Passage** all employ Cape Island fishing vessels but each run different routes of different durations. Budget from 2 to 4 hours for one of these cruises. *Mariner Cruises: Westport Brier Island;* ☎ *800/239-2189 or 902/839-2346; www.nova scotiawhalewatching.ca; cruises C$27–C$49 adults. Pirate's Cove Cruises: Tiverton, Long Island;* ☎ *888/480-0004 or 902/839-2242; www.piratescove.ca; cruises C$23–C$45 adults. Petite Passage Whale Watch: 3450 East Ferry (at the end of Digby Neck);* ☎ *902/834-2226; www. ppww.ca; cruises C$28–C$65 adults. Ocean Explorations: Tiverton, Long Island;* ☎ *877/654-2341 or 902/839-2417; www.oceanexplorations.ca; cruises C$40–C$59 adults.*

★★ Whale-watching off Cape Breton. Bay St. Lawrence, at the stony tip of Cape Breton, is home to several good whale-watching outfits. Family-owned Oshan Whale Watch operates a 13m (42-ft.) lobster boat, on which deep-sea fishing tours are also offered. Captain Cox's Whale Watch offers a different experience: Its cruises are aboard a 7.6m (25-ft.) inflatable Zodiac craft with a microphone to hear the whales. You'll get wetter, perhaps, but it's a right-there-in-the-sea experience. No whales? Cox's will book you on another tour. For free. *Oshan: 3384 Bay St. Lawrence Rd., Bay St. Lawrence;* ☎ *877/ 383-2883 or 902/383-2883; www. oshan.ca. Tours C$25 adults, C$20 seniors, C$12 children; July–Oct 3 tours/day. Captain Cox's: 578 Meat Cove Rd., Capstick;* ☎ *888/346-5556 or 902/383-2981; www.whale watching-novascotia.com; Tours C$45 adults, C$25 children 6–17 (4-person minimum required); mid-June to Sept 2–3 tours/day.*

Hiking on **Cape Breton Island**

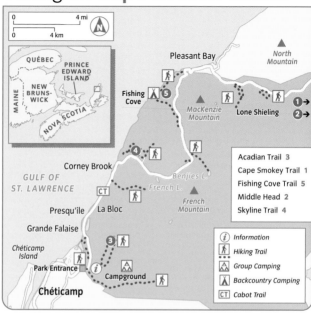

Acadian Trail 3
Cape Smokey Trail 1
Fishing Cove Trail 5
Middle Head 2
Skyline Trail 4

(i) Information
🚶 Hiking Trail
⛺ Group Camping
⛺ Backcountry Camping
CT Cabot Trail

I f it's spectacular hiking you want, **Cape Breton Island** is the place for you. The island possesses the most spectacular views and most thorough network of trails in the Maritimes. Here are a few hikes to start you off; some are easy, some are for expert hikers only. (I've noted shorter, easier parks and walks elsewhere in this book.)

★★ **Acadian Trail.** This 8.5km (5.3-mile) hike is no day at the beach—it's steep and difficult, and only veteran hikers should try it. But the consistently tough slog is rewarded up top with a long view back down taking in the Chéticamp River, the Atlantic, and the forested heart of the national park. 🕐 *3–4 hr. Trail head at park visitor information center (p 102), Chéticamp.*

★★★ **Cape Smokey Trail.** From the Cape Smokey parking lot, most travelers don't get past this trail's first lookout, which is pretty

impressive. But the trail actually continues 11km (6.8 miles) to Stanley Point, with its impressive headland views. (If you can make out Newfoundland 160km/100 miles across the strait, though, you've got better eyes than I.) It's a tougher hike than the Skyline; make sure you're in good shape, and wear good footgear. It's a fairly strenuous test, with some iffy footing and nervy views in spots. 🕐 *4 hr. Trail head at Cape Smokey Provincial Park (p 168) parking lot, 6km (3¾ miles) south of Ingonish Harbour.*

★★ **Fishing Cove Trail.** A 350m (1,148-ft.) descent to a secret beach? Sign me up. But the hike is not for amateurs—you must pack all your water for this moderate-to-strenuous, 6 to 10km (3.7–6.2-mile) walk, which you can do from either the north end or the south (both are equally steep and tough going). On the plus side, you can swim when you get there, or even camp: The park's only sanctioned wilderness camping (pre-registration required) is here. ⏱ *5–6 hr. Trail head on Cabot Trail, 11km (6¾ miles) beyond the French Mountain parking lot.*

★★ kids **Middle Head.** Just beyond the Keltic Lodge, this easy 4km (2.5-mile) hike out to Middle Head and back is good when you want views without the hard work or danger. The dramatic, rocky peninsula thrusts out into the Atlantic; the trail is wide and mostly flat, crossing open meadows with wonderful views both north and south. The tip of the peninsula is grassy and open, a good spot from which to watch for passing whales or see waves crashing in after a storm. ⏱ *1–2 hr. Trail head at Keltic Lodge Resort (p 117), Keltic Inn Rd., Ingonish Centre.*

★★★ **Skyline Trail.** This 10km (6.2-mile) loop isn't too exerting but offers some of the best walking-trail views in the province. From a parking lot, the hike runs out to an awe-inspiring point of land capped with blueberry bushes and a stunning cliff-top view of the ocean surf pounding far below. Remember that bears, moose, and coyote do live in the area of this trail—steer clear if you see any of them. (A hiker was sadly killed on this trail in 2009 by a coyote, though it is incredibly rare for a coyote to attack.) Don't be afraid of wildlife; simply keep your distance and travel in groups. ⏱ *2–3 hr. Trail head halfway btwn. Chéticamp & Pleasant Bay, from parking area atop French Mountain (follow signs).*

A gorgeous view from a lookout on the trail to Middle Head.

The Fundy Trail Parkway

1 Fox Rock Lookout
2 Fownes Head
3 Melvin Beach
4 Pangburn Beach
5 Davidson Lookout
6 Big Salmon River Interpretive Centre

One of Eastern Canada's unsung natural attractions, this park sits on the wildest stretch of the Bay of Fundy about 65km (40 miles) east of Saint John. You can see whales, seabirds, and islands; photograph terrific ocean views; cross a suspension bridge; wade a river; or just soak up the beauty from a car or wheelchair. This tour follows the 10km (6¼-mile) paved road; a 16km (9.9-mile) hiking/cycling trail (with the same name) parallels it, wiggling up and down the ravines and breaking into overlook views. START: **From Saint John, take Rte. 111 to St. Martins. Turn right at the XTR station (Main St.) & travel 10km (6¼ miles) to the guardhouse.**

Travel Tip

The Fundy Trail Parkway (☎ 866/386-3987 or 506/833-2019; www.fundytrailparkway.com) is privately owned and charges a small admission fee for entry (C$4 adults, C$3.50 seniors, C$2.50 children 12 and under, C$13 families). A paved road touches on most of its key points (except the Fundy Footpath), and a free weekend shuttle also runs from the entrance through most of the park. Cycling and pets are allowed. Plenty of guided walks and bike rides are also offered from the Big Salmon info center (see p 172, ⑥).

① ★★ **Fox Rock Lookout.** Just beyond the park's entrance, around the first bend, is the first parking area, on top of a promontory head looking out onto the sometimes-foggy coastline. It's a pretty good introduction to what will come later: a long view back onto cliffs and the park's westernmost tip. 🕐 *15 min.*

Continue about .3km (¼ mile) to the lookout over

② ★★★ **Fownes Head.** The Fownes Head lookout is spectacular, with eastward-sweeping views up the coastline. Seabirds are often seen here, and there are also easy side-trail hikes from the parking lot, each about .8km (.5 mile) long: A set of stairs leads down to weirdly carved

Flowerpot Rock and the **Flowerpot Rock Scenic Footpath** that follows the shoreline to Melvin Beach. Meanwhile, another trail veers inland to the so-called **Sea Captains' Burial Grounds,** the cemeteries commemorating the Fownes and Melvin families who farmed this land and built more than 30 wooden ships here during the mid-19th century. 🕐 *45 min.*

Continue .8km (½ mile) to the parking lot at

③ ★ **Melvin Beach.** There are more views from this cliff-top parking area, which leads to a set of stairs. Follow the stairs down the cliffs to the scenic beach at the bottom.

The weirdly shaped Flowerpot Rock at the bottom of the Fownes Head lookout.

Pangburn Beach is a lovely pocket beach wedged improbably between points of rugged cliff rock.

Impressive cliffs stretch from here east to the next crescent beach. You can hike .8km (.5 mile) to Fuller Falls from here, if you like, or wait for the next stop to do it. ⏱ *45 min.*

The paved road loops inland, passing through forest, then back down toward the sea. After 2.4km (1½ miles), turn into the parking lot at

❹ Pangburn Beach. Just beyond the turnoff is a cable ladder leading 1.2km (¾ mile) down to skinny Fuller Falls (which are not huge and spectacular, but rather nicely pastoral) and Pangburn Beach. It's still another lovely pocket beach, similar to Melvin Beach, wedged improbably between points of rugged cliff rock. ⏱ *30 min.*

Continue about 2.4km (1½ miles) along the cliff-top road to

❺ ★★ Davidson Lookout. Some of the very best photo opportunities on the entire paved road can be found at Davidson Lookout, where the bay dominates the panoramic view. You can even see the western coast of Nova Scotia—the Annapolis Valley region—from here. Really. ⏱ *15 min.*

Continue 1.7km (1 mile) to a final cluster of three parking lots; the last one is closest to the

❻ ★★ kids Big Salmon River Interpretive Centre. The park's visitor center is at the very end of the parkway, where once sat a tiny logging town. From here, you can sign up for guided walks among the paths and beaches; rent a bike (C$11 per hr., C$40 per day); visit Big Salmon River Beach and its waterfowl observation deck; view a video on the park; and stock up on snacks and souvenirs. Just past the center is an 85m (279-ft.) suspension bridge that's good for snapping scenic photos, a bouncing and swaying stroll across the river, and right-on-top-of-the-water views. A hiking trail, the **Pioneer Scenic Footpath,** runs .8km (.5 mile) to the **Hearst Scenic Trail,** which then takes you 2.4km (1.5 miles; no car access) to the Parkway's own **Hearst Lodge,** a wood-paneled former fishing lodge (with two nearby cabins, built by the famous Hearst newspaper family when they owned this land), offering rustic overnight accommodation. ⏱ *2 hr. Short walks free to C$3 adults; full-day adventures C$15–C$30 adults. Scheduled guided walks Mon–Fri 1–3pm. Hearst Lodge $125 adults per night w/breakfast & dinner; closed Oct–May.* ●

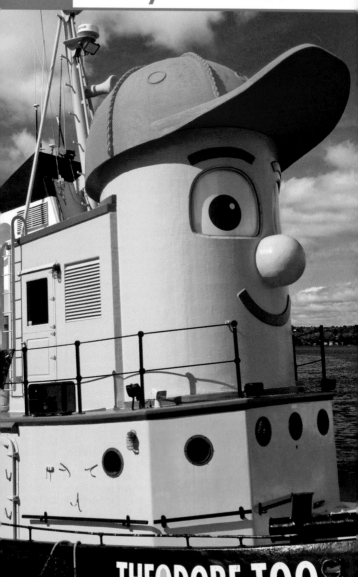

THEODORE TOO

Before You Go

Tourist Offices

All three provinces run helpful **Visitor Information Centres (VICs)** at key access points, including the main roadways running into the provinces and major cities. Expect friendly staff and well-stocked racks of menus, brochures, and booklets. Excellent road maps are also available from all provincial tourism authorities—just ask. The official provincial tourism offices are located at:

- **Nova Scotia Department of Tourism,** Culture & Heritage, World Trade Centre, 6th Floor, 1800 Argyle St. (P.O. Box 456), Halifax, NS B3J 2R5; ☎ 800/565-0000 or 902/424-5000; www.novascotia.com.

- **New Brunswick Department of Tourism & Parks,** P.O. Box 12345, Campbellton, NB E3N 3T6; ☎ 800/561-0123; www.tourismnewbrunswick.ca.

- **Tourism PEI,** P.O. Box 2000, Charlottetown, PEI C1A 7N8; ☎ 800/463-4734 or 902/368-4444; www.tourismpei.com.

The Best Time to Go

The weather in the Atlantic provinces is much like that of New England in the United States or the northern parts of Great Britain.

Spring is damp, cool, and short, though it can get warm and muggy as it eases into summer. If the attractions you're seeking are open, it can be a good time to visit—just don't expect warm temperatures and clear weather because winter often hangs on late in this part of Canada.

Previous page: The Theodore Too tugboat in Halifax Harbour.

Note that many attractions, tourism offices, and restaurants open on a *partial* schedule in Atlantic Canada (3 days a week or weekends only, for instance) during the "shoulder" months of April and May; check ahead if you have your heart set on a particular dining experience, hotel, or attraction. One big advantage to coming during spring: Daylight lasts incredibly long, sometimes as late as 10pm, so you can tackle the long driving distances between points in full illumination.

Summer is compact (high season here runs from early July to early Sept) but definitely one of the two best times to visit the region. That's when the great majority of travelers take to the road, enjoying the bright, clear days and warm temperatures. The upside? The weather is normally very pleasant (if a bit rainy at times), and you can expect *all* restaurants, inns, attractions, and tourist offices to remain open 7 days a week from July through August, often through September. The down side? This short, short summer season means that everybody *else* will be coming here, too—you'll possibly wait in lines for tables at a restaurant, for tickets to a theater production, or to get gas at the gas station. If you don't mind dealing with a little bit of crowding (it's all relative) in what's normally a *very* uncrowded place, it shouldn't be a problem.

But that's why **fall** can be just as great a time to visit the region, even if it's usually fairly chilly. The crowds are all gone by mid-September, but the ocean and beaches are still here. The first blushes of fall color are sometimes visible as early as September and really take off in October, especially in the highlands of Cape

Breton. Bring winter sweaters and a heavy coat. I've found that most seasonal attractions and tourist offices close down in mid-October, but some places sometimes hang on into November and even through Christmas. I have listed open seasons for attractions throughout this book.

And **winter?** I'd give it a pass. If you do go then, you need to seriously prepare for the frequent blustery storms that sweep in off the Atlantic. Ice, sleet, and/or snow are a possibility any day of winter, and they can blow in suddenly; if you're driving, make sure your car (or rental car) is equipped with good snow tires and antifreeze windshield wash (you can also buy it from any gas station). And drive cautiously: Outside the major urban areas, most of this region's high-speed arteries are two-lane roads without medians. Watch for drivers coming your way. If you're coming in winter, be prepared—most of the key attractions, restaurants, and accommodations will be closed. That's why few travelers venture here during the season, and I definitely advise against it—with a single exception. If you're visiting Halifax, you can be confident that all the key restaurants and some (but not all, due to weather) of the city's key attractions remain open through winter.

Festivals & Special Events

WINTER   To be honest, Atlantic Canada mostly shuts down its public face during the winter months, which stretch roughly from November through March here. But there are a few options—the **Charlottetown Winter Carnival** (☎ 902/892-5708), held annually in early February, is one. It's said to be the biggest winter festival east of Quebec City and involves 3 days of food, fun, ice sculpting, and sports—albeit mostly inside the city's civic center. If you happen to be visiting St. Andrews, New Brunswick, late

in the year, there's a wonderful month-long **Winter Festival** (☎ 506/529-3555) of events, music, art shows, decorated Christmas trees, and more. The event, held in many venues around town (but centered at the Fairmont Algonquin hotel, p. 163) begins in late November and runs through Christmas.

SPRING   May 18 is celebrated as **Loyalist Day** in Saint John, New Brunswick, because that's the day the city charter was signed in 1785. Watch for events, readings, and a real 21-gun salute by the 3rd Field Artillery Regiment—Canada's oldest (almost as old as the charter). If you're on Prince Edward Island during late May, look for the **Spring Wine Festival** (☎ 902/368-5710) at the end of May or in early June, held at the Delta Prince Edward hotel (p. 144) in Charlottetown. It's a series of Friday and Saturday tastings of the finest local and regional wines. The **Cape Breton International Drum Festival** (www.cape bretoninternationaldrumfestival. com) in late May is, supposedly, one of the planet's biggest (and, I'd add, least-known) drumming festivals. It's held way, way up on the wild north tip of Cape Breton in the community of Glace Bay in the town's Savoy Theatre.

SUMMER   The **Royal Nova Scotia International Tattoo** (☎ 902/420-1114; www.nstattoo.ca) is one of Halifax's summer centerpieces, when military and marching bands descend upon the Halifax Metro Center each July. Also in July, the annual **Atlantic Jazz Festival** (☎ 902/492-2225; www.jazzeast.com) features performances ranging from global and avant-garde style to traditional jazz in various Halifax nightclubs and on outdoor stages around town. The **Highland Games** (☎ 902/863-4275; www.antigonishhighlandgames.ca) have been staged in Antigonish continuously since 1861. Mighty feats of strength predominate the tartaned proceedings. On PEI, Charlottetown's **Festival of Lights** expands on the annual Canada Day holiday (July 1), blowing it out to a full week of al fresco concerts, fireworks, food, and games. Buy a weekend passport.

The 10-day **Halifax International Busker Festival** (www. buskers.ca) is a sort of world summit of street musicians, jugglers, fire-eaters, and the like. Performances take place continuously along the waterfront during August, and all are free (donations accepted, of course). Also check out the **Halifax Seaport Beerfest** (☎ 902/453-5343; www. seaportbeerfest.com), a fun August brewfest on the waterfront. One ticket gets you a 118mL (4-oz.) glass with which you can sample all the beers you like. Bring a picture ID. In New Brunswick, **Chocolate Fest** (www.chocolate-fest.ca) is an August St. Stephen tradition celebrating the town's local chocolate factory with stories, sweets, pony rides, tours, and the like.

FALL The **Atlantic Film Festival** (☎ 902/422-6965 or 902/422-3456; www.atlanticfilm.com) is one of Canada's best, with more than 150 films screened in theaters around Halifax over a 10-day period during September. The focus is largely on Canadian filmmaking. Panel discussions with movie-industry players are also a big part of the festival. The September **PEI International Shellfish Festival** (www.peishellfish.com) is one of two fall food fests in Charlottetown; this one showcases local lobsters, fish, those gorgeous mussels, plus the Eastern Canadian Oyster Shucking Championship. Then, around harvest time in late September, **Fall Flavours** (www.fallflavours.ca) takes over Charlottetown and the finer restaurants of rural PEI; there are more

than 100 events scheduled each year, such as potato-picking and clam-digging demonstrations.

If you're in Nova Scotia in mid-October, absolutely don't miss **Celtic Colours** (☎ 877/285-2321 or 902/562-6700; www.celtic-colours. com), which takes over much of Cape Breton Island during this time. Great Celtic music from local and international stars, plus great foliage, in a wide variety of venues: an unbeatable combination.

The Weather

Being in Eastern Canada means dealing with changeable weather on a regular basis; resistance is futile. The Atlantic tends to bring lots of moisture and wind ashore, fast, so things tend to happen (or change) dramatically here: Snow or rain could ashore suddenly, in sheets and buckets, with horizontal winds. Winter storms sometimes wash waves up over the beach and across access roads or parking lots. Hurricanes have even been known to graze the coast occasionally in summer. On the other hand, the ocean also serves as a sort natural air-conditioner during the hottest, most humid dog days of summer: Walk to water's edge, and you'll almost certainly feel cooling breezes wafting off it.

Spring is chilly, late to arrive, and often soggy. On the other hand, if you hit a good year, those long days provide ample sightseeing opportunities well into the warming evenings.

Summer here is flat-out wonderful, full of long days of late light and moderate temperatures. The average daily high in these three provinces is around 25°C (77°F). There's no "typical" summer here, though, so you're just as likely to experience warm, sunny days as you are a sudden rainstorm—maybe even on the same day. But you'll almost *never* experience an uncomfortably hot,

HALIFAX'S AVERAGE MONTHLY TEMPERATURES

	JAN	FEB	MAR	APR	MAY	JUNE
High (°F)	31	30	37	46	55	65
(°C)	−1	−1	3	8	13	18
Low (°F)	16	15	23	31	39	48
(°C)	−9	−9	−5	−1	4	9

	JULY	AUG	SEPT	OCT	NOV	DEC
High (°F)	71	71	65	55	46	36
(°C)	22	22	18	13	8	2
Low (°F)	55	56	50	41	33	21
(°C)	13	13	10	5	1	−6

humid day here; the constant sea breezes see to that.

Autumn in Atlantic Canada is colorful, arriving in a rush of cold air and bringing lovely foliage with the crispness. It's blissfully quiet. Days are getting shorter, though, and it can get dark before dinnertime.

The worst thing about autumn? It portends **winter,** which is almost invariably long and wet in Atlantic Canada, with frequent (and sometimes heavy) snows, sleet, hail, rain—not the sorts of conditions conducive to smooth traveling. People here simply grin and bear it. The city of Saint John, New Brunswick, even built a linked maze of enclosed passages called "the Inside Connection" to shuttle people around town without having to face winter head-on. Elsewhere, though, you'll need to don your warmest scarf and bravest face.

Cell (Mobile) Phones

Most cellphones work in Canada, though you'll pay roaming and long-distance charges that can push call costs above C$1 per minute. Most major U.S. carriers offer **Canadian roaming** plans that reduce these charges. Check with your carrier and make sure there's no penalty for switching it back off after you get back home.

Remember that you won't be able to use your cellphone everywhere in

Eastern Canada. Coverage is spotty, though it's getting better, and even on the Trans-Canada Highway, you pop in and out of coverage zones. In the major cities, you'll be reliably connected; in smaller towns, it's hit-or-miss; and in national and provincial parks, assume you *don't* have service.

Canada uses GSM (Global System for Mobile Communications), requiring a GSM phone or "multi-band" phone. In the U.S., **T-Mobile** and **AT&T Wireless** use GSM, but **Sprint** and **Verizon** do not. All **European** and most **Australian** phones are GSM-ready. If your cellphone doesn't work in Canada, you can rent a Canadian cellphone. It's usually cheaper to rent before leaving home; check a big-city phone book or the Internet for wireless rental companies operating in your area. Buying a Canadian cellphone is another option. Stop by a shop in Halifax and ask about the cheapest package; you'll probably pay less than C$100 for a phone and starter calling card.

Keep a phone on hand at all times for emergencies, but don't expect it to work anywhere and everywhere. Charge your battery every night, if you can. And definitely ask park rangers about local cell coverage before venturing into backcountry areas.

Getting **There**

By Plane

Most travelers to Eastern Canada fly into **Halifax,** Nova Scotia, the region's major air hub. The city's **Stanfield International Airport** (airport code: YHZ) is 34km (21 miles) north of the city center. Nova Scotia's notorious fogs mean it's always a good idea to call your airlines before heading out to the airport to make sure your flight will depart on time. There are also small and mid-sized airports in places such as Fredericton, New Brunswick; Charlottetown, Prince Edward Island; and Saint John, New Brunswick, though, as a rule, these airports are generally quite a bit more expensive to fly into.

The main air carrier serving Eastern Canada is **Air Canada** (☎ 888/247-2262; www.aircanada. com), with flights from North America and Europe. Several North American carriers, including **Continental** (☎ 800/231-0856; www.continental. com), now also offer flights into Eastern Canada. Canada's **WestJet** (☎ 888/937-8538; www.westjet. com) connects Halifax with Toronto and a few other Canadian cities.

By Car & Ferry

From within Canada, it's easiest to reach Atlantic Canada by car via the Trans-Canada Highway (about 9 hr. from Montréal to Fredericton). You can also enter the U.S. at any of a number of small border crossings in Vermont, New Hampshire, and Maine, work your way east, and re-enter New Brunswick—in theory, about the same amount of driving if there are no backups at the borders. If you do this, make sure to bring your passport for the two border crossings.

Overland access to Atlantic Canada from the United States is through Maine. The most direct route to New Brunswick is to drive to Bangor (about 4½ hr. from Boston), then head east on Route 9 to Calais, Maine (about 2½ hr.). Here, you can cross into St. Stephen, New Brunswick, and pick up Route 1 to Saint John and beyond.

If you don't plan to stop until you hit Moncton or points east of Moncton, a slightly faster alternative is to continue northeast on the Maine Turnpike to Houlton, then cross the border and pick up the Trans-Canada Highway. Remember that the Maine Turnpike is a toll road for a stretch (the toll is US$5 maximum one-way for a passenger car), although it becomes completely toll-free beyond exit 113 at Augusta.

Travelers headed from New Brunswick to Nova Scotia can save significant driving time by taking a ferry: A year-round ferry connects Saint John, New Brunswick (about a 4-hour drive from either Bangor or Bar Harbor, Maine), with Digby, Nova Scotia.

The ferry sails daily year-round, with two sailings per day during peak travel periods. The peak season one-way fare (charged June–Oct) is C$40 adults, C$30 seniors and students, C$25 children 6 to 13, and C$5 children under 6. Your car itself costs an additional C$80 (more for trucks, vans, and buses), plus a variable fuel surcharge (currently C$20). Fares are a bit cheaper outside the peak travel months, and if you walk on and return within 30 days, there are also discounts available on the round-trip. Note that AAA and CAA members receive discounts on the automobile portion of the fare. Complete up-to-the-minute schedules and fares for the *Princess of Acadia* can be found by calling

Useful Websites

- **www.thechronicleherald.ca:** *Halifax Chronicle-Herald* (daily newspaper)
- **www.thecoast.ca:** *The Coast* (Halifax free alternative/ arts weekly)
- **www.pc.gc.ca:** Parks Canada (administration of national parks)
- **www.theguardian.pe.ca:** *Charlottetown Guardian* (daily newspaper)
- **www.nationalpost.com:** Canadian national daily newspaper
- **www.411.ca:** Canadian Yellow Pages (phone directory)

☎ 888/249-7245 or visiting www. nfl-bay.com.

Road maps can sometimes be deceptive, so keep in mind that these provinces (and especially Nova Scotia) are bigger than they look on a map. Budget plenty of time for driving. I have noted driving distances or driving times in this book wherever possible, but a good rule of thumb to follow is that 80km (50 miles) of rural driving takes 1 to 1½ hours, even if there's little traffic. And most of your driving in these provinces *will* be rural driving. (In summer, passing through a string of busy towns, it might take even longer.)

By Train

Interprovincial rail service is a shadow of its former self. Prince Edward Island lacks rail service completely, as does southern New Brunswick (you can no longer travel by train to either Fredericton or Saint John), and there's now just a single train line connecting the provinces: **VIA Rail** (☎ 888/842-7245; www.viarail.ca), the national rail carrier. Its trains run once daily (except Tues), stopping in a handful of towns along an overnight route between Montréal and Halifax. In New Brunswick, the train stops at Campbellton, Charlo, Jacquet River,

Petit Rocher, Bathurst, Miramichi, Rogersville, Moncton, and Sackville—none of which are covered in this book. In Nova Scotia, you can get on or off the train at Amherst, Springhill Junction, or Truro: again, not areas I've covered here. The journey from Montréal to Halifax takes about 22 hours.

Fares for the trip depend on which class of seat you buy—anything from an economy seat (sleep sitting up) to various configurations of cabins. A non-discounted economy seat costs about C$250 each way from Montréal to Halifax or back. Sleeping berths and private cabins are available for an extra charge—the cheapest bed, in a double-bunked cabin, is about twice the cost of the no-bed fare—and VIA has also added an extra luxury tier of summer services known as Sleeper Touring class. It gets you better beds, presentations from an onboard guide, and access to a private dome car if you pay the extra charge.

Discounts for buying tickets at least a week in advance are sometimes offered.

By Bus

Bus service into and out of the region tends to be slow and cumbersome. Most buses from the United

States will take you to Montréal, where you need to connect to another bus line to Halifax—an 18-hour trip.

Greyhound (☎ 800/231-2222 or 214/849-8100; www.greyhound. com) offers service from diverse points around the United States to Montréal's bus station (☎ 514/843-4231), from which buses run to Atlantic Canada.

Acadian Lines (☎ 800/567-5151; www.smtbus.com) offers service from Bangor, Maine, to New Brunswick several times weekly and reliable daily service within Nova Scotia, New Brunswick, and Prince Edward Island. It's actually possible to circumnavigate the key points in the provinces entirely using Acadian buses.

Getting **Around**

You'll need a car, plain and simple, as public transit between and even within the provinces is limited. Fortunately, Eastern Canada's road networks are extensive and usually well maintained. But travelers expecting to find six-lane highways with high-speed on- and off-ramps will be in for a surprise. With few exceptions, the highway system here is on a far smaller scale. Even main arteries, such as the inland route from Yarmouth to Halifax, are often just two lanes (one coming, one going). The Trans-Canada Highway is the main road running through this region. Numerous feeder roads connect to the Trans-Canada.

A few rules of the road: As in the United States and continental Europe, drive on the right in Canada. You may make a right turn at a red light, provided that you first stop fully and confirm that no one is coming from the left. (At some intersections, signs prohibit such a turn.) Radar detectors are prohibited in all the Atlantic Provinces. Drivers and all passengers are required to wear seat belts.

If you're arriving by plane, the usual suspects offer car rentals at major airports. Despite the number of rental outfits, however, it can be difficult to reserve a car during the short summer season, when

demand soars. It's best to reserve ahead. See p 189 for a complete list of rental car providers.

There's also an inter-provincial ferry that can considerably shorten the slog around the Bay of Fundy. The year-round ferry, known as the *Princess of Acadia,* links Saint John, New Brunswick, with Digby, Nova Scotia. The ferry sails once daily year-round, with two crossings per day during peak travel periods. In 2009, a peak season one-way fare (charged June–Oct) cost C$40 adults, C$30 seniors and students, C$25 children 6 to 13, and C$5 children under 6; the car itself costs C$80 (more for trucks, vans, and buses), plus a C$20 fuel surcharge.

Fares are a bit cheaper outside the peak travel months, and if you walk on and return within 30 days, there are also discounts available on the round-trip. Note that AAA and CAA member receive C$10 discounts on the car fare. Tariffs on this route haven't budged in several years; nevertheless, up-to-the-minute schedules and fares can be found by calling ☎ 877/762-7245 or going to www.nfl-bay.com.

Traffic in Eastern Canada is very light compared with that in urban and suburban areas of the East Coast. Only in Halifax at rush hour or on a highway with construction work will you ever get into anything like a traffic delay.

Remember that Canadian gas prices are higher than those in the U.S., though lower than they are in Europe.

If you'll travel by car, you may be able to avoid costly car-rental insurance. Some credit cards offer free collision coverage for card holders' rental cars; ask your credit card issuer before departing.

Fast **Facts**

ATMS ATM machines, sometimes referred as "cash machines" or "cashpoints," are widely available in Eastern Canada. ATM networks here are usually compatible with international banks, allowing travelers to use their home ATM or credit cards for withdrawals. ATMs often offer the best exchange rates in Canada; your home bank will convert the withdrawal at the prevailing rate. Memorize your personal identification number (PIN) and your daily withdrawal limit before arriving in Canada. Remember that many banks impose a fee when you use a card at another bank's ATM, higher for international transactions (up to US$5). Ask your bank about fees before traveling; members of the Global ATM Alliance usually charge no fees for withdrawals at Alliance member ATMs, which include Bank of America in the U.S. and Scotiabank in Eastern Canada. If your card uses the **Cirrus** (www.mastercard.com) and **PLUS** (www.visa.com) networks, check those websites to locate ATMs in Eastern Canada that connect to your bank.

BANKING HOURS Banks usually open early (8 or 9am) and keep lobby hours until 3 or 4pm, with limited or no open hours on weekends. In cities, these hours might extend later, especially on Fridays, and banks in cities are more likely to open on weekends, though you can't count on that.

BED & BREAKFASTS AND COTTAGE RENTALS Nearly every town of size in the eastern provinces has at least one simple bed-and-breakfast, though in rural areas, this can mean sharing a bathroom and/or sleeping above the owners' own bedroom. Renting a seaside or lakeside house or cottage is much closer to the ideal Eastern Canadian experience, though prices can range all the way from C$600 (for a plain studio cottage with no view) to C$5,000 (for a multi-bedroom home in a key area) per week during peak season. Your first stop should be the ultra-helpful website of **Canada Select** (www.canadaselect.com), Canada's official rating agency for inns, hotels, motels, and rental cottages. There's a wealth of information available here, including pictures, prices, and those all-important star ratings. Local tourist offices may also have lists of additional cottage and home rentals.

BUSINESS HOURS Business hours in Eastern Canada are similar to those in the rest of North America. Most offices are open from 8 or 9am until 5 or 6pm Monday through Friday, and are closed on weekends. Shops may open around 10am and stay open until 6pm, later during summer. Expect longer hours in larger cities (including a few 24-hr. groceries and pharmacies), but shorter hours in smaller towns and villages. Many stores are closed on Sundays.

CONSULATES & EMBASSIES   All foreign embassies in Canada are in Ottawa, the national capital, a few hours' away from Halifax by plane. If you're a U.S. citizen and have an emergency, there's also a **U.S. Consulate General** (a sort of branch office) in Purdy's Wharf Tower 2, Suite 904, 1969 Upper Water St., Halifax, NS B3J 3R7 (☎ 902/429-2480). The **British Consulate** (☎ 902/461-1381) is located at 1 Canal St. in Dartmouth, across the harbor.

CREDIT CARDS   Credit cards are widely accepted in Eastern Canada, and you *must* use one to rent a car or hold a hotel room in advance. Most businesses take **Visa** (Barclaycard in Britain) and **MasterCard** (Eurocard in Europe, Access in Britain). Far fewer take **American Express, Diners Club,** or **Discover.** And a handful of establishments here—fast-food eateries, simple B&Bs—do not take *any* credit cards. Foreign travelers to Canada may return home to find an extra fee on all credit card charges that were made abroad (usually 1% to 3% of the purchase values), so be prepared for that.

DENTISTS   Dentists are readily available in the eastern provinces, but often booked weeks in advance. In an emergency, they will fit you in if possible, but they also might not have enough staff. Your best bet for getting seen quickly is in Halifax, at one of the city's dental clinics; check a local phone book or ask your hotel concierge. He or she will know where to point you.

DOCTORS   The major cities in Eastern Canada all maintain good hospitals with a high level of care, but smaller towns in rural areas rely on clinics that probably won't be open 24 hours. If health is a serious issue for you, check ahead with your accommodations (or consult the phone book when you arrive) about the nearest emergency-room service or 24-hour clinic.

ELECTRICITY   Canada uses the same electrical current as the United States: 110 to 115 volts and 60 cycles. Travelers coming from Europe, Australia, and New Zealand (where the standards are 220 to 240 volts AC and 50 cycles) will need a converter, which is easiest to pick up in your home country, as it may not be widely available in Atlantic Canada.

EMBASSIES   See "Consulates & Embassies," above.

EMERGENCIES   For fire, police, and ambulance, find any phone and dial ☎ 911. If this fails, dial ☎ 0 (zero) and report an emergency.

EVENT LISTINGS   The *Halifax Chronicle-Herald* is Halifax's daily newspaper, with an arts section and decent listings; but the free *The Coast* has better listings and reviews of local concerts, clubs, films, restaurants, and art shows in that city. In Charlottetown, look for the daily *Charlottetown Guardian*. A few other cities in the region—Saint John and Fredericton, for example—also support daily newspapers. In other areas of these provinces, you'll need to seek out small local weekly papers and their event listings. And in *really* small towns, head straight for the local grocery store, cafe, and/or pub: Tacked up on a wall, you'll usually find announcements of the latest *ceilidh* or art showing.

GAY & LESBIAN TRAVELERS   Canada, as a whole, is considered extremely friendly to gay travelers. Eastern Canada varies from place to place in the warmth of the welcome, but the cities are uniformly accepting. **Destination Halifax** (www.destinationhalifax.com/rainbow) is a good online guide to that city's gay events. Ask locally or check online for resources in smaller cities and towns in the region.

HOLIDAYS   Public holidays include New Year's Day (Jan 1), Islander Day (PEI only; third Mon in Feb), Good

Friday (Fri before Easter Sun), Easter Monday (Mon following Good Friday, only for federal employees), Victoria Day (Mon before May 25), Canada Day (July 1), Natal Day (first Mon in Aug, Nova Scotia and PEI only), Labor Day (first Mon in Sept), Thanksgiving Day (second Mon in Oct), Christmas Day (Dec 25), and Boxing Day (Dec 26). Note that Natal Day is *not* an official holiday—but it's celebrated by bars and communities in those two provinces anyway.

INSURANCE   I always recommend carrying some form of travel insurance, no matter how rudimentary, even when traveling to a place as incredibly safe as Eastern Canada. Check your insurance policies (especially with credit cards) before you purchase extra insurance to cover trip cancellation, lost luggage, medical expenses, or car-rental insurance. The cost of travel insurance varies widely, depending on the destination, the cost and length of your trip, your age and health, and the type of trip you're taking, but you can usually expect to pay between 5% and 8% of the total cost of the trip itself. Make sure it covers against "carrier default" for your specific travel provider. If a major airline goes bust mid-trip, the law in most countries requires other carriers to take you to your destination (on a space-available basis) for a fee of no more than US$25, provided you rebook within 60 days of cancellation. You can get estimates from various providers through **InsureMyTrip.com**. Enter your trip cost and dates, your age, and other information, for prices from more than a dozen companies.

Medical Insurance: Although it's not required of travelers, health insurance is always a good idea. Many health insurance policies cover you if you get sick away from home—but check your coverage before you travel to be sure. As a safety net, you may want to buy travel medical insurance from providers like **MEDEX Assistance** (☎ 410/453-6300; www.medex assist.com) or **Travel Assistance International** (☎ 800/821-2828; www.travelassistance.com). (Canadians are covered when traveling within Canada, but many U.S. health plans do *not* provide coverage for travel to Canada.)

Trip-Cancellation Insurance: Trip-cancellation insurance typically covers you if you have to back out of a trip (due to illness, for example), if your travel supplier goes bankrupt, if there's a natural disaster, or if your government advises against travel to your destination—which isn't much of a worry for Atlantic Canada. Some plans cover cancellations for any reason. **TravelSafe** (☎ 888/885-7233; www.travelsafe.com) offers both types of coverage. **Expedia** (www.expedia.com) also offers any-reason cancellation coverage for its air-hotel packages. Other recommended insurers include **Access America** (☎ 866/807-3982; www.access america.com), **Travel Guard International** (☎ 800/826-4919; www.travelguard.com), **Travel Insured International** (☎ 800/243-3174; www.travelinsured.com), and **Travelex Insurance Services** (☎ 888/457-4602; www.travel ex-insurance.com).

Lost-Luggage Insurance: If your airline loses your luggage, immediately file a lost-luggage claim at the airport, detailing the luggage contents. Most airlines require that you report delayed, damaged, or lost baggage within 4 hours of arrival. On international flights, baggage coverage is limited to approximately $10 per pound, up to approximately $700 per checked bag. If you plan to check items more valuable than what's covered by the standard liability, see if your homeowner's policy covers your valuables or get baggage insurance as part of your comprehensive travel-insurance package.

INTERNET ACCESS Many of Eastern Canada's public libraries maintain computer terminals with free public Internet access, enabling travelers to check e-mail on the fly. Most inns and hotels now offer Wi-Fi with your stay, usually (but not always) for free; ask when booking. Any reasonably hip coffee shop in this region is also very likely to offer free Wi-Fi with your java.

LIQUOR LAWS In Canada, drinking age is set individually by each province. The legal age for purchase and consumption of alcoholic beverages in New Brunswick, Nova Scotia, and Prince Edward Island is 19 in each case.

LOST PROPERTY Most bus and train stations, stores, and hotels in Eastern Canada keep lost items for a decent period of time, waiting for the owners to call and reclaim them. If your *credit card* disappears or is stolen, however, contact your credit card company immediately. (If theft was involved, also call police and get a printed police report.) Visa's emergency number is ☎ 800/847-2911; MasterCard's is ☎ 800/307-7309; and American Express is at ☎ 800/221-7282.

MAIL & POSTAGE Canadian cities and towns of size all have at least one post office apiece (smaller ones may; check the local grocery store first). At press time, first-class postage rates for a normal-sized letter sent from Canada were C54¢ to Canada, C98¢ to the United States, C$1.65 to any other country in the world. Postcards cost less; packages and express services cost more. Remember to fill out a customs form and possibly pay taxes if you're mailing something back home from Canada. For full information on rates and postal requirements, go to **www.canadapost.ca**.

MONEY Canadian currency comes in graduated, multicolored denominations of dollars and cents. The dollar and two-dollar exist only as coins, called the loonie (because of the picture of a loon engraved on it) and toonie (pronounced "two-knee"), respectively. At press time, the Canadian dollar was worth 97¢ in U.S. currency and 64p in U.K. currency. Visit www.xe.com for the latest exchange rates. Always carry some cash in medium and small bills for small items, tips, and establishments that don't accept any credit cards. Be prepared for a bit of sticker shock during summer: Even simple motels might charge C$100 or more a night for a simple room during peak summer season. But other daily expenses, including dining, are very reasonable—in fact, you can dine extremely well on a budget in this region.

PASSPORTS Every visitor to Canada needs a passport to enter the country, including people arriving from the United States. Visas are required only of selected nationals (visit the Citizenship and Immigration Canada website at www.cic.gc.ca for the list). If your passport is lost or stolen, contact your country's consulate immediately (see "Consulates & Embassies," above). If you're a foreign traveler, *always* make a backup copy of your passport's first page and keep it somewhere safe; if you lose your passport, this will be invaluable. Keep your passport numbers, and your embassy and consulate phone numbers, too.

PHARMACIES Chain drugstores and independent pharmacies are located throughout Atlantic Canada. Check the phone book under "Pharmacy." Stores in larger cities and towns are likely to be open later than those in more remote villages. One of the larger national chains is **Pharmasave** (www.pharmasave.com), with about 70 stores in the four provinces (although most of them are located in Nova Scotia).

SAFETY Eastern Canada must be just about the safest place I've traveled on Earth. The odds of anything bad happening are extremely remote. Still, travelers should take all the usual precautions against theft, robbery, and assault. Avoid unnecessary public displays of wealth; store laptops and valuables in safes, if possible; try not to travel very late at night; stop in well-lit, busy areas; don't venture out alone at night (bring a friend or family member); don't leave anything in plain view in the seats of your car; lock valuables in the trunk. If you have an electronic security system, use it.

Finally, when traveling on a boat, always wear life vests or other provided safety gear. Bring warm, dry clothing in your bag—pants, a sweater—even for a sunny summer cruise; weather on the sea can turn windy, chilly, or unpredictable fast.

SENIOR TRAVELERS Except for the long driving distances, Eastern Canada is very well suited to older travelers. Senior travelers usually get reduced or free admission to theaters, museums, national parks, and other attractions, plus discounted fares on public transit.

SMOKING The minimum age for legal purchase of tobacco products is 19 years in all of Canada's eastern provinces. Smoking is not allowed in workplaces, interior public spaces, and some exterior public spaces *anywhere* in Canada (with only occasional exceptions for ventilated smoking rooms in certain types of facilities). Individual provinces also enact tougher, more specific laws: In Nova Scotia, for instance, it is illegal to smoke inside a private vehicle in which a person under the age of 19 is riding. (In New Brunswick, the cutoff age is 16.)

TAXIS There are exactly 1,000 licensed taxis in greater Halifax, and you get one just like you'd guess: by stepping to the curb and hailing one that's empty with its service light on. If you need to book a taxi in advance, try **Maritime Taxi** (☎ 902/456-4248) or **Casino Taxi** (☎ 902/429-6666). Outside of Halifax, though, you'll be hard-pressed to find a taxi quickly; some small towns sometimes have a local service. Once again, check the phone book.

TELEPHONE The area code for New Brunswick is ☎ 506, while Nova Scotia and Prince Edward Island both share the area code ☎ 902. For local directory assistance ("information") in Canada, dial ☎ 411 (not a free call). For toll-free directory assistance, dial ☎ 800/555-1212. You can also check numbers online from many sources, including **www.411.ca**. A local call from a pay phone (increasingly difficult to find) costs 50¢. The United States and Canada are on the same long-distance system. Canada's international prefix is 1.

TAXES Two of the three provinces covered in this book—New Brunswick and Nova Scotia—use the so-called **HST (Harmonized Sales Tax).** The HST rolls provincial and federal sales taxes into one flat tax charged on *all* goods and services, keeping things simple. New Brunswick's HST remains at 13%, but Nova Scotia raised its HST to 15% beginning in July of 2010. (Local cities sometimes apply a small additional tax for hotels.) On **Prince Edward Island,** it's different: the national **Goods and Services Tax** (5%, called GST on your bill) is folded into the hefty PEI provincial tax of 10%—the highest in Canada—for a 15.5% total tax on most items (it's higher than 15% because there's also a tax on the federal tax). Footwear, clothing, books, and groceries are exempt from the 10% PEI portion of that tax, however.

TIPPING If service is good, tip bell-hops C$1 or more per bag (C$2–C$3 for a lot of luggage) and maids a few dollars per day (more if you have a large suite). Tip a doorman or concierge if some specific service was performed (calling a cab, booking theater tickets). Tip valet-parking attendants C$1 to C$5 each time you get your car. In restaurants, bars, and nightclubs, tip servers 15% to 20% of the bill (pre-tax), tip bartenders 10% to 15%, tip coatroom attendants $1 per garment. Tip cabbies 15% of your fare; tip skycaps at airports C$1 per bag (C$2–C$3 if a lot of bags); and tip hairdressers and barbers 15% to 20%.

TOILETS In Eastern Canada, they're called washrooms or restrooms. ("Bathrooms" is used, too, though less commonly.) Find them in hotel lobbies, bars, coffee shops, restaurants, fast-food places, museums, department stores, train stations, and some gas stations. Sometimes, you will need to ask a cashier for a key or make a purchase before getting that key, but usually not.

TRAVELERS WITH DISABILITIES Canada has made tremendous efforts toward eliminating barriers to mobility for its citizens and, by extension, visitors. City pavements feature curb cuts for wheelchair travel, and larger hotels and airports sport wheelchair-accessible washrooms. A growing number of restaurants and tourist attractions are now designed for wheelchair accessibility, though room for improvement remains.

The **Canadian Paraplegic Association** (www.canparaplegic.org) runs a helpful website and maintains an office in each of the Atlantic provinces. In New Brunswick, call ☎ 506/462-9555; in Nova Scotia, call ☎ 902/423-1277; in Prince Edward Island call ☎ 902/626-9523.

Travelers with disabilities headed for Nova Scotia can also ask locally about accessible transportation and recreational opportunities by contacting the **Nova Scotia League for Equal Opportunities,** 5251 Duke St., Suite 1211, Halifax, NS B3J 1P3 (☎ 866/696-7536 or 902/455-6942; www.novascotialeo.org). The organization maintains a useful network of contacts throughout the province.

Eastern Canada: A Brief History

16,000 BC A mile-high pile of ice begins receding from Canada, scratching mountaintops and depositing boulders and mud in its wake.

5500 BC–2000 BC Native peoples begin arriving in waves and populating the coves and rivers of Canada's eastern provinces.

1000 AD Vikings sail across the Atlantic from Scandinavia, land in Newfoundland, and establish a colony. They leave after just a few years.

1497 Italian explorer John Cabot (1450–1499), seeking to establish trade for England, sails along Cape Breton Island and probably lands near Cape North (p 103).

1604 Explorer Samuel de Champlain (1567–1635) moves north from the Maine border and establishes a colony at Port Royal (near present-day Annapolis Royal).

1749 In a harbor that had previously been visited by European fishermen, Colonel Edward Cornwallis (1713–1776) establishes a military post at Halifax.

1783 Fredericton, New Brunswick, and Digby and Shelburne, Nova Scotia are all founded by Loyalists fleeing the establishment of the American nation.

1842 A treaty with England establishes Canada's long-disputed southeastern border with Maine and the U.S.

1864 Delegates from the Ontario area and three eastern provinces meet in Charlottetown to confer about the idea of confederating, or creating a single larger nation from their territories.

1908 Author Lucy Maud Montgomery's (1874–1942) book *Anne of Green Gables* is published. It will eventually sell more than 50 million copies worldwide.

1912 The *Titanic* ocean liner sinks offshore from Nova Scotia, and rescue boats are dispatched from Halifax. They also ferry back the dead, who are buried in three city cemeteries.

1917 A huge explosion caused by two colliding boats in Halifax harbor levels much of the city's waterfront and kills an estimated 2,000 local residents.

1922 Telephone inventor Alexander Graham Bell (1847–1922) dies at his summer home in Baddeck, Nova Scotia, on Cape Breton Island, age 75. He is buried on the property grounds.

1936 Cape Breton Highlands National Park is established, the first national park in Canada's eastern provinces.

1998 A new high-speed ferry service from Bar Harbor, Maine, to Yarmouth, Nova Scotia, debuts. Overnight service from Portland, Maine, to Yarmouth (later trimmed to a half-day's time) follows soon afterward.

2005 Nova Scotia native Sidney Crosby (1987–) is drafted by the National Hockey League's Pittsburgh Penguins. A star is born.

Eating & Drinking in **Atlantic Canada**

The eastern provinces of Canada are many things—tranquil, wild, friendly, wave-swept—but one thing they *aren't* is gourmet. Yet there are a few local tastes that might catch your fancy.

Fish 'n chip shops certainly aren't unique to Eastern Canada, but they do the chippie proud here. Check around the Halifax area or the shoreline just to the south. Order cod, if you can.

North-central Prince Edward Island is famous for its church-sponsored **lobster suppers.** The typical supper might include a lobster or two, a hunk of blueberry cake, and some corn on the cob for one all-inclusive price. See chapter 6 for a few suggestions. You can also buy **live lobsters** right off the boat at many lobster pounds on the coasts of these three provinces (especially Nova Scotia).

Some say you won't find better **mussels and oysters** anywhere in the world than those harvested in the shallow waters on, and offshore of, Canada's Prince Edward Island. Restaurants from New York to Tokyo covet (and pay big money for) the prized PEI mussel. You can get them on the relative cheap at local seafood houses and shacks; sometimes, you can even buy a bag off the docks.

Foodies in search of obscure-eats rapture might indeed feel they've died and gone to heaven when they reach the southwestern shore of Nova Scotia and discover **rappie pie,** a staple of true Acadian cooking. It's a rich, potato-stock-and-onion casserole which is then topped with a pile of pork or pork rinds and baked.

The waters off Digby Neck (on the western shore of Nova Scotia) produce some of the finest **scallops** in the world; I like them pan-fried. They're ubiquitous on the menus of restaurants along the western shore of Nova Scotia, and show up in lots of fine kitchens around the rest of the province, too.

Here and there, particularly along the Atlantic shore of Nova Scotia, you'll come across the odd **fish-smoking shack.** That's not really surprising, given the huge supply of smokeable fish just offshore. The most organized and commercialized operation is the J. Willy Krauch & Son's operation in the village of Tangier, Nova Scotia (see chapter 2). Krauch & Sons' "hot-smoked" herring is a classic example of the form.

You can even find locally made **whisky** (no "e" for the Scottish version, please) in the highlands of Cape Breton, at a distillery producing "Scotch" (it can't be *called* Scotch, this not being Scotland). So, "single-malt whisky," then. It's fantastic, crafted from the pure local water. See chapter 5.

Finally, drink the **beer** here. Eastern Canadians do love their beer, and the quantity and quality of locally microbrewed beer is amazing given how thinly populated these provinces are. See my "Halifax for Beer Lovers" tour, in chapter 4, for a sampling of the wares.

Toll-Free Numbers & Websites

Airlines

AER LINGUS
☎ 800/474-7424
in the U.S.
☎ 01/886-8888 *in Ireland*
www.aerlingus.com

AIR CANADA
☎ 888/247-2262
www.aircanada.com

AIR FRANCE
☎ 0820/820-820
in France
www.airfrance.com

AIR NEW ZEALAND
☎ 800/262-1234
in New Zealand
www.airnewzealand.com

AMERICAN AIRLINES
☎ 800/433-7300
www.aa.com

BRITISH AIRWAYS
☎ 800/247-9297
☎ 0345/222-1111
☎ 0845/77-333-77
in Britain
www.british-airways.com

CONTINENTAL AIRLINES
☎ 800/525-0280
www.continental.com

DELTA AIR LINES
☎ 800/221-1212
www.delta.com

NORTHWEST AIRLINES
☎ 800/225-2525
www.nwa.com

PORTER AIRLINES
☎ 888/619-8622
www.flyporter.com

QANTAS
☎ 800/227-4500
in the U.S.
☎ 612/131313
in Australia
www.qantas.com

UNITED AIRLINES
☎ 800/241-6522
www.united.com

US AIRWAYS
☎ 800/428-4322
www.usairways.com

WESTJET
☎ 888/937-8538
www.westjet.com

Car Rental Agencies

ALAMO
☎ 877/222-9075
www.alamo.com

AVIS
☎ 800/879-2847
www.avis.com

BUDGET
☎ 800/268-8900
www.budget.com

DOLLAR
☎ 800/800-3665
www.dollar.com

ENTERPRISE
☎ 800/325-8007
www.enterprise.com

HERTZ
☎ 800/263-0600
www.hertz.com

NATIONAL
☎ 877/222-9058
www.nationalcar.com

THRIFTY
☎ 800/847-4389
www.thrifty.com

Hotel & Motel Chains

BEST WESTERN INTERNATIONAL
☎ 800/528-1234
www.bestwestern.com

COMFORT INNS
☎ 800/228-5150
www.comfortinn.com

DAYS INN
☎ 800/325-2525
www.daysinn.com

DELTA HOTELS & RESORTS
☎ 877/814-7706
www.deltahotels.com

FAIRMONT HOTELS
☎ 800/257-7544
www.fairmont.com

HILTON HOTELS
☎ 800/HILTONS
(445-8667)
www.hilton.com

HOLIDAY INN
☎ 800/HOLIDAY
(465-4329)
www.ichotelsgroup.com

HOWARD JOHNSON
☎ 800/654-2000
www.hojo.com

HYATT HOTELS & RESORTS
☎ 800/228-9000
www.hyatt.com

MARRIOTT HOTELS
☎ 800/228-9290
www.marriott.com

RADISSON HOTELS INTERNATIONAL
☎ 800/333-3333
www.radisson.com

RITZ-CARLTON
☎ 800/241-3333
www.ritzcarlton.com

SHERATON HOTELS & RESORTS
☎ 800/325-3535
www.sheraton.com

WESTIN HOTELS & RESORTS
☎ 800/937-8461
www.westin.com

Index

See also Accommodations and Restaurant indexes, below.

Index